TEARS OF DISINHERITANCE

Revisiting the Maasai Historical and Contemporary
Land Injustices in Kenya

Ben R. Ole Koissaba

Ilkiyio Lenjun'go

Nsemia

First Edition: May 2021

Published by: Nsemia Inc. Publishers (www.nsemia.com)
Oakville, Ontario, Canada

Edited by: Rose Keya
Cover Concept by: Author
Cover illustration by: Author
Cover Design by: Linda Kiboma
Layout Design: Bethsheba Nyabuto

Note for Librarians:

A cataloguing record for this book is available from Library
and Archives Canada.

ISBN: 978-1-989928-09-7

DEDICATION

My gratitude that is beyond description goes to my understanding father the late Sironka Lendapana Koissaba (RIP) who despite having not had the privilege of going to school, valued education and believed that by allowing me to go to school; will not only be an investment in the family but it will be an example to many Maasai families who would rather have their sons look after livestock and become coveted warriors.

I dedicate this to my family, who had to feel my absence and missed my humble time with my father due to my education workload, and supported me in succeeding in school. Roine, Rianto, Rarin, Rotiken, and Riyies deserve praise for bearing with my absence. This dedication also goes to Serena Wilcox for her patience with me and the support she gave me and my children during this process. Josephine Santetwa Kindi, for her support when I was in ill health and for her companionship during the last stages of completing this book.

This dedication also goes to the late Marima Ole Sempeta for his tireless efforts to dig into the annals of history for information that informed the Maasai movement. The late Hon. William Ole Ntimama, for his steadfast protection of Maasai land rights, the late Ntinaai Ole Moiyiare, Saisa Ole Kipury, Ole Kunkuru, Ole Mpoye, and many others who gave their lives for the Maa Nation. The late Justice Moijo Ole Keiwua was mainly recognized for his financial, material, and intellectual contributions to liberating the Maa Nation. This dedication also goes to the late Vincent Ole Ntekerei Matura ole Karia for the massive and invaluable knowledge about the Maasai history they have gone to rest with. I also dedicate this to my friend and mentor, the late Dr. Hassan Ole Kamwaro, who taught me how to navigate a treacherous life of being involved in human rights in a country where you are constantly viewed as a threat to the status quo. I also dedicate this to Moses Ole Marima and the Maasai Council of Elders for the wisdom and encouragement they gave me during the struggle of seeking opportunities to redress Maasai land grievances. Finally, I dedicate this to all the people who believe that all human beings are equal and that they all deserve justice and have stood firm to become the voice of the voiceless in their work for justice for all in a world where might is considered right, as opposed to living in a world where right is might.

ACKNOWLEDGMENTS

In the long quest for justice for the Maasai on historical and contemporary land loss, and the dissertation process, I was fortunate to have benefited from the academic support and professional guidance of some very thoughtful people. The encouragement, direction, redirection, and gentle nudges were all delivered at the right time. In this treacherous and risky journey of advocacy and human rights, I was fortunate enough to have interacted with individuals and organizations that provided opportunities to learn and propel the Maasai agenda to the political sphere in Kenya. I acknowledge the role played by Mainyioito Pastoralist Integrated Development Organization (MPIDO), Kenya Land Alliance, Centre for Minority Rights Development (CEMIRIDE), the Kenya National Human Rights Commission (KNHRC), the Independent Medico-Legal Unit (IMLU), the Kenya Human Rights Commission (KHRC), and RECONCILE. In the international arena, I acknowledge the support provided by the United Nations Office of the High Commissioner on Human Rights through the United Nations Permanent Forum on Indigenous Issues (UNPFII).

In developing my research proposal, I never dreamed I could complete a project of this nature until I met Dr. Bonnie Holaday. She answered my plea for care; I never felt alone from then on. This remarkable woman is gifted with accurate perception, truthful delivery, and faith that allows others to make mistakes and learn from them. Under her guidance, I have been able to publish several papers.

I also acknowledge Dr. Mark Small for his role in ensuring that I think out of the box and, through his legal studies background, I could critically analyze issues and arguments during my study and research. I thank Dr. Kenneth Robinson for his constant encouragement, even when I almost gave up. I also wish to acknowledge the patience of Dr. Betty Baldwin in ensuring that I understood qualitative data analysis. I appreciate the role that Dr. Martie plays. Thomson played a key role in secondary data analysis, which was key to my research project. I acknowledge Lemomo Ole Kulet for contributing content about the Maasai cultural practices.

I recognize the role played by many Maa-speaking people who have come together under the auspices of the Maa Civil Society Forum for the great work they have done in educating, informing, and empowering the Maasai to be able to speak and demand their rights. I acknowledge the significant role played by the research participants in voluntarily accepting to participate in this study and for the time they put into contributing to the study's outcomes. This acknowledgement goes to the following people: - Moses Ole Marima, the late Vincent Ole Ntekerei, the late Matura Ole Karia, Dr. Clement Lenachuru, Michael Ole Tiampati, Daniel Salau Ole Rogei, Nicholas Ole Soikan, Jackson Ole Shaa, Rahab Kenana, Lemayian Ole Taiko, John Kisimirr, Julius Lemanken, and Fredrick Kamakei. I also acknowledge late Jason Ole Sein, the Late John Ole Tameno, the late Ole Karariet, and the late Ole Ntokoti for the narratives they shared with me during formative years of growing up which led to this book having a section on the mythology about the Maasai, as well as the untold story of how the Maasai were politically manipulated both by the colonialist and post independence regimes.

I acknowledge the roles played by my colleagues who have weathered the storm of seeking justice for the Maasai: Francis Ole Sakuda, Margaret Lesuuda, Kimaren Ole Riamit, John Ole Legei, and the team from Osiligi, Godfrey Ole Ntapayia, Saitabao Ole Kanchory, Lukas Ole Naikuni, and Soipan Tuya (Kudate). Much appreciation to Joseph Ole Simel, Mathew Lempurkel, and Daniel Ole Tenaai. Mary Simat, Caroline Ncharo, and many other Maa heroines who bore the brunt of teargas during the Nairobi processions. I also acknowledge the roles that Odenda Lumumba, formerly of Kenya Land

Alliance, Michael Odhiambo, formerly of RECONCILE, and Yobo Rutin of CEMIRIDE played in helping to make the Maasai voice audible.

Among supporters from the international community, I acknowledge the role played by the International Work Group for Indigenous Affairs (IWGIA) and Cultural Survival, which have identified with the Maasai struggle and have helped in one way or another to facilitate processes aimed at enabling the Maasai to address issues of land, disinheritance, and marginalization. For those who ought to have contributed, but for one reason or another, they did not. I acknowledge your support and willingness to take this project forward; where you did not, I still appreciate that you know about it. It is essential to mention all those who spent their valuable time participating in the research about Maasai land appropriation. Without your participation, this work would have been nought. Thank you to Pastor Elistan Supeyo, who hosted me in Seattle when I needed a roof over my head and food as a new immigrant in the United States. Thank you also to Ellen Graben at Clemson University for your help with editing and formatting part of this work.

I also acknowledge Lemareka Kibasisi's contributions to Maasai and biblical traditions on God and its origins.

FOREWORD

Embedded in this book is a rich history of a community land rights activist and academic researcher who has spent several years discussing, learning, and accumulating data on his people's land dispossession. I have been fortunate to collaborate with his community and himself in producing this book. It is the first of its kind since the promulgation of the Constitution of Kenya, 2010, that provides the mechanism for redressing historical land injustices. In Article 67 (2) (e), the National Land Commission is established as a Constitutional organ to investigate historical and contemporary land injustices and recommend appropriate redress on its own initiative or on a complaint. I hope that this book will become a reference material to complement indigenous knowledge of the Maasai people who wish to seek redress for the century-long colonial and post-colonial land issues.

The desire of the Maasai to undo a century of dispossession became a subject of debate in 2004 as the community, in commemoration of 100 years since the Anglo-Maasai Agreements, turned up in Nairobi to petition for restitution of their land. Since then, the community has never tired of reminding itself of the history that shaped and continues to shape its present. *Tears of Disinheritance* is undeniably a chronicle of events of dispossession that have shaped the community's contemporary culture and economics, particularly as they relate to power relations.

Finally, I wish to reiterate that this kind of study serves as an exemplary effort to put together a community's experience that hopefully will inspire everyone to move forward with the agenda of community land rights. Thus, I look forward to the wide use of this book to improve the understanding and address historical land injustices to secure a community land tenure regime in Kenya.

Odenda Lumumba Land and Agrarian Studies Fellow, University of the Western Cape, SA.
[2019-2021].

ODENDA LUMUMBA is a Land Rights Activist, a founder and co-ordinator of the Kenya Land Alliance, Policy, and a Network Advocate on land laws and institutional reforms. He has enrolled for PhD studies in Land and Agrarian Studies and holds a Master of Philosophy in the same field from the University of the Western Cape. He has co-authored book chapters on *Land and Sustainable Development in Africa* and *The Global Land Grab*

PREFACE

The title of this book in the Maa language is *Ilkiyio Lenjun'go,* meaning *Tears of disinheritance.* According to the Maasai, this is translated to mean "the last tears a man can shed," when all is lost; loss of the plate that God provided for him to eat from, that is, the land. It is about people with no hope for a future, a life full of lamentation and regrets. It is about how the Maasai have been crying over time to seek redress over land that was expropriated through forced acquisition, laws, policies, and self-inflicted losses, that despite having become the hosts of all ethnic communities in Kenya, the communities they hosted have turned against them by demanding control of the resources that are available on their land. The issue here is intertwined: It is about a century-long cry of grievances of a people who once occupied, controlled, and used the plains of East Africa, but because of the loss of the land, all that remains is their name with no territorial control. It is also a tale of the Maasai being disinherited by design or default. It is about people who have fond memories of places. Places are the locations that matter to people because they return to them, build memories around them, write their histories, and call them home. Unfortunately for the Maasai, the places they called home have been taken over by others; they cannot return and claim most of these places, but the fond memories of places they called home still linger in their minds, thanks to the stories that have been passed on from generation to generation.

The book is divided into nine parts. The first part is about my personal river of life, as it flowed through different life terrains, I was able to look, listen, and learn about life's intricacies, which motivated me to get involved in human rights and advocacy. This journey took me through a spectrum of events that affected the Maasai people in Kenya.

Part two of the book is about who the Maa speakers are from their own perspectives and narratives. In this part, I also address the mythology: about their origin, their religion, social structure, rites of passage, leadership structure as it was historically constructed, the historical intra-Maasai wars, as well as their pre-colonial geographical localities.

In part three, I revisit the issue of the Maasai and colonization. This section examines Europeans' perceptions of the Maasai before they came to Africa and the arrival of European settlers in Kenya. In this part, I examine events regarding the Maasai, including the infamous Maasai agreements often referred to as the Anglo-Maasai agreements of 1904 and 1911. Since the subject of the book is about how, for more than a hundred years, the Maasai have continued to lose their land, I reviewed the Kenya Land Commission Report, commonly referred to as the Carter Commission of 1933-1934 Report, the Million Acre Scheme, and the deliberations of the Lancaster Independence Conference of 1962.

Part four examines post-independence government regimes and how they have contributed to Maasai land appropriation. This part is informed by my doctoral research titled *A Critical Analysis of Factors that Contribute to Maasai Land Appropriation: A Case Study of Narok and Kajiado Counties in Kenya*: To understand the underlying factors about Maasai land appropriation, this section examines laws, policies, and decrees that have been issued by the successive government regimes which have contributed to continued loss of land by the Maasai in Kenya.

In part five, I examine the possibilities and potential legal structures and systems that the Maasai may use to contest past and future land appropriation. By reviewing local legal regimes related to land and subjecting them to the Maasai claim, I discuss how such can be used by individuals and communities who have land claims to seek redress. In this part, I also examine regional and international mechanisms and case laws that the Maasai can leverage to seek redress. Part six looks at the emergence of the Maasai civil society, the events that led to its vibrancy, and its objectives. In this section, I focus mainly on those civil society groups whose objectives were human rights, advocacy, and land rights. I enumerate their goals and objectives, strategies, and the challenges they faced during their work. Part six also looks at how the Maasai Civil Society Forum (MCSF) built local, regional, and international networks and how the networks built their capacity to raise their voices in advocating for land rights in Maasai land.

Part seven examines the real and perceived manifestations of land appropriation in the lives and livelihoods of the Maasai. This part looks at how land appropriation has impacted the cultural and spiritual values of the Maasai as well as the economic and political aspects of the community. Part eight is a discussion on lessons learned from the case studies and interactions I have had over a long period with people who provided key details that have contributed to the content of this book.

Part nine contains the conclusion, findings, and recommendations. The resources I used for writing this book were both primary and secondary. I used a systematic review of available literature about the Maasai and their historical places, culture, and social structure in secondary sources. Primary sources included narratives from people who observed events about the Maasai as they evolved or were told such stories by others who took part in the events or were told about certain phenomena. I was privileged as a child to hear stories from such wise people as the late Meiriapie Ole Seno (my uncle, whom I referred to as grandfather because of age group- Ole Seno's first wife was my father's elder sister), the late Mpaeki (Mpaayei) Ole Kinayia, the late Ole Karariet (Ole Karariet was a seer who was consulted by many Maasai), the late Jason Ole Sein, the late Dr. John Ole Tameno, and many others who passed this knowledge to me in narration.

I also intended to introduce the lesser-known word in academic circles: Indigenous Humanities. Humanities have been linked with European traditions as a source and foundation for scholarly knowledge; the idea of linking the humanities to indigenous people has not been fully embraced in the African literary world. From my experience, I have found that some Western scholars still consider African scholars inadequate, less informed, and seldom referenced in research done by Western scholars. Hence, in my thoughts, I acknowledge the colonial system that has entrenched indigenous trauma and disconnected indigenous people from their languages and cultural fabric that held them together and made them a community. Their local narratives in their own languages gave them identity. Since every scholar must use a certain theoretical framework, all known frameworks are alien to indigenous communities, and none of their theories is accepted in any academic argument.

From this perspective, I am looking at post-colonialism from a positivist perspective instead of the common perspective that post-colonialism is the time or era after colonialism. For me, it represents more of an aspiration, a hope yet to be achieved. It constructs a strategy that responds to the experiences of colonization and imperialism. Therefore, as I write this content, I intend to look at the past and current events in the Maasai history from the Maasai perspective by critically interrogating all processes and actions that contributed to Maasai land appropriation.

Further, I agree with the sentiments that: -

> "When we speak about colonization, we might speak of it as an event—that is, in terms of people (colonists) coming, conquering, and dominating other people at a moment, and administering people colonially, until the colonized fight and push them back. This definition of colonization can be dated, in terms of when it started and ended" [1](Sabelo J. Ndlovu-Gatsheni).

I understand that, as I speak about colonization, I view it as a complex power structure that transformed a people's way of life. It is an asymmetrical and colonial inter-subjective relation between the colonizer (citizen) and the colonized

---

1   See Sabelo J. Ndlovu-Gatsheni. Decolonization, Decoloniality and the Future of African Studies

(subject), and it economically instituted dispossession and transfer of economic resources from those who were indigenous to those who were conquering and foreign. It claims to be a civilizing project, as it hid its sinister motives. This thinking has been replicated in academia, where scholars from the former colonies are subjected to a secondary role. In contrast, Eurocentric scholars are perceived as custodians of indigenous knowledge. It is my informed opinion that African scholars are the best storytellers of their own stories because they speak from their hearts, their daily lived experiences, and their interactions with their environment.

To borrow from Ngugi wa Thiong'o's famous title, *Decolonizing the Mind*, politics, economics, and other structures of human interrelation cannot be decolonized without decolonizing the minds of people on all sides of the colonial relation, compradors, colonials, colonized, and post-colonized alike. Decolonizing the mind involves a rejection of diffusionism, the notion that knowledge spreads one way from ancient Egypt to Greece and Rome, then Europe, and from there to the rest of the world. Decolonizing the mind means recognizing a wide array of knowledge systems, operating in a global ecology of knowledges, that, like other ecological systems, involves interdependency, competition, and contestation. It means learning enough of the heritage and trajectory of different systems of knowing so that the Eurocentric tradition cannot continue to reaffirm its totalizing claims. Interest in and respect for different knowings means consciously turning to different knowers as authorities and sources of knowledge. It means a conscious politics of citation, which refuses to recite the same authorities endlessly while maintaining motivated ignorance and silence around alternative authorities. It means a different bibliography. Ironically, perhaps, it means marshalling traditional tools of humanistic studies for alternative purposes, including studies of how philosophies of mind are conveyed not only in the very languages we use but even more so in the languages we tried to exterminate.

This decolonization process does not only affect academia, it impacts all facets of life in that the traditional aspects of the former colonized, have been demonized in religion, while its leadership structures were dismembered to suite the colonizers aspirations of centralized authority, selection of representation in the name of democracy; which ended up weakening the traditional leadership structure that was based on sound ethics, moral, and accountability to the people that one was selected to lead. I also intended to write with some in-depth Maasai narratives to inform and educate literate Maasai about events, terminologies, history, idioms, and many social Maasai dynamics that have since ceased to be practised due to changes that have occurred over time.

In discussing Maasai land appropriation, I use a critical theory approach (Harbamas, 1996 and 1989). Critical Theory (*Aibiribirr*) seeks the emancipation of society and the liberation of human beings from circumstances that oppress them. It aims to contextualize philosophical claims to truth and moral universality without reducing them to social and historical conditions, preventing the loss of truth about past knowledge and actions in any society (Harbamas, 1996). By examining the historical problems of marginalization, dispossession, alienation, and political domination, critical theory enables me to study social institutions and how they have transformed over time and their contributions to the critical reflective processes aimed at empowering the community (Creswell, 2007). It is a critical thinking approach aimed at empowering people using the extrajudicial concept of fairness, focused on exposing and ending social inequalities.

Jürgen Habermas is one of the leading critical theorists from the Frankfurt School. Since Habermas's theory is known for its complexity, this book will focus only on those aspects of his theory that relate to the book's narrative. This includes themes and concepts in legitimization crises (Habermas, 1995), structural transformation of the public sphere (Habermas, 1989), between facts and norms (Habermas, 1996), and the theory of Communicative Action in volumes 1 and 2 (Habermas, 1984, 1987). Critical theory is also interested in those social facts and circumstances that constrain the realization of the ideal democracy and force people to reconsider its normative content (Harbamas, 1996). Habermas asked critical questions about modern society's nature, its problems, and the place morality, language, politics, and the law play in it.

The discussion in this book used the above Habermas concepts to analyze legal, regulatory, and policy frameworks in Kenya that have contributed to continued land appropriation, as well as their challenges. I also use the concepts to make recommendations for policy actions for future considerations. By critically analyzing the legal and policy frameworks within the context of facticity and validity, the study sought to draw parallels with Habermas' argument that states:

"A justified truth claim should allow its proponents to defend it with reasons against the objections of possible opponents; in the end, she should be able to gain the rationally motivated agreement of the interpretation community as a whole (Harbamas, 1996, p. 14).

Critical theory, therefore, helped create a framework for both recognizing the role of social structures in creating and sustaining social inequalities and provided for understanding and acting upon the effects of these structures in individuals' personal lives and everyday experiences (Reisch, 2014).

Therefore, this becomes the goal of the narrative in this book: to speak from a Maasai context and understanding of the processes that contributed to land appropriation to engage others in a dialogue that will result in a common understanding of the history of dispossession and Maasai contestation of land appropriation. I seek to challenge what has been generally accepted by the Kenyan society's social order that legal statutes of a country represent the generally accepted norm by engaging in communicative action. Such communicative action agrees with Habermas' arguments that legal validity has a relationship with how legal systems have developed, becoming instruments of coercion and impediments to freedom and democracy. According to Harbamas, it is generally assumed that any legal system has a higher level of legitimacy over and above individual legal norms (Harbamas, 1996). This became the force that drove Kenyan policy processes, where laws were enacted to create and facilitate nationhood. Based on the above arguments by Harbamas, it could be argued that the legal systems used to dispossess the Maasai of their land were contrary to the socially accepted norms and thus ethically unjustified (Harbamas, 1996). The laws disregarded the interests of the Maasai. Therefore, they were morally and legally illegitimate from the Maasai context, as they lacked adequate consultation and were deliberately enacted with the primary goal of appropriating Maasai land. While such laws derive legitimacy from legislative processes based on state sovereignty, their inability to secure the rights and political autonomy[2] of their citizens (subjects) denies them legitimacy as they deprive individuals and entire communities of the rights to own land and practice traditionally accepted land-use systems.

To put Habermas's critical theory in the context of how governments impose laws and rules, you must be aware that in 1885, several European imperial powers met in Berlin, Germany, to discuss the partition of the African continent amongst themselves. The meeting led to the signing of the Treaty of Berlin, under which arbitrary boundary lines were drawn on a map of Africa and territories were created and allocated to the participating European powers. Under this arrangement, Kenya was assigned to Great Britain. The boundary lines were drawn without any consideration of the position of the local tribes, such that sections of tribes like the Maasai of East Africa found themselves belonging to two different countries, namely Kenya and Tanganyika. Following the partition, each European power sought to implement the Treaty of Berlin. In this regard, Great Britain's Attorney-General advised his Government that from then onwards.

---

2   The rights enjoyed by citizens should be evident across the whole structure, as those rights that grant free opportunities of free choice to the citizens. See Harbamas 1996, p. 83.

Kenya was part of the British Empire, and therefore part of the King's territories; thus, the Crown or King could deal with the land in the territory as he or she pleased.

This legal interpretation of the treaty assumed that no indigenous people existed in the territory. If there were people, their rights were irrelevant to Great Britain's expansion plans. To alienate or allocate individual pieces of land in the new territory, the Government enacted the East African (Lands) Orders in Council of 1895, 1897, and 1901. These orders in the Council were later re-enacted as the Crown Lands Ordinances of 1902 and 1915. The Ordinances dealt with and governed land allocation for agricultural, residential, commercial, and other purposes. In these statutes; *Crown Land" was defined to mean all public land within the East African Protectorate which, for the time being, was subject to the control of His Majesty.* In other words, the entire territory known as Kenya was declared Crown Land.

To attain independence, Kenya inherited and adopted the entire set of colonial land laws enacted to address the interests of the white settlers. The principle of these laws was the Crown Lands Ordinances of 1902 and 1915. I will refer to these statutes, under which the British Monarch was empowered to allocate land to whoever the Monarch wished and, on such terms and conditions as the Monarch pleased. As a result, depending on who the allottee was, the land would be granted on freehold tenure or leasehold term for periods ranging from 99 to 999 years. The independent Government made superficial amendments to the laws inherited from the British, such that ordinances were simply renamed Acts. The term Crown was substituted with President, Crown Land was renamed Government Land, and where Crown referred to the British Monarch as an institution, it was substituted with Government.

TABLE OF CONTENTS

LIST OF TABLES

Table 1:	Iloshon, Clan names, and Clan Identity
Table 2:	Participating organization during the M.C.S.F. Strategic Planning Workshop
Table 3:	Summary of Strategies and Activities
Table 4:	Implementation Plan
Table 5:	Ontological and epistemological questions

LIST OF FIGURES

Figure 1:	Maasai Territory before Colonization
Figure 2:	Maasai Mara National Game Reserve and Conservancy areas.
Figure 3:	MMWCA Conservancies Administrative Structure
Figure 4:	Total Area Under the MMWCA
Figure 5:	Summary of Benefits Accruing from the Conservancy Model
Figure 6:	Magadi Concession Area and adjacent Group Ranches.
Figure 7:	Kajiado County Governor Joseph Ole Lenku with other Maasai leaders addressing press regarding the displacement of the Maasai in Kedong on November 12th, 2019.
Figure 8:	Environment and Forestry Cabinet Secretary Keriako Tobiko, Narok North MP Moitalel Ole Kenta, and Maasai leaders appreciating the efforts made to preserve the MaasaiMau Forest.
Figure 9:	The Author leading a discussion about how the demonstrations by the Maasai will be conducted.
Figure 10:	Maasai protesters marching along Nakuru-Nairobi highway in Maai Mahiu demanding the returnof Maasai land.
Figure 11:	Maasai demonstrate in the streets of Nairobi demanding back their land.

LIST OF ABBREVIATIONS

ACPR	African Commission on Human and Peoples' Rights
AFC	Agricultural Finance Corporation
CBOs	Community Based Organizations
CBNRM	Community Based Natural Resource Management
CEO	Chief Executive Officer
CEMIRIDE	Center for Minority Rights in Development
CLMB	County Land Management Board
CMS	Church Missionary Society
CSO	Civil Society Organizations
EACJ	East African Court of Justice
ECF	East Coast Fever
FAO	Food and Agricultural Organization
FBOs	Faith-Based Organizations
GOK	Government of Kenya
HRC	Human Rights Council
ICCPR	International Convention on Civil and Political Rights
IEBC	Independent Electoral and Boundaries Commission
IGAD	The Inter-governmental Authority on Development
IRB	Institutional Review Board
IMPACT	Indigenous Movement for Peace Advancement and Conflict Transformation
IMLU	Independent Medico Legal Unit
ILO	International Labour Organization
IRIN	Integrated Regional Information Network
IWGIA	International Working Group for Indigenous Affairs
KANU	Kenya African National Union

KADU	Kenya National Democratic Union
KNBS	Kenya National Bureau of Statistics
KNHRC	Kenya National Human Rights Commission
KLDP	Kenya Livestock Development Project
KLA	Kenya Land Alliance
KWCA	Kenya Wildlife Conservation Association
LDSB	Land Development and Settlement Board
LRA	Land Registration Act
MCSF	Maa Civil Society Forum
MMWCA	Maasai Mara Wildlife Conservation Association
MRC	Minority Reforms Consortium
MPIDO	Mainyioto Pastoralist Development Organization
MUF	Maasai United Front
NGO	Non-Governmental Organization
NLC	National Land Commission
NLP	National Land Policy
NSF	National Science Foundation
OLPADEP	Olmaa Pastoralist Development Project
PDNK	Pastoralist Development Network of Kenya
KEPACO	Keekonyokie Pastoralist Community Organization
RECONCILE	Resource Conflict Institute
ROK	Republic of Kenya
TJRC	Truth Justice and Reconciliation Commission
UN	United Nations
UNDRIP	United Nation Declaration on the Rights of Indigenous People'
UNDP	United Nations Development Program
UNPFII	United Nations Permanent Forum on Indigenous Issues
WGIP	Working Group on Indigenous People

PART I
MOTIVATION FOR THE BOOK

The Motivation of the Book

The contents of this book are informed by the experiences and knowledge I acquired over 25 years in civil society in Kenya, Africa, and the United States. It is also from my life experiences as a child from a poor Maasai family whose livelihood depended on my father's earnings from being employed as a herdsman at both the White ranches in Naivasha and Nakuru in the mid-sixties, and that of the late Ernest Letoya Ole Mpaayei at Olooltepes, in Kajiado County. I am the firstborn of the late Sironka Lendapana Ole Koissaba and the late Nariku Kitaika. I was born at Enkutoto in Nairagie-Enkare-Enkare-Enkare-Enkare-Enkare, where the family of Ole Soyiantet currently lives. The date of my birth is not known since both my parents were illiterate. Still, I am told it was during the time of *Olgesherr Loo Ilnyangusi* (a time when the right and left circumcision group of Ilkalikal and Ilkamaniki had the ceremony to make them one age group called Ilnyangusi).

My formative years growing up in such environments and being the only child under the care of my father exposed me to situations where I came face-to-face with a cruel and an unjust world, an unequal world, and a world where when you do not have, you will not get, more so, you too loose the little you have to those who already have. This led me to undertake intensive studies to try to understand the phenomenon.

As a very young child, I got my firsthand experience of the government's ruthlessness. One afternoon at our home in Intikin, I suddenly heard loud voices speaking in a language I could not comprehend (I later learned that it was a mixture of Kiswahili and English) as they raided our home. They were not carrying ordinary sticks or clubs, which I was used to seeing men carry. They had with them what I learned later in life were guns. They were dressed differently and acted unusually compared to what I was accustomed to. They started pulling down the roof of our house. I heard my mother cry and saw several of them beat my father and take him away. Our house

3

was set on fire because my father resisted arrest. My mother and I had to sleep in a neighbour's home for several nights. The next thing I knew was that my step-uncles had married off my mother to another man when my father was in prison, because it was said that he would never be released because his crime was serious. Both of us moved to my mother's new matrimonial home in Ilmelili. My mother and I became part of the Family of Ololdapsh. We stayed over time (I could not remember how long, and nobody bothered to let me know how long it was) until I found myself on a bus heading to Narok Town.

The trip was long, and as I looked around the bus, I saw my father and attempted to go to his seat. My mother held me tight until we got to Narok. I later learned that we went to court because my father had filed for my custody. I was scared to death because I was not allowed to go to my father, and the presence of the police made it even worse. I could not understand the language, and all I remember is that I jumped from my mother's hands and ran to my father. I heard a bang on the table and clung to my father. The next thing I saw was my mother crying and my father carrying me out of the building. I later learned that my father had won my custody. That was the last day I saw my late mother.

My father had sold most of his cows to meet the custody case cost, so he had to search for employment. The best employment for a Maasai who had not gone to school was as a herdsman or shepherd, and the best employers were the white settlers in Naivasha and Nakuru. My father was employed as a herdsman in Naivasha by the Delameres and other white ranchers, and I always had to be with him. Two men and a woman lived in each *boma* (sheep enclosure). The role of the men was to look after the flock, and the role of the women was to clean the boma. In the evenings, my father would tell stories about how that land was historically owned by the Maasai. He described how the white men moved them from Olomuruti (Rumuruti), and how they had to walk for 10 days to get to Suswa, where the rest of his relatives now lived.

His narratives were filled with bitterness and anger because of the experiences that he went through as a child. He witnessed my grandfather's cows and sheep being slaughtered by white men on horses, the dogs that accompanied the white men feeding on the carcasses of their livestock, and women being raped in front of their children and husbands. I found the stories very disturbing, and I became curious. I had my father retell the story every night as we slept in the little V-shaped tin hut. I remember names such as Esoit Sampu, Olmarura, Morintat, Kiraka, and Kirgil (Gilgil), as some places where my father worked. I remember one occasion, a white man came to pick up my father and me and took us to his home. In the house were several Maasai people, one of whom I learned later was the late Matura Ole Karia, who translated to my father what the tall white man was saying. He told my father that because of his good work, he was promoted to a *Nyapara* supervisor (pronounced Olmunyaparai in Maa). My father was not the only Maasai employed by the white men; I recall the names of Ole Supeyo, Ole Sayiorri, and Ole Napieirag, whom I met later in life.

In that place, various risks ranged from lions, leopards, and cheetahs that would invade the enclosures made from wire mesh. The worst of all were the warriors who made random raids. I remember one night when our camp was raided by men who were speaking in Maa. They held all of us hostage as others drove off the sheep towards Oldonyio Opiru (Eburu). I later learnt that they were called Olkioma Le Baati.[1]

In 1969, my father and I moved to Kajiado. I later learned that he was persuaded to go and work for one of his clansmen as a shepherd. The walk from Naivasha to Kajiado took us several days. We walked during the day and slept in people's homesteads (*Inkangitie*) on our way, in a journey that took us 5 days (*Ilkiragarien Imiet*). We arrived at the present-day Kiserian, where we were hosted by the late Manyoike Ole Maloi. He had prepared a place for us because he came from the same place as my father, from the same clan and age

---

1   This was a group that consisted of a mixture of young Maasai who tried their luck in getting rich by stealing from the European Settlers

group, and we had known each other before. A ram was killed, and the local brew (*Esuguroi*) was available for the elders. That is where I met Shompole Ole Leroka, a respected Maasai teacher who also lived in the neighbourhood and who became one of my mentors later in life. We spent two days because I was fatigued and needed a rest.

On arrival at Olooltepes, my father and I were shown a small iron sheet house by an old man from Ilkisonko called Ole Nkitoria. I was the only child among the three men. Then there was a woman from Ilkisonko called Ngoto Namelok (the mother of Namelok) who had a daughter who could not speak the Maa language. I later learned that she had adopted her daughter from a Kalenjin family in Naivasha, so the daughter could not speak the Maa language. Since the area was sparsely populated with the nearest homes being those of the late Jason Ole Supeyo and that of William Ole Mopel on the Keekonyokie side and on the Ilkaputiei side, the nearest homes were that of Jason Ole Sein and the late Ole Kisoso; I had to accompany the person tending the calves and lambs because the area was by then inhabited by lions, rhinos and other dangerous wild animals. Ernest Ole Mpaayei, now my father's employer, worked as the Principal of the Maasai Rural Training Centre in Isinya. I was therefore taken into their home at Isenya, where I started my education at Isenya Primary school in 1970. All three other landowners were working class; hence, they did not live on their land but left their workers, herdsmen, to care for their livestock. In charge of the livestock were two men, namely Ole Sayiorry and Ole Napieirag, who, I later learned, worked as herdsmen for the European farmers in Nakuru, and they knew my father. It was from their recommendations that my father was convinced to come and work for Ole Mpaayei. This is where I first heard about individual land ownership by the Maasai. The trio were among the elite Maasai and had embraced the individualization of land, and each had acquired a particular ranch. Arising from their position in the community, they could be allocated as much land as needed. At that time, there were few people, so there was not much pressure on the land.

My real engagement with land issues began in 1984 when the Olchoro-Onyori Group Ranch was subdivided. During this time, I was a teacher at Ilmasin Primary School, and most of the school children came from the Group Ranch. When the subdivision was underway, many community members complained about not being included or being given smaller pieces of land than they deserved by the Group Ranch Committee. A group of young men (Iran Girang and Irampaun) approached me to draft letters of complaint since I was among the educated individuals in the area. After that, I drafted the letters and attended a meeting where I acted as a translator, as most complainants did not speak Kiswahili. This is where I discovered the highest level of corruption in the registration and allocation of land. The Group Ranch Committee allocated multiple pieces of land, registered their underage children, allocated the private surveyors and the lands officers' tracks of land, and left more than 100 *bona fide* members unregistered and without land. Unfortunately, as a civil servant, I was forced out of my teaching job because the elites and the committee used their connections in government to imply that I was involved in politics. During the process, it dawned on me that clanism (*enegilat*) and age-groupism (*eneporori*) were key underlying factors of land allocation. Two camps emerged at different levels. The first camp was led by Chairman Ole Mureisi, who came from Ilikumae vis-à-vis Ilmolelian and Odomongi[2]. The other camps were those of Iseuri and Indifferences Ilkitoip. They were so intense that it created enmity amongst the camps to a point where the Head Teacher of Ilmasin Primary School was convinced by his agemates(who were in the committee) to find ways of eliminating me from my teaching job. The Headteacher made my work so difficult that I had to quit the job at Ilmasin Primary School and transfer to Olooseos Primary School. I did not last long at Olooseos Primary School because of the local politics, which made me forego the job to pursue further studies.

The second time I got involved with land issues was in

---

2   See the Maasai social structure section for the meanings

1985 when President Moi set aside a 400-hundred-meter strip on Ngong Hills (Olteyani) to resettle the Maasai who had settled there in 1974. The Provincial Administration under the Provincial Commissioner, Hezekiah Oyugi, and the District Officer in Ngong, Mr. Oreta, and the Paramount Chief Idi Malambu took it upon themselves to dish out land to non-Maasai and non-residents. Most land officials, employees of the Provincial Administration, and their friends were the primary beneficiaries. As a community, we mobilized ourselves and held several demonstrations where some of us were arrested for illegal demonstrations and others faced trumped-up charges. This marked the beginning of the Maasai renaissance. This became a wake-up call, and the Maasai started agitating for their land rights.

On the heels of the Ngong Hills land scandal was the Iloodoariak Group Ranch subdivision. By Section 114 of the Constitution of Kenya, the Iloodoariak was vested in Olkejuado County Council as a Trustee. The County Council was to hold the land in question for the benefit of the persons whose original residence was thereon. The adjudication process at Iloodoariak proceeded until 1989 when it was pronounced complete. The adjudication register was published for inspection, and objections were invited within sixty (60) days of the publication. Consequently, 459 objections were lodged and determined by 1990 (MPIDO, 2000). Soon thereafter, those recorded as owners of the parcels of land in the section were registered as absolute proprietors and hence issued with the title deeds regarding the provisions of the Registered Land Act (Cap. 300).

However, the adjudication process was marred by greed, abuse of office, acts of arbitrariness, and corruption exhibited by the officials from the Ministry of Land and Settlement who were ostensibly facilitating the adjudication process. During the alleged adjudication, available evidence indicated that many Government officials were recorded as the owners of the land in this area. Further, a great deal of the land was demarcated to people, friends, and relatives of these officials who were not original residents. This did not happen for free or by accident. The non-residents made hefty payments to these government officials and Land Adjudication Committee members.

According to the records, 362 persons who were (still are) neither residents nor members of any of the existing group ranches of this area were nonetheless recorded as owners of the land in the section. They were allotted land and issued title deeds. A significant number of these non-residents were and still are highly placed politicians, adjudication officials, other senior government and local officials, and their relatives, friends, business people, and associates who had no connection with the area. These people were paying bribes to lubricate the process. The officials took advantage of the ignorance and the illiteracy level of the members of this community. Over 2,000 legitimate and indigenous Maasai families and inhabitants were deliberately, and through fraudulent means, left out of the adjudication process and were declared to be squatters on the land allotted to other people. These residents were not aware of the demarcation and recording taking place. The community was not made aware of these matters. The same was never effectively communicated to them as required by section 14 of the Land Adjudication Act. The Maasai residents of Iloodoariak from the then Kajiado district undoubtedly lived on this ancestral land for many generations. Their case was to protect the land being taken away through unfair, arbitrary, and gross abuse of power perpetrated by Government officials. The rightful and laid-down land adjudication procedures were not applied. There was neither a publication nor a notice to this effect.

The Maasai quest to have land injustices addressed has been a historical issue since the Maasai agreements, and, as will be elaborated in part two of this book, it is important to take cognizance of how the Maasai have continuously strived to have this issue heard. The Maasai wrote several memoranda to both the Njonjo and Ndungu commissions on land (MCSF 2004). In Baringo, the Ilchamus community had filed a constitutional case for a constituency. All these efforts necessitated the need for a unified front for the Maasai to agitate for their rights. This led to the formation of a Maasai social movement called the Maa Civil Society Forum (MCSF). When I became the Chair and National Coordinator of MCSF, I fully engaged myself in advocating for the land rights of the Maasai in Kenya. This led to a people's movement that made strides in raising awareness among the Maasai people about their rights and entitlements as a community.

My engagement with issues of Maasai land grievances placed me in a confrontation with the government and local Maasai political elites. The government saw that the compulsion of the Maasai land rights was an incitement to ethnic violence, while the local politicians perceived that MCSF had a political agenda. While some founder members like Mathew Lempurkel, Joseph Ole Simel, and Daniel Ole Tinaai ended up vying for political positions as members of parliament, my story was different. I was arrested on several occasions and forced into exile in the United States. My greatest enemy was the late Professor George Saitoti, who by then was a very powerful Internal Security Minister who perceived me as a potential political enemy. There were also reservations by some Maasai political leaders who, while knowing that I did not have an interest in any political position, believed that I might be grooming persons of interest who were members of the forum. Within the forum, some members who had dominated the Maasailand rights sphere were not as excited as I was in mobilizing the Maasai; some, despite being founder members, ended up sabotaging the activities of the forum.

PART II:

WHO ARE THE MAASAI?

The Maa Speakers

According to available literature (which has mostly been written by the Maasai), the Maasai are a Nilo-Hamitic people and one of the several groups of Maa-speakers in East Africa today whose ancestors came into this region from southern Sudan during the first millennium, AD. (Cartwhite, 2019). The Maasai are all the descendants of Maasinta, hence their dialect Maa. Maasinta is also referred to as Naiteru Kop (the beginner of the earth). Known in Maasai as Iloshon, the Maasai subtribes include the Ildamat, Ilpurko, Ilkeekonyokie, Iloitai, Ilkaputiei, Ildalalekutuk (*Ilkankere*), Isiria, Ilmoitanik, Iloodokilani, Iloitokitoki, Ilarusa, Ilmatatapato, Ilwuasinkishu, Kore, Ilparakuyu, and Ilkisonko[1]. The name Maasai, which is commonly used to describe Maa speakers, is interchangeably used by the Maa speakers with Olmaa or Ilmaa- this is frequently used by the Samburu. Apparently, according to the Maa-speaking communities in Kenya, the Isampur (Samburu) and the Ilchamus are part of the larger Maa community, but were separated during colonization, and separation has been maintained by post-independence Kenyan regimes. Unfortunately, these differences have been exploited for political interests, where a lack of historical knowledge about how the Isampur (Samburu) and Ilchamus (*Njemps*) are part of the larger Maa community, statistics have isolated them from the bigger Maa Community and are projected as a different tribe, yet they are part and parcel of the Maa community.

As currently constituted, the Maa-speaking people in Kenya are mainly found in Samburu, Kajiado, Narok, Baringo, Nakuru, and Laikipia Counties. In the 2019 National Census, the total Maasai population in Kenya was projected at 1,189,522[2]. That of the Samburu (Isampur)

---

1   Some others, like Isalei, are also sometimes referred to as Maasai, but I have not confirmed that from reliable sources.
2   See Ministry of State for Planning, National Development and Vision 2030.

was 310, 327, and the population of Njemps (Ilchamus) was 35,000 (ROK, 2019). Despite being counted separately in national statistics, the total number of Maa speakers is about 1,535,848 in Kenya. As previously indicated, the Maasai society is comprised of 16 sections or sub-tribes[3]. More details about the Maa-speaking people are found in the other section on the Maasai social structure.

Historically, the Maasai were a pastoral community (due to land subdivision and subsequent sale of land, some have turned into agropastoralists in the recent past) who were well known for keeping large numbers of livestock such as cattle, goats, and sheep, which were the primary source of their income[4]. Families moved with their livestock from place to place in search of water and pasture for their large herds of livestock, using seasonal-rotational patterns. For this reason, the Maasai required large tracks of land for grazing their animals. Since the Maasai lived under a system of communal ownership, where land traditionally belonged to the entire Maasai community, this system of seasonal rotation was not a problem. They had grazing patterns that were dependent on weather and climatic conditions, and had rules for how the pasture was accessed and used.

Mythological Origin of the Maa Speakers

The mythological origins of the Maa people are shrouded in conflicting stories depending on the current geographical locations of the Maasai as they are now. One common narrative of the origin of the Maa speakers is that God sent the Maa with a sliding hide from heaven. The other narrative is associated with the Maasai, who originated from Palestine and mainly Israel. This is affirmed by some names of certain places in ancient Palestine (Pasinaai, which is Mount Sinai, Mesiri, pronounced Misri in Kiswahili, currently called Egypt, Ongata oo Sidan, current Sudan), Egypt, Sudan, and Kenya. According to the former myth, once on earth, the Maasai

---

3   Known in Maasai as Iloshon, they are the Ildamat, Ilpurko, Ilkeekonyokie, Iloitai, Ilkaputiei, Ildalalekutul (Ilkankere), Isiria, Ilmoitanik, Iloodokilani, Iloitokitoki, Ilarusa, Ilmatatapato, Ilwuasinkishu, Kore, Parakuyu, and Ilkisonko.

4   Maasai Association Website: http://www.maasai-association.org/maasai.html (last accessed January 20, 2019).

found themselves in a desolate land that had no food, so God decided to send cows to them. This is told through the story of *Enkeene-E Nkai* (the rope of God). Several myths recount the lowering of *Enkeene-Enkai*, the rope of God, from heaven to support humanity in its predicament. To address the needs of the Maasai, God sent through *Enkeene E Nkai* the tamed animals, which were mainly the cows, goats, and donkeys, to be sources of milk and for other purposes for the people.

Mythology also has it that the cattle were supposedly meant to be sent to *Iltorobo* (hunter-gatherers), but Maasinta prayed and the cattle were sent to him instead; Maa seized the opportunity by making a required burnt offering to God. This made the Maa and his posterity the beneficiaries of God's blessings, in that God lowered many cattle through a leather thong in a flow that stopped only when the Maa loudly expressed astonishment. Oltoroboni was jealous and shot an arrow at the rope of God, which cut it and stopped the flow of the cattle to the Maasai.

Mythology also has it that the Maasai may be the lost tribe of Israel. According to Maasai myths, and on reflecting on the Bible's Old Testament, narratives of similarities in ancient Babylon have been narrated by the Maasai. Narratives about the experiences of Mount Sinai are still embedded in the Maasai language as a lamentation of when the Maasai broke away from the rest of their people, hence the common phrase *Pasinaai.* This denotes the remembrance of the tragedy on Mount Sinai when the Biblical Moses broke down stone tablets containing the Ten Commandments, scattered the Israelites, and, unfortunately for the Maasai, they travelled down through the Rift Valley. Other similarities with the ancient Jewish practices are the sacrifices, circumcision of men, the use of olive trees during the rituals, and child naming ceremonies. There are stories about similarities in the Jewish and Maasai calendars[5]. Proponents of the mythology have used the Bible verse below to justify their claim:

---

5   This is elaborated further in the section about the Maasai religion.

"Adaiah son of Jeroham, the son of Pashhur, the son of Malkijah; and *Maasai* son of Adiel, the son of Jahzerah, the son of Meshullam, the son of Meshillemith, the son of Immer" (1 Chronicles 9:12).

The land that the Maasai found themselves in was crater-like, surrounded by high escarpments. In remembrance of the Biblical narrative of Moses and the children of Israel, Maasai mythology has it that at one time there was a severe drought that led to suffering. The Maasai observed birds coming down from the steep escarpments with green grass to build their nests. The elders met and decided to send *Ilaikitalak* (spies/ scouts) to go up the steep escarpment and see what the land looks like. It is said that spies had difficulties climbing up the steep escarpment and at times had to crawl or walk sideways. Upon reaching the top, the spies were mesmerized by the green, lush grass, vegetation, and the fertility of the land.

The spies lived in the beautiful country for a few days. They collected different fruits, grass, some soil, and the seeds of all the plants they found, wrapped them with leaves before starting to descend the escarpment. On arrival, the spies were accorded a great reception, and the people celebrated upon seeing what they had brought as evidence of the existence of some good and productive land. After that, the elders deliberated on how to take the people and their livestock to the newly discovered land. They finally decided to construct a bridge. After the bridge was built, the great ascent began. All the people started going up the bridge.

As hundreds of people and their livestock in thousands were climbing the bridge, with half of them having ascended to the top of the plateau of the new land, suddenly, the bridge collapsed. Half the population fell back into the crater. The people who had already ascended could not reach down to help, and those who fell back to the plains in the crater could not ascend because the bridge had collapsed. It is said that many of them died as the bridge was collapsing, but no one among those who had ascended could tell the casualties because they fell so far below that their cries could not be heard. Those that were left behind became *Ilmeek*, non-Maasai.

Once on top of the plateau, the Maasai flourished as their population increased, and their cattle increased in numbers. They lived for many years, and as the population of people and livestock increased, they started spreading over the land. As the expansion of grazing land continued, the Maasai were confronted with people known as *Ilarinkon* who lived on the land. Ilarinkon were said to be tall and fiery people. They were ruled by a giant called *Olarinkoi*. Ilarinkon did not welcome the Maasai but rather instructed them to go away or they would force them back with a fight. The Maasai feared Ilarinkon because they were big, numerous, and had superior weapons. The Maasai tried to negotiate by giving Ilarinkon cattle to appease them, but the Ilarinkon refused to take any cows from the Maasai.

Because the Maasai population had grown and their livestock had increased in numbers, they needed more pastureland for grazing their livestock. They became persistent and went ahead to beg Olarinkoi. To dismiss the Maasai request, Olarinkoi decided to demand gifts that seemed ordinarily impossible to get. Olarinkoi told them to go and get warm, fresh milk that had just been milked from a cow and had the froth[6]. Olarinkoi did this because he knew the Maasai lived far away with their cows, and so there was no way the Maasai could bring fresh, warm milk with froth as requested. The Maasai elders met and hatched a plan; they moved milking cows at night near where Olarinkoi lived, milked the cows very early in the morning[7] , and dashed the warm milk to Olarinkoi. Upon realizing that the Maasai beat him in his own game, Olarinkoi gave the Maasai another challenge. This time, he challenged them to bring a whole guard (calabash) full of fleas. Once again, the Maasai hatched a plan. They cut hair from a donkey's tail into miniature sizes and filled the calabash. When the day to meet Olarinkoi came, the Maasai delegation chose to sit

---

6   This translates in Maa as Kule e Kaiyiam nairowuo naaruko Olaburra."
7   Emanaa enanyokie- First light.

on the side where the wind blows so that when the calabash is opened, the small pieces of donkey hair would be blown away by the wind. As they sat, Olarinkoi demanded that he be given the fleas, since there was a strong wind; once the calabash was opened, the miniature donkey tail hair flew with the wind. This convinced Olarikoi that the Maasai had brought with them real fleas.

During the entire negotiation with Olarinkoi, the Maasai prepared their warriors to fight Ilarinkon. The preparation involved choosing several warriors who were considered strong. They were then fed with meat, milk, and herbs. They practised war games, and finally, one of the warriors was chosen to face Olarinkoi. A meeting was planned between Ilarinkon and the Maasai. As they were sitting to deliberate on what needed to be done and deliberately delaying the talks with Olarinkoi, the warrior who had chosen to kill Olarinkoi was allowed to address the meeting. He paced from end to end during the meeting and came close to Olarinkoi as he was being guided by the elders. They said, *'Tenaa Ira Oloitieu, toosho tiabori enkaluana, naa tenimira nilimu pee kiarr Oloboru Ngotonye*[8]*'*. The warrior jumped and hit Olarinkoi below the ear as instructed and killed him instantly. It is said that the club the warrior used to kill was from Oletukat in the current Narok County. With Olarinkoi dead, the Maasai won over Ilarinkon and took over the land and livestock.

The Maasai and their livestock then grew in numbers and conquered many tribes in East Africa, and it is believed that they travelled south across Tanzania, Malawi, and Zambia until they were stopped by the Zulu from South Africa. The Maasai were pushed back, and along the way, some of them remained in some parts of Zambia and Malawi. The last of their group is currently the Ilparakuyu, who live in the southern part of Tanzania.

The other narrative about the origins of the Maasai is that the Maasai came from some place in the Middle East. This has tales of ancient wars in the Middle East in the ancient

---

8   If you are brave enough, hit him below the lower lobe of the ear, and if you are not, let us know so we can run for our lives.

Mesopotamia. During that time, the Maasai are said to have discovered cooking gas, which *Imotiok Nayier ate* (Pots that cook themselves). During the wars, the Maasai were said to have hidden in caves to escape their enemies, and they developed a code to open the caves (*soit bolo, soit ripa*), the equivalent of *open sesame*. Reminiscence about today's technology may be the first time a man has begun using a password like the one used in today's world. It is said that they migrated to the west and ended up in the current Palestine, where they were faced with long droughts. They settled around Mount Sinai, and as they got tormented by the droughts, they kept asking: *Kanu Kenya esha Pasinaai?* As a way of asking when it will rain.

In reverence to God's manifestation, they looked upon Mount Sinai during their prayers and sacrifices. It is also on Mount Sinai that there was a dispersal of Maasai, where some Maasai clans moved to the west. According to the Maasai oral tales, this is how Mount Sinai (Pasinaai is the cry of desperation when Moses came down from Mount Sinai and dropped the Ten Commandments). Due to droughts, the Maasai moved further west, where they lost all the cows and had no milk to drink and mix into the herbal drinks they were taking. They called the land Mesiri (*the land where waters cannot be coloured with milk*). According to this narrative, this is the current Egypt, which in Kiswahili is called *Misri*. The talk between them was all about where they were going. (*Kaji Ilo*) It is said that the natives of that land translated that to what is now known as Cairo.

As the drought persisted, the Maasai stumbled upon a very big river with waters that were very clean and glittering. They named it *Naitiil Inkariak"(the waters that shine)*. It is said that the River Nile got its name from *Naitiil*. Since they lived in the desert, they decided to find the source of the river by following it southwards. As they moved southwards with few livestock that survived from the drought in *Mesiri*, they found themselves on a very fertile plain that had many ostriches. They called the land *Ongata oo Sidan* (the land of ostriches). This later came to be named Sudan. As they kept on moving southwards in search of the source of the river, they encountered some steep mountains and veered off the course of the river. They ascended to some dry land where they found people who grew crops. Since they needed food, they sought to exchange grains for their livestock. However, they could not speak the local language, so they kept asking the residents whether they could get some grains, *"katum pasa"* (*Will I get grains?*). The term was adopted by the local communities, who pronounced it Khartoum.

The Maasai kept on moving southwards, and some of them veered eastwards and found themselves mingling with people called Ilabashi (the people from Habashia, in the current Ethiopia). There they intermarried and out of them became *Isampurr* (Samburu). The Isampurr also moved to the south, and with them was a group of people, a mixture of people from the Habashia and Iladoru (Somali). Later, these people came to be known as *Irantile* (Rendile). As the Maasai kept moving southwards, they got to a place that had lush grass, a good supply of water, and a good place to settle down. As a sigh of relief, they all said, *"kitabautua kenya"* (we have ultimately arrived). It is said that this is how Kenya, as a country, got its name: Kenya. Therefore, each man was supposed to choose a site to build their homestead because there was plenty of good land and pasture, water, and it became like 'where does one settle?' In the planning, each man was asking themselves which place to settle. In their discourse, each man asked *Kitalate* (We are confused). This place came to be named Kitale.

The Maasai flourished with their herds growing in numbers, which necessitated the need for expansion of grazing land. They expanded their territory in all directions; others went towards *Oldonyio Keri* (Mount Kenya). This is how the Maasai came to occupy Laikipia in Kenya. Because of the increase in their population and that of their livestock, others continued southwards and settled in Kinopop, while others saw a huge mountain with a white peak, *Oldonyio Oiborr,* which came to be called Kilimanjaro. During these moves, the Maasai conquered other tribes, possessed their land, and married their women. The conquests increased their livestock, which necessitated more land. It is said that the Maasai conquered many tribes in Africa until a few of them were stopped from expanding their territory by a warlike tribe that had small spears, small shields, and fought in very close-quarter battles that the Maasai could not challenge with their large shields and long spears. From the local narratives, the tribe meets the description of the Zulu. That is why we have Maasai remnants in southern Tanzania, Zambia, and Malawi.

The Maasai Beliefs and Religion

In describing the Maasai religion, I deliberately use past tenses because a lot has changed due to the influence of education and Christianity. Secondly, I write about God, not god as commonly used by Christians to depict other faiths, which, according to me, demeans other faiths. Just to express my personal philosophy about religiosity, faith, and culture, I posit that it is unfortunate that, other than Professor Mbiti, there are no African scholars who have deconstructed the influence of the new and unknown faith called Christianity that demonized other faiths and was used as a tool for conquests. I grew up witnessing how the Maasai God answered and responded to prayers, so according to me, the Maasai never worshipped a lesser God. The Maasai culture and religion are synonymous, and God was referenced in many instances of the Maasai daily life. It was a common practice that, during sunrise, the elders would wake up to greet God by saying a prayer. Women also used the first drops of milk from the cows they milked to appease God. They threw drops of the milk to the north (*Moikuape*), south (*Kopikop*), east (*Oloosaen*), and west (*Oloontoluo*) as a sign of reverence to God. When warriors were in their meat-eating camps (*ilpuli*), they would wake up before sunrise to pray (*enkipolosa*).

The Maasai diligently observed their religiosity through offering sacrifices to their deity (*Enkai*). The Maa believed in an omnipresent God who was in their daily lives, would answer their prayers, and reveal himself to them by responding to their prayers in times of need. When the community was faced with difficult situations that required divine interventions and in times of prolonged drought, Enkai (God)[9] was offered sacrifices to appease him for rain. The Maasai were monotheistic (Hodgson, 2005). Enkai was a single deity with a dual nature: Black God (*Enkai Narok*), who was benevolent, compassionate, kind, and helpful and Red God (*Enkai Nanyokie*), who could be vengeful and harmful (Hodgson, 2005). The Black God and the Red God represent different aspects of Enkai; they were not two separate deities (Hodgson, 2005). These were the literal names given to Enkai, but Hodgson argues that they should be translated as meaning the divine red and the divine black (p. 23) because people cannot see God with their naked eyes. The Maasai believed that Enkai was the originator and creator of everything on earth. In their prayers, Enkai was perceived as the one who was unique and universal, inherent and transcendent, powerful and righteous, and yet personal and helpful to humankind (Hillman, 1993). The Maa creation story starts with Enkai's conflict with the Entiamasi (the dragon), an enemy who reappears after the fall in other forms, associated with ghosts and all creature threats to life.

In social relations, God had a role as depicted by the many names that the Maasai call him. God among the Maasai was associated with all manner of good tidings. Children grew up with the knowledge and the fear of God. One could hear children say *Maas amu kaadol Enkai* (I will not do wrong because God is seeing me). To entrench God through various names used to refer to Him made the name of God present in everything about the Maasai life. These names include Enkai, Olaitoriani's ruler, Enkoteyiai's mother, Napik Neitayu "puts and removes" (one who is in charge), *Naori Oriki Ai* (the distributor/allocator of gifts and resources). According to the

---

9   Note that I am capitalizing the name God to denote my own believe that contrary to some Christian beliefs; any belief in any other divine name denotes a lesser god. As a Maasai, and having observed the Maasai faith, I am convinced that the Maasai worshiped a true God and not a small god.

Maasai, Enkai was like a parent who had many children. Enkai, who watches over the stars (heavenly children), can similarly keep his earthly children. The Milky Way is sometimes referred to as the cattle of God, or sometimes the entourage of warriors with cattle coming from the raid. In addition, *Leken* is an evening star while *Kileken* is the harbinger of the morning. *Enkakenya sirwa*,[10] the 'light of morning', is a daytime pointer name for God, when everything in creation comes to life. So, all the time, day and night, Enkai was ever-present.

According to Kibasisi (2011), the Maa theology of God was built on a pattern like that of Biblical narratives, where God's glory and interaction with Israel happened through appearances (theophanies) forecasted audio-visually in the arena of atmospheric manifestations[11]. The divine masculine and feminine terms were employed in an acknowledgement of the origins of the Maa as well as of a parent-child relational idea. God in the Maa language was referenced in the many other names that show His manifestation in everyday language among the Maasai. Such references include manifestations of His glory, such as peaceful ones. Enkai Narok, 'the divine black God, is the blue serene sky without any trace of clouds and is the same as *Empus Oshoke,* that is, 'God of the blue stomach'_ God's skydome. *Parmuain,* which means 'God of many colours, is an appearance when the rain is over; the sky displays a proliferation of clouds with a zebra-pattern of colours (i.e., *enkoitiko,* literally a zebra) and *Olosira nkumok* ("God of many colours")[12]. This accords with references to God,

---

10 Enkakenya sirwa is God's name in feminine form but masculine in its function, and it was the name of the ideal time chosen for the confrontation of the Maa armies. This may correspond with entoros, a feminine word depicting supreme warriors.

11 The term Theophanite refers to the manifestation of the Abrahamic God to people; the sensible sign by which His presence is revealed. Only a small number of theophanies are found in the Hebrew Bible, also known as the Old Testament.

12 It is interesting to note that the thought of feminine attributes can also be described in masculine names and variants as Mol puts it: "olosira kumok: he of many stripes, God is indescribable [my translation would be 'God of variant colors' (glory)] oloonmuain kumok: he of diverse colors, God is indescribable" [here I would translate 'God with multiple glory']. Mol, MAA: A Dictionary of the Maasai Language and Folklore, p. 75. This applies also to the rainbow, which the Maasai girls would call olkila le papa "the cloth of my father!" Because the father who offers blessing to the young members of the family is highly respected, his robe is an icon that reflects the covenant bond of Maa with Enkai symbolized by the rainbow "There is something which the Masai call the rainbow (Olokirr

such as Tepisia ("wearer/creator of adornment chains"), *Noosaen Ai* ("one with bracelets"), etc.

It was hard to put a dichotomy between God and the Maasai culture. The religious and socio-cultural structure of a society is a visible means of ascertaining the divine revelation and message to that society. This was to say that the Maasai culture was their religion and their religion was their culture. The past historical actions and current revelations of Enkai through nature and experience form the basis of the Maasai knowledge about God. Understanding the concept of God in Maa is key to interpreting the myths of their origin and religious practices, given their economic and socio-cultural dimensions.

According to available literature, the Maasai traditional religion was one of the purest monotheistic religions in the world (Hauge, 1979).[13] The Maa also used masculine and feminine metaphors to describe God. Such masculine examples include *Olmagilani* ("almighty" as a warrior with war armoury and a shield); *Partulusoo* (the over-generous, the transcendent – the beyond human comprehension, "God is all-wise, etc.); *Parmasio, Oldapash* ("the great one", "the wide one"), which metaphorically applies to an elder's chest surrounded with the family, it is about the greatness and omnipresence of God in the universe; *Oloikurrukur lai* ("my thundering one"). Feminine metaphors are: *Enkai Pasinaai* (the merciful one who sees my trouble), *Pasai* [Parsae] (one worshipped), *Noonkipa* (one with embryonic fluid- provider of fertility), *Parmuain* (God of many colours), *Noolopir lai* or *Noonkopir ai* (one who shelters under the feathers like an eagle), *Enkakenya Sirwa* (my bright one of the morning), and *Nalakua Etaana Ai* (my too far yet so near).

Ai), and if one is seen in the heavens whilst rain is falling, it is a sign that the rain will shortly cease. Children call a rainbow 'Father's garment' on account of its many colors, one part being red, another white, and a third variegated. They also say: 'I will give it to father for he will like it.'" Hollis, The Masai, p.277. Furthermore the word "olkila le papa" is a sacred name used by girls in oath-like confirmation of truth.

13 Hans-Egil Hauge, Maasai Religion and Folklore, Nairobi: City Print Works, 1979), p. 42. The Maa stand on the side of God while cannibalistic monsters were fought against and detested as enemies of God and humanity. On monotheism and the religion of Olmaa see Merker, Die Masai 195-203; 249-251; Vincent J. Donovan, Christianity Rediscovered, p. 21.

The Maasai Social Structure

There are several Maasai sections (sub-tribes of Maasai or Iloshon) based on their socio-territorial and geographical locations and dialect (See figure 1). The Maasai speak the Maa language (Mol, 1996). The Maa language has two internal subdivisions. North Maa includes the Isampur (Samburu) and Ilchamus (Njemps). The South Maa includes the Ilarusa, Ilmoitanik, Isiria, Ilwuasinkishu, Iloodokilani, Ildalalekutuk (Ilkankere), Ildamat, Ilkaputiei, Ilmatapato, Ilkisonko, Iloitai, Ilpurko, Ilparakuyo, and Ilkeekonyokie (Vossen, 1988). Some of these Iloshon are very close linguistically but independent politically.

The focal point of Maasai social institutions was based on clans, and each member of the Maasai people belonged to a clan. Men from a clan address each other as brothers, and there exists a very strong bond and responsibility for each other. Every family is identified by its clan. Maasai clans are believed to have originated in the ownership of cattle. This is derived from the two major pillars of Maasai society: *Oodo Mongi* (the Red Cow) and *Orok Kiteng* (the Black Cow). The Maasai clan system played a significant role in providing leadership and maintaining and sustaining relationships. The clan system specified how marriage and other intimate relationships were supposed to be within the Maasai society (Hodgson, 2005). Historically, men did not marry within their clan because this was seen to be incest and could lead to curses. Similarly, men never married girls who were born in their age group.

The clan also played a crucial role in mending the relationship between clans or even within clans. Clans were viewed as a safety net for not only the clan members but also for the whole community. If, for instance, a clansman lost his livestock, the whole clan met and contributed livestock to their clansperson. They would also raise cattle to pay dowry if a poor member of the clan wanted to marry. In case a member of the clan committed murder, the clan would raise the required forty-nine cows as a requirement/penalty for murder.

The clan system began with the Maa patriarch Naiterukop (Maasinta), the founder of the world, or Oledukuya (the first one). From folklore, Naiterukop is believed to be the founder of the Maasai community. He had two wives. The first wife lived on the right side of the gatepost known in Maasai as *Entailoshi e Tatene,* while the second one was placed at the left-hand (*Entaloishi e Kedienye*) gatepost at the homestead enclosure. The first wife had cattle that were all red. That's why her house was called " Maa Odomongi, " meaning "the one of which the calves and oxen are red". This wife gave birth to three sons, namely Lolkesen, Lelian, and Losero. The descendants of the three sons became Ilmakesen (of baboon), Ilmolelian (of elephants), and Il-taarosero (of the hyena) clans, respectively, which are together known as Odomongi.

The second wife, who lived on the left side of the gate post known as Orokiteng, had calves and oxen that were black in colour. Her house is called "the one of which the calves and oxen are black" in. This wife gave birth to two sons, namely Lukum and Naiser. The descendants of the two became the Ilukumai and Ilaiserr clans, which are represented by the raven and rhinoceros, respectively. Together, Ilukumai and Ilaiserr are known as Orokiteng. The five sons are the founding fathers of the five major clans in Maasai society. Clans are very important among the Maasai, as clan members have a very strong communal support/obligation. The members normally have the same branding of their cattle. Clans also have a very important role in the Maasai political system. They are known in Maasai as *Olgilata* (Ilgilat in plural). Clan members help each other settle disputes and matters related to marriage, including negotiations and obtaining bride-price.

Among the Maa-speaking communities, other small sections lived among them, but due to the nature of their work, they were considered people of a lower caste. These were *Ilkunono* (the blacksmiths*),* *Iltorobo* (the hunter-gatherers), and *Inkidongi* (the medicine men). Due to their roles, they were absorbed or adopted into the various Maasai clans and are still identifiable today among the Maasai clans. The *Ilkunono* were known to be secretive, unlike the other sections of Maasai, and they mainly lived among the *Ilkeekonyokie* and *Ilpurko* subclans.

They were feared among the Maasai since they were seen to be merchants of death as they made things like arrows, spears, swords, and many other warfare equipment and weapons. They were despised, and their girls were not married by the main clans. When they slept in people's homes, the cowhide that was spread on the bed was overturned. Later, as communities progressed, they were assimilated into the other Maasai communities. Many of their families are found around Oloirowua among Ilkeekonyokie and Leshuta among Ilpurko, but they are also widely spread among other Maasai Iloshon (sub-tribes). Iltorobo, on the other hand, were also despised for their way of life as they did not have livestock, but they had roles to play among the Maasai. They supplied honey, which was used to make liquor. This liquor was used in almost all Maasai ceremonies. They also supplied special monkey skins (Ilkoroin and Indeeri) that were worn by elders and warriors. Some of them were also the circumcisers. They had a dialect of their own and lived around Mau, Enoosupukia, and other forests in Laikipia, where they are known as Iltorobo Lolchoki.

Mythology of the origin of Inkidongi says that the Inkidongi are descendants of Saei Kidongoe. Saei Kidongoe was said to have been a male child who was found by shepherds in the Ngong Hills (Oloolaiserr). Saei Kidongoe was said to have had some supernatural powers, where he could foretell events, and as young as he was, he started giving the elders advice on various events, including when it was going to rain, when the next drought was expected, and many others. He was adopted, and as he grew up, he trained others on his "magic". Inkidongi were known to be medicine men and seers. They were also known to produce *Iloibonok,* who were consulted by each Olosho. It is believed that Inkidongi are all descendants of Oloiboni Mpatiany, who was a descendant of Saei Kidongoe.

They are mostly concentrated in Kisokon, where Chief Oloiboni, who is a descendant of Senteu and son of Mbatiany, is. The descendants of Olonana are found around Kirarapon, Ooloolua, and Enoomatasiani, as well as other parts of the Maasai land. Some were assimilated by other Maa clans, and the Kikuyu around Ngong and Kiambu were mostly assimilated due to intermarriages. According to Maasai narratives, it is said that Jomo

27

Kenyatta had some relationship with Inkidongi and, at one time, lived in Naroosura, which is currently Narok County. It is suggested that the Kenyatta family, by virtue of this relationship, came to live in the current Lenana and Karen areas in Nairobi.

Inkidongi were feared by the rest of the Maasai because some of them practised witchcraft. They had special powers that created fear among many who did not understand them. Contrary to what present Christians portray Inkidongi as witches, Inkidongi are not witches, even though there were a few of them who practised witchcraft, like in many other African communities. The demonization of Inkidongi should be seen from the perspective of the conquests of the heathen and demonization by Christians concerning people of other faiths and cultures, which is still evident in the world we live in today, in the form of racism. The true Oloiboni was a seer, a defender, and an advisor to the community. All such prejudices against the Iltorobo, Ilkunono, and Inkidongi have since ceased due to modernization and what has commonly come to be known as *maendeleo* (modernization), Christianity, and other globalization processes that have influenced the lifestyle of the Maasai.

Central to the Maasai social structure was the age group (age-set). The age group is constituted over time. A new age-set (*Olporror/Olaji*) was established every seven or so years, a successive pair of age-sets (*Olaji*) on a fourteen-year cycle (Spear and Waller, 1993)[14]. I am using the terms age group and age sets interchangeably because of how and when both terms are used. This system was very important in the life of a Maasai because it provided an opportunity for the young men who were expected to take over from the elders to build a sense of brotherhood and solidarity. It is also in this age group that the Maasai had warriors who played the role of the army and defended the community. Each age group has left and right components, which are divided into seven-and-a-half-year periods after their circumcision[15].

---

14 This has since changed a lot since many Maasai communities have abandoned warriorhood. In some cases, many young Maasai men do not even know their age group or clan because circumcision has become more of a family affair.

15 This is mainly done by the rest of Maasai Iloshon except for Ilkisonko and Ilkaputiei who have their warriors stay for longer periods of warriorhood.

Each age group lasted between seven and fifteen years. The relationship between the members of each age group was almost closer than that of the blood brothers. If a member of the age group lost his livestock to theft or sickness, he would be given other animals to start over by his comrades. This group's social system lasted throughout their lives. It was during occasions like age group festivals, ceremonial groups (*Olamal*), circumcision ceremonies, weddings, and passage to junior elders that young men got to learn *Inkoon* (stories about their past and culture).

They also got to learn the great deeds of their ancestors and the myths and legends of the past generations. One of the major cultural values that anchored the life of a Maasai was respect for oneself, others, and society. The age sets instilled respect among their members. Disgracing acts were punishable within the age-set system. One could be fined dearly by their age-mates or the age-set leadership, or mentors if found guilty of a dishonourable act that might dent the image of the age-group[16]. The role of women in the age-set structure was that of being wives to the age-set that they are married to, and mothers to the age-set that their sons and daughters belong to. No man married children from their age-set or clan[17]. Many times, the members of the age group would organize for *Olpul* (meat-eating hideout), where each member was expected to contribute an ox for slaughter. Those who were not able to contribute were incorporated into groups in the spirit of comradeship, which was a cardinal virtue of the age-group system. Due to the many changes that have happened over time, the Olpul system is now organized by friends, relatives, and neighbours, but it is not as elaborate as it was in the past.

It is within the age set that young men, under the supervision of elders, were trained to be responsible adults. Each age group had its own group of leaders called *Inkasisin*, who facilitated age group ceremonies. The Inkasisin were divided into four leadership positions: the

---

16 The fines ranged from a heifer which is the highest price one would pay to a goat depending on the nature the act that one performed.

17 Lately, this has greatly changed due to the influence of school, and the decline of adherence to the Maasai culture by younger generations.

Olaiguenani, Olotuno, Oloboru Enkeene, and Olopolosi Olkiteng. Each of these leaders had their own specific roles and responsibilities. The Olaiguenani (chief) was the first position to be filled as a new age group develops. He was secretly selected by *Olpiron* from a family that was known to have no blemish. He was chosen as a chief because of his skills and abilities to handle disputes and mediate conflicts in the age group and the larger community, as well as to consolidate consensus in community decision-making. He was also chosen because of their family background. Before Olaiguanani was selected by the elders, they investigated the family lines of each potential candidate, and the one among them who had the best family background and was of good moral and social character was chosen. He was expected not to rule as a dictator or in a traditional hierarchical position but as a mediator in the conflict. Traditional Maasai society had no centralized political structures; hence, governance relied heavily on the age-set system.

As each boy was circumcised, he was incorporated into a generational category, or age-set. He and his cohorts passed through the stages of warriorhood (*murrano*), junior elder, senior elder, and retired elder, each stage lasting about 15 years[18]. The senior elders held their meetings under certain trees; their meetings were referred to as *Ilkiushin* (*Olkiu*-Singular), and their deliberations or meetings had the primary responsibility for the traditional administration in Maasailand. Same age groups from across all Maasai sections shared a name, and their leadership was known to each other. Decisions regarding the naming of age groups were made by senior elders in consultations with the traditional seer (*Oloiboni*), who performed rituals to bind the age groups; by performing traditional rites which were strictly observed by all who belonged to the age group. Families and children from the same age group consider themselves related, and that girls from that age group will never be married to men from their father's age group, as it is considered incest and punishable.

---

18 This has since gradually changed but one can still find some pockets of communities maintain the practice, but the time periods has drastically reduced to between 3-4 years.

While this is the general case for all the Maa speakers, some of the Maasai clans have specific names that are neither included in the main *Ilgilat* (Clans). According to S.S. Ole Sankan (1971), these include the Iloshon as shown in Table 1 below.

Table 1: Iloshon, Clan names, and Clan Identity

Oloshon (Sub-Tribe)	Clan name	Clan Identity
Isampur (Samburu)	Ilpusi Kisu Iloig'geli Ilmasula Iloorrok Kishu Ilukumae Iloimisi Ilanat Ilnyaparrai Ilguesi	Ilmakesen-Odomongi Ilmolelian-Odomongi Iltaarrosero-Odomongi Ilaiserr-Orok Kiteng Ilukumae-Orok Kiteng Orok Kiteng Orok Kiteng Orok Kiteng Orok Kiteng
Ildalalekutiuk (Illkankere)	Ilkarat Ilmakuperiani Ileparsiria Ileshoi Ilkupere Seroikineji Ilpojoos Ilmoshoho Ilporre Ileparmootian Ilmakarau	Ilmolelian-Odomongi Ilmakesen-Odomongi Iltaarosero-Odomongi Odomongi Odomongi Ilaiserr-Orok Kiteng Ilukumae-Orok Kiteng Orok Kiteng Orok-Kiteng Orok-Kiteng Orok-Kiteng
Ilwuasi Nkishu and Ilmoitanik	Ilparsaman Ilnyayia Isaikong Ilmasarunye Ilkoitileni Iloiborrsampin Ilkokoyo Ilkisamoot	Ilmakesen-Odomongi Iltaarosero-Odomongi Ilmolelian-Odomongi Odomongi Ilaiserr-Orok Kiteng Ilukumae Orok Kiteng Orok Kiteng

Adopted from S.S. Ole Sankan, 1971.

The Maasai Rites of Passage and Ceremonies

A rite of passage is a ceremony that marks the transition from one phase of life to another. Rites of passage among the Maa-speaking people are milestones that mark the progression from one stage in life to another. They were key in defining one's identity, association, and place in society. When a Maasai child was born, the child was given a pet name. When the child reached a certain age, and depending on the clan they came from, the child was given another name. This ceremony, which was synonymous with Christian baptism, is called *Enkitupukunoto Tiaji*. By this time, the child, both boys and girls, would have undergone the removal of the two front lower teeth (*Embuata*). This was done so as to facilitate feeding in case one got sick of lockjaw, which was a common disease. This was followed by the piercing of the upper ear lobes (*Orkitipet*). It is also during this time that they were subjected to leg marks or tattoos (*Ilkipirat),* which were done on both thighs using fire.

Upon reaching puberty, both girls and boys were subjected to another signature event, the piercing of the lower earlobes (*Esegerua*). At this stage, the girls would have been receiving training from the elderly women on how to become good wives and responsible mothers. The boys, on the other hand, received training in fighting and protecting the herds, families, and the community. All these were minor acts in preparation for the main rites of passage. These rites of passage between boys and girls were different in that girls got circumcised and given out as wives, while boys had to go through a series of rites of passage to make them protectors of the community against external aggression and responsible fathers. This was so because it was boys who established age groups (Olporror).

Key among the many ceremonies and rites of passage events in Maasai society were *Enkipaata*(senior boy ceremony), *Emuratta* (circumcision), *Eunoto* (end of warriorhood), and *Olgesherr*(end of junior eldership). Other rights of passage were *Enkiama* (marriage), *Eokoto e-kule* (milk-drinking ceremony), and *Enkang Oo-nkiri* (meat-eating ceremony). Circumcision of boys among the Maasai was associated with their origins in the Middle East (Mesopotamia), which, according to the myths, was a command from God. The Maasai never used to circumcise girls until a time when spies from an enemy tribe befriended a girl and she gave them secrets about the location of Maasai warriors. As a way of punishing the women for setting the warriors up through intimate relationships with the enemies, they started circumcising girls.

For the boys, their first initiation ceremony is Enkipaata (pre-circumcision ceremony) and was organized by the fathers of the new age set (*Olpiron*). Enkipaata happened only when the senior warriors were settled. A fraternity of boys, aged fourteen to sixteen years, travelled across their section for about four to six months, announcing the formation of their new age-set. The boys were accompanied by a group of elders spearheading the formation of a new age-set. Men would form age-sets, moving them closer to adulthood. As I alluded to previously, despite sharing the same dialect and many traditional practices, the rites of passage are celebrated differently, especially among Ilchamus and Isampur.

The Maasai Leadership Structure

As opposed to the current leadership structure, the traditional Maasai leadership structure emanated from the age-group (*Olporror*). Traditional Maasai society had no centralized political structures, and governance relied heavily on the age-set system. As each boy was circumcised, he was incorporated into a generational category, the age-set. As indicated previously, the boy and his cohorts passed through the stages of a warrior (*murrano*), junior elder, senior elder, and retired elder, each lasting about fifteen years. The senior elders led all deliberations in which the family sat at the top of the heap in leadership and was primarily responsible for the traditional administration in Maasailand.

As explained in the previous section, every age group succeeded another upon graduation into junior eldership; they handed the leadership mantle to the upcoming age group. Each age group had its own group of leaders called *Inkasis*, who facilitated age group ceremonies. Also, as indicated before, the Inkasis were divided into three offices: the *Olaiguanani, Olotuno, Oloboru Enkeene,* and *Olopolosi Olkiteng.* There was also another set of unofficial leaders called *Inkopirr.* They played roles that were designated by Inkasis. The Olaiguanani was honoured with a specially chosen female cow and a special black club (*Orinka*), which was blessed by *Olpiron.* Oloboru Ekeene was honoured with a leather strap and a knot that symbolized his age set. By the end of warriorhood, this knot would be untied to free the warriors from their isolated world. The knot allowed warriors to do things independently of their age mates. This stage of life was a transition to being an elder. As alluded to in the previous section about the Maasai leadership structure, each of the leaders had a specific role that guided how the community was to conduct its affairs in consultation with elders and the spiritual person, Oloiboni.

Historical Intra-Maasai Wars

The Maasai history is characterized by wars among several Maasai Iloshon (clans). Arising from intra-sub-clan wars, some of the Maasai clans that ruled East Africa are now extinct, and some of their remnants were assimilated into existing Maasai sub-clans or other Kenyan ethnic communities that they sought refuge in. Most of these wars were carried out by a combined force of other Maasai for territorial control and the amassing of livestock. The earliest known intra-Maasai war was in *Iltaarmodoon.* The narratives of how this Maasai Olosho (sub can) was annihilated are very sketchy and narrated by the Iltareto, Ilterito, and Ilnyankusi, who, unfortunately, are almost all dead[19]. Narratives have it that, after being defeated, the Iltaarmoddon ran to the forest and became Iltorobo Lolokirisiai. It is said that afterwards, they left the forest and joined the Ildamat sub-clan. Among Ildamat, they are now known as *Ilpedees.*

Iloogol Ala was another Maasai sub-clan that was fought

---

19 As the case of Iltareto and Ilterioto are all dead, while the living Ilnyankusi have gone senile at the time of writing the manuscript.

and vanquished by other Maasai subclans. According to oral narratives, the Iloogol Ala were a very powerful section of the Maasai. The Iloogolala, who occupied Purka, were attacked and wiped out by the combined forces of the IlMaasai and the Iloikop, leaving the whole area between Entorrorr and Kipaya almost empty. They were defeated, and the remnants were absorbed by the conquering Maasai clans. It is important to note that during the intra-Maasai conquests, the Maasai believed in *Kiyela,* the act of adopting or assimilating the remnants of the conquered people. The remnants were assimilated by all the Maasai sub-clans that conquered them, and families were separated since the conquering Maasai were from different Iloshon. They ended up belonging to different Maa sub-clans and different *Ilgilat.*

Another Maasai sub-tribe that was fought and vanquished by the Maasai were the Ilosekelai. After their defeat, the Ilosekelai were absorbed (*aayel*) by Ilaikipiak. They were adopted and became part and parcel of the Ilaikipiak clans, and they ceased to exist as a sub-tribe. Ilosekali were also the beneficiaries of an earlier conquest of Ilkoki, who, because of their inferior numbers, were fought and defeated by the other Maasai sub-tribes, and their remnants absorbed by the Ilaikipiak.

Another Maasai Olosho that was vanquished was the Idikirri. After their defeat, the remnants are said to have moved into the forest and became Iltorobo. The remnants are now found in Laikipia County and call themselves the Laikipia Maasai, but, according to the Maasai, they were considered Iltorobo, which is probably the cause of the conflicts between Isampur and the Laikipia Maasai(who are commonly referred to by the Samburu as Iltorobo).

The last major Maasai group that was collectively fought by a combined force of other Maasai groups was Ilaikipiak. Ilaikipiak were known to have very strong and brave warriors who waged wars with almost all the other Maasai groups. They had superior fighting skills and outnumbered the other groups. Their raids were mainly to extend their grazing territories and to acquire more cows, and often they would take with them the most beautiful girls. Then, the Ilaikipiak, using their superior power, turned on their relatives, the Ilwuasinkishu and the Isampurr, and reduced them to minimal numbers. The Isampurr were lucky because they had the vast dry land towards Lake Turkana to resort to. The Ilpurko took this opportunity to disable the Ilwuasinkishu. They killed Oloiboni Lolgos and annihilated the whole family and seized all the tribes' belongings, taking away domestic animals together with young wives and girls. Only a few families were lucky enough to escape from Nakuru to Mao Nanyokie, and they settled in Ang'ata Nanyokie. Ang'ata Nanyokie is probably the area between the Mau summit and Entebes (Intepes) in the Kitale area.

Ilaikipiak turned their wrath on other Maasai subclans, harassing them and annexing their lands to expand their grazing area. The Ildamat, Ilpurko, Ilkisonko, Ilkeekonyokie, Ildalalekut, and Ilkaputiei were subjected to frequent attacks by Ilaikipiak. All the other Maasai subclans were rendered poor, necessitating a strategy to counter the Ilaikipiak menace. With the advice from the elders and blessings from Mpatiany, warriors from each Maasai section started attacking from different fronts. It is said that, for the warriors who may be filled with fear not to run back, dry grass was tied with a long leather rope, and a fire was lit such that the warriors were dragging the burning grass as they advanced. The fire spread from all directions, further confusing the Ilaikipiak warriors who were caught unaware by the invading warriors. Entorrorr was surrounded by armies from all the Maasai clans, and within a short time, the Ilaikipiak were defeated. Their possessions were plundered, and a few lucky families were rescued by relatives. These lucky ones were scattered throughout Maasailand.

One of the Maasai subclans that escaped annihilation is the Ilmoitanik. Originally, Ilmoitanik were part of the two houses of Ilwuasinkishu. Initially, Ilwuasinkishu were one house, but there came a time when there was a split to form two houses, the Orange (*Enkaji Mugie*) house and the Blackhouse (*Enkaji Narok*). Before the split, Muneria ole Kantai was their seer (*Oloiboni*). After the split, Ole Kantai became the seer for the Black House. Since cattle raids had to have the blessings of the seer, warriors from the Orange House went to seek blessings from Ole Kantai. The warriors were successful and brought back many cattle after raiding neighbouring tribes.

On hearing that their seer had blessed the warriors from the Orange House and their raid was very successful, warriors from the Black House were bitter with Ole Kantai, who was their seer. They hatched a plan and killed him. The killing of Ole Kantai angered the Orange House, and they decided to avenge his death by fighting the Black House. They organized and gathered their forces and set out to punish the Black House for the killing of Ole Kantai. The latter were defeated, and the remnants migrated to settle at a place called Moita (Mumias). Later, they came back, but upon their return, they were named Ilmoitanik, meaning those who hailed from Moita.

Since independence, there have been some conflicts that have resulted in the loss of lives among several Maasai Iloshon. These conflicts still portend high risk since the main cause of such conflicts is land. Recently, in Transmara in Narok County, there was a major clash between two clans, the Ilwuasinkishu and the Isiria, who have had a long-standing dispute over the land boundary. There has always been a potential for conflict between the Keekonyokie from both Narok and Kajiado and Ilpurko over a disputed boundary at Endarkalal and Oldepe. There were also conflicts in the early 1970s between Ilmatapato and Ildalalekutuk, as well as Ilpurko and Iloodokilani, where many lives were lost. In Ntulele in Narok County, a conflict over land involved the Ildamat, Keekonyokie, and Ilpurko in the late 1980s and early 1990s. The Ilpurko and Iloitai have had boundary-related conflicts in such areas as Osupuko and Ongata E Loita.

While this is the case in the inter-Maasai conflicts, it should be noted that the Maasai have had conflicts with other ethnic groups that border the Maasai country. Most of the conflicts between the Maasai and other communities arise from expansionist strategies by other ethnic groups and political domination. The Ilchamus in Baringo have had perennial battles with the Pokots, resulting in the loss of life and destruction of property. The Maasai who live in Nakuru have had several conflicts with both the Kikuyu in the general Maa Mahiu area and the Kalenjin at Olchurai. In Narok, the conflicts between the Maasai and the Kipsigis have been recurring, and, more recently, because of the evictions in the Mau forest. The Kisii have also had running battles with the Maasai due to livestock thefts. In Kajiado, the Ilkaputiei have had conflicts with the Kamba due to unsettled boundary claims along the Mombasa- Nairobi railway line, which was the historical boundary. The Ilkisonko have also had conflicts with the Taita in the Njukini area, but this has been recently addressed by the Kajiado County Governor, Ole Lenku, and his Taita counterpart.

The Maasai and their Pre-Colonial Geographical Localities

By the mid-19th century, the Maasai territory was at its largest, extending over pretty much the entirety of modern-day Kenya and half of Tanzania. In the 19th Century, the European powers were fighting for colonies. They occupied several regions that were divided by multiple international borders between British Kenya and German Tanganyika. In 1885, during the Berlin Conference, the Maasai land was divided between the British and the Germans.

An interview with Marianyi Ole Kertela conducted by Gerald Hanley at the studios of the Kenya Broadcasting Corporation in Nairobi, about 1970, is probably the only available written Maasai narrative about the lands occupied by the Maasai. According to Ole Kertela's interview, which was corroborated by other Maasai narratives, the Maasai territory extended to Ilorroki (Lorogi) and Kisima in the current Samburu County_ all through the Rift Valley, and covered land up to parts of the current Taveta County. Iloodokilani occupied the land on the floor of the Rift Valley in the present Kajiado County, bordering Ilmatapato to the east and extending all the way north between Endonyio Narok, Esonorua, and Inkurman escarpment all the way to Mosiro. The Iloitai occupied all the land west of Enkare Ngiro (River Wuaso Ngiro) in the present-day Narok County, extended all through Loita (Loita plains), Osupuko Oirobi, Entatsikira, and right across to Ongata e Sirinket (Serengeti plains) in Tanzania. On the western side, their boundary was Enkare E Nkipai (the Mara River).

The Ilkaputiei occupied the whole of Ngong, Ooolaiser (the Ngong hills), including Rura, Kukuya, Narok Omon (where the Kenya Defence Forces 7th Battalion is located). All those areas include Inkariak (Nairobi), Naresho (Ngong Forest), Ilkejek Onyokie, Olmanie Loo Nkoben, Kapete (Kabete), Enteijia (Ndeiya), and Lemorog (Limuru). Among them were the Inkidongi who lived in Kerarapon, Oloolua, Olepolos, and Enoomatasiani. Their land extended towards Oldonyio Sapuk and the Ongata E Kaputiei (Kapiti Plains) past Ololtibili (the hills near the current Daystar University). The Ilkisonko (Iloitokitoki) occupied all the area around Oldoiyo Oibor (Mount Kilimanjaro), Oloitokitok, Osilalei, Lolpenyet, Ongata e Kinyawa (the Simba Plain), right up to a place called Oloitilai le Mosonik and Ildoiyo Lolkirosion. They lived side by side with Ilkaputiei. Their land extended southwards, where they bordered on Iltupeita (the Taita), Kenya, and Chaga, Tanzania. On the western side, their land extended to Olgulului to Olkeju Leselenkei, where they bordered Ilmatapato. Ilmatapato occupied all the land extending from Oldonyio Orok and northwards towards Olkejuado (Kajiado) and bordered Ilkaputiei from Oloontulugum to Indonyio Enkorika.

The Ilkeekonyokie were at Kinopop (Kinangop) until the Maasai were forced to leave that area by the colonialists after the signing of the Maasai agreements of 1904 and 1911 (the agreements will be discussed in detail later). They were at Kinopop, Sision, Imunyi, and extended westward and bordered Ilpurko at Olomuruti. Their land extended from Olenkijape (Kijabe), Kitilikini, and all through the peaks of the Aberdare Ranges (Enkushuai E Simel, and Enkume) to Enaiururr (Nayhururu). Ilkeekonyokie lived side by side with Ildalalekutuk (Ilkankere), and their land extended to a place called Karat (Karati). Ilpurko occupied all the northern land. Their land extended southwards towards Ongata-Olbartan (The Plains of Horses), Ongata Pus, and extended eastwards to Enkutoto E Purko towards Oldonyio Keri (Mount Kenya). The Isampur (Samburu) occupied the lower drier parts of the country (*Olpurkel*), the whole area of Oldonyio Le Ngiro (Mount Nyiro), and northward towards Marsabit. On the southern side, Ilpurko lived side by side with Ildamat, who occupied the land around Enaiposha (Naivasha), Morintat, and all the way to Nakuro (Nakuru). They occupied all the land on the East side of Engare Ngiro, including Engare Narok (Narok River), Siyapei River, all the way to Enesampulai, Enaiborr Ajiik, and all the land towards Enaiposha.

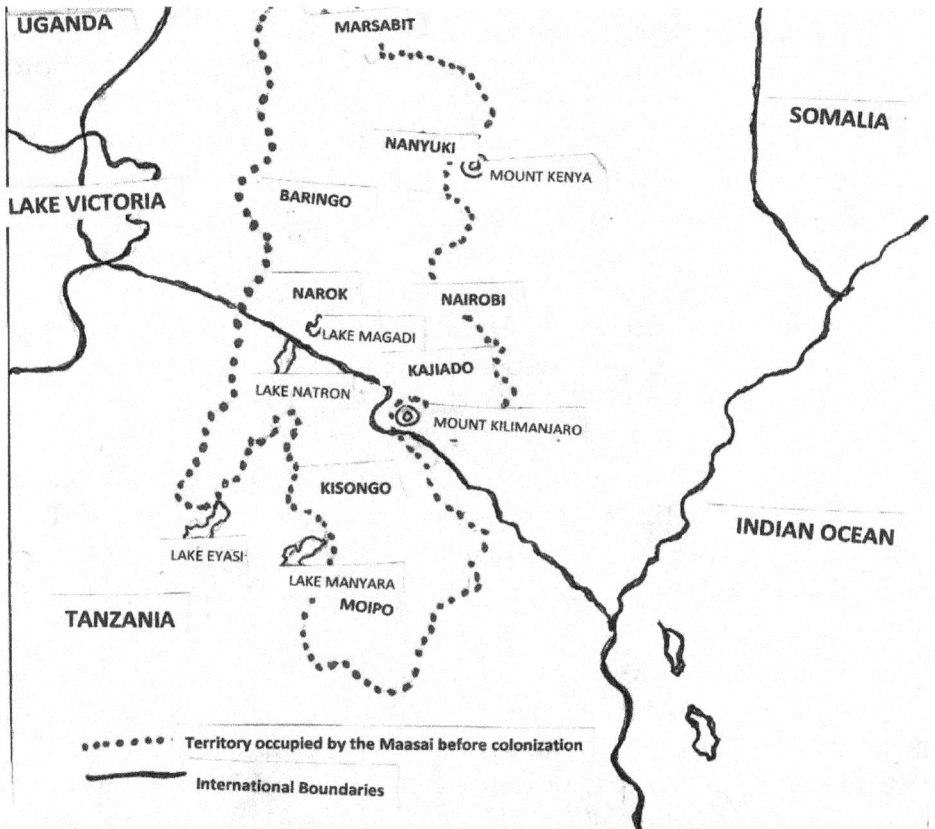

Figure 1: Perceived Maasai Territory before Colonization

The map by the author is based on narratives and personal travels around most of the areas previously occupied by the Maasai.

40

PART III:

THE MAASAI AND COLONIZATION

The European Perceptions of the Maasai

There is little literature about Maasai contacts with the external world before the Europeans came to Africa by the Maasai themselves. While this is the case, local narratives suggest that before the Europeans, the Maasai had contact with Arab traders. A lot has been said about the Maasai being a barrier to the slave trade due to their geographical location in Kenya, which created a hindrance for Arab slave traders. According to narratives, the Arabs interacted with the Maasai for the Ivory and salt trade. The Arabs were said to use the Kamba as couriers, and in the process, they employed some Maasai who ended up being slaves once they arrived at the coast. It has been said that there are Maasai families that have silky hair because they were born of the Arab traders.

Available old and new literature includes details of how early European and modern Western scholars started stereotyping the Maasai. The European perceptions of the Maasai and other African communities were informed by early explorers and missionaries who came to East Africa. Such explorers included the likes of James Bruce (1790); Mungo Park (1799); Richard Burton (around 1856); David Livingstone (1857,1866, 1874); John Speke (1864); James Grant (1864); and Henry Morton Stanley (1872, 1878). These scholars provide sources for this information. These explorers and missionaries mainly wrote about their encounters with the Maasai. Among the explorers was Joseph Thompson, who wrote a book titled: *Through Maasai Land.*

Thompson's writings about the Maasai and other pastoralists portrayed them as wandering people with no fixed abode. Joseph Thomson was sent by the Royal Geographical Society in 1883 to find a direct route between the coast and Lake Victoria and is credited as being the first European to cross Kenyan Maasailand in the 1880s (Thomson, 1885). In some of his writings, Thompson was quoted thus:

"We soon set our eyes upon the dreaded warriors that had so long been the subject of my waking dreams, and I could not but involuntarily exclaim, what splendid fellows as I surveyed a band of the most peculiar race of men to be found in Africa' (Thomson, 1885).

These writings and others contributed to the stereotyping of the Maasai as a bloodthirsty, martial race that had prevented European commercial exploitation of upcountry East Africa. The thinking was probably a result of tales from the coastal people who had historical Maasai raids and feared the Maasai. Stories by Arab slave traders who were prevented by the Maasai from venturing into some parts of the East African hinterland for the ivory and slave trade also helped to propel this narrative.

This stereotyping was also expressed by early missionaries Johannes Rebmann and Ludwig Krapf, who were sent by the British Church Missionary Society (CMS). Both Rebmann and Kraft explored the Kilimanjaro, Ukambani, and Usambara regions between 1847 and 1852. In his journals, Kraft stated this about the Maasai:

"They are dreaded as warriors, laying all waste with fire and sword, so that the weaker tribes do not venture to resist them in the open field, but leave them in possession of their herds, and seek only to save themselves by the quickest possible flight" (Krapf 1860, 359–60).

To add emphasis to his perceptions, he recorded in his journal, stating that:

"These worst of heathen; these truculent savages who conquer or die, death having no terrors for them; and further said they do not make slaves of their prisoners but kill men and women alike in cold blood" (Krapf 1860, 365–66).

This stereotyping of indigenous people is affirmed in the 'Doctrine of Discovery', which provided a framework for Christian explorers, in the name of their sovereign, to lay claim to territories uninhabited by Christians. If the lands were vacant, then they could be defined as "discovered" and sovereignty claimed. According to Steve Newcomb: -

"The Doctrine of Discovery established a spiritual, political, and legal justification for colonization and seizure of land not inhabited by Christians. It has been invoked since Pope

Alexander VI issued the Papal Bull 'Inter Caetera' in 1493" (Newcomb, 2008).

The Doctrine of Discovery created the principle of *Terra nullius*, a Latin expression derived from Roman law meaning *"land belonging to no one"*. It is used in international law to describe territory which has never been subject to the sovereignty of any state, or over which any prior sovereign has expressly or implicitly relinquished sovereignty. Sovereignty over territory that is *terra nullius* may be acquired through occupation. This is how the new narratives facilitated and continue to facilitate the gentrification of Africa's "empty lands". The concept of Terra nullius has been variously used by post-colonial governments in Africa to appropriate land from many indigenous communities. This has been the case in Kenya, where land occupied by pastoral communities has commonly been referred to as "idle land"; hence, the government and investors in land-related development need to have access to undertake development.

Unfortunately, the notion/perspective of Europeans about the Maasai, as portrayed by most of the scholars who have written about the Maasai, can be transcribed as an attitude of ownership, authenticity, and superiority of their written narratives. This has been done to the extent that they look down upon literature that is written by the Maasai themselves. They perceive themselves as the custodians of the Maasai story to levels where they have entrenched historical narratives from the early European explorers and missionaries, and their publications, to demean the real Maasai narratives. However, there is limited literature by the Maasai themselves to deconstruct this narrative, and the Maasai elites have accepted and embraced these narratives and speak with the voice and tone of the Euro-centric and Western scholars whose interests are not about the Maasai, but to distort the story so they can gain leverage in the literary world. As well and regrettably so, the stereotyping of the Maasai is still rife in Kenya, where other non-Maasai communities perceive the Maasai as backward just because they have stuck to their culture.

The Arrival of the European Settlers

In Africa, like elsewhere in the world, at the dawn of the 18th century, the British used deception and, more importantly, their military strength to alienate land for British settlers at the expense of the local populations (Vambe, 1972). The arrival of the colonialists in Africa in the late 1800s and the beginning of the 1900s ushered in a new and devastating century-long governance and economic system that was not in tandem with indigenous systems. From the advent of colonialism to date, this has made colonial history one that is characterized by the infringement of the rights of the native communities in Kenya.

The scramble for Africa, which culminated in the Berlin Conference of 1884-1885, when the Europeans partitioned Africa into spheres of political, military, and economic influence, led to the colonization of the African continent. This marked the beginning of more than a century-long grievance by Indigenous African communities (Michalopoulos & Papaioannou, 2012). The Europeans divided the territories and drew boundaries on their maps, without considering the local geographic conditions or the ethnic composition of the territories. African leaders were not invited to attend the conference. The literature has argued that the exercise was arbitrary. For example, Asiwaju argued that the study of European archives supported the accidental rather than a conspiratorial theory of the marking of African boundaries, and was purely unfair (Asiwaju, 1985).

It has also been argued that most of the conflicts in Africa today arose from the partitioning of Africa and the exploitation of resources by the colonial governments, and post-independent regimes that adopted the colonial governance systems (Asiwaju, 1985; Wesseling, 1996; Wimmer et al, 2009; Englebert et al, 2002; Miguel, 2007; Bates, 1981, and Herbs, 2000). Kenya was officially declared a British Protectorate on June 15th, 1895. The declaration marked the beginning of a massive land takeover from the natives to create settlements for the British settlers (Syagga, 2011). With the Declaration of Protectorate, the stage was set for the systematic expropriation and exploitation of native lands.

By the time the British administration was established in the 1890s, the Maasai were recovering from devastating blight rinderpest (bovine pleuro-pneumonia), smallpox, and drought. Blight rinderpest disease was first recorded in 1891 in Maasailand on the slopes of Mt Kilimanjaro. Raiders brought diseased cattle back to the interior from the coast at the end of 1890, and within months, the Oloitokitok cattle were destroyed. Efforts to replenish stocks by raiding the herds of the neighbouring Kamba proved fruitless since they were also suffering from the effects of the scourge. By the early 1990s, the disease had reached the Maasai settlements of the Kinopop and Kedong valley. With rinderpest destroying the economy and weakening the fighting ability of the Maasai, the British were able to extend their rule over the area.

The European settlers coveted the land occupied by the Maasai as it provided a good environment that suited their economic endeavours. The early Europeans recommended the Laikipia highlands because of the climatic conditions and encouraged those willing to settle to come and take over the land. The settlers were mainly the Boers (*Ildashi*) from South Africa and the British. The Maasai nomadic way of life that required them to move from place to place further encouraged the Europeans to covet the land, which they deemed vacant. While nomadism portrayed the Maasai as people of no fixed abode, it also created a challenge because their movement constrained government control.

To facilitate acquisition of land from the African natives, the Land Acquisition Act of India (1894) was extended to Kenya and used to appropriate all the land situated within one mile of either side of the Ugandan Railway for the construction of the railway as well as the compulsory acquisition of land for government buildings in 1897 by the Commissioner of the Protectorate (Okoth-Ogendo, 1991). In 1902, all land within the protectorate was declared Crown Land, whether the land was reserved for the natives or occupied by the same, which in the effect made all Africans become tenants of the Crown (Okoth-Ogendo, 1991).

According to Okoth-Ogendo (1991), Crown Land was defined as all public land within the East African Protectorate that, for the time being, were subject to the control of His Majesty by virtue of any agreements or treaties, and all lands that had been or may have been acquired by His Majesty under the Land Acquisition Act of 1894. The Crown Lands Ordinance No. 21 of 1902 gave powers to the Commissioner to identify and sell freehold land to desiring European settlers without giving due cognizance to customary and indigenous land tenure systems (Kanchorry, 2006). Further, in 1915, the Land Ordinance empowered the Commissioner to give the European settlers freehold leases of up to 999 years without due consideration of the African natives who inhabited the same land. According to Mortensen (2004), by 1914, nearly five million acres (two million hectares) of land had been taken away from Kenyan Africans, mostly from the Kikuyu, Maasai, and Nandi communities (Okoth-Ogendo, 1991).

The Maasai Agreements

The first Maasai land alienation was made possible by two treaties or agreements commonly referred to as the Maasai Agreements of 1904 and 1911. The British, having found the Maasai weakened by inter-clan war and both human and livestock diseases, used the opportunity to convince the Maasai to sign agreements to move from their traditional lands to give room for European settlement in 1904 and 1911 (Sena, 1986). This argument is further captured by Saibul and Carr (1981), who argued that the British tricked the Maasai after civil wars and droughts had weakened them. They claimed that the Maasai Laibon (Oloiboni) named Olonana had signed an agreement in 1904 and 1911 with His Majesty's Commission for the East African Protectorate, giving away Kenya to the British.

Under the terms of those two agreements, the Maasai ceded their territory in the central Rift Valley to move to two reserves, one to the north of the newly constructed Kenya-Uganda border. Railway, and the other south of it to create room for European settlers (Kantai, 2005). Economic and social factors, in favour of the settlers, were at the root of the agreement.

As noted previously, the Rift Valley settlement was excellent and productive, and this attracted the settlers for economic reasons. The area was suitable for ranching and was close to the railway. From a social perspective, the agreements helped the British by giving them a social control tool to manage the Maasai (Galaty,2013).

Notably, Maasai oral narratives say that in 1890, Mbatiany, the Maasai Oloiboni (the ritual expert), died, leaving his succession in dispute between his two sons, Senteu and Olonana. The two brothers were divided between rival sections of the Maasai, which was still the case when the settlers came and saw the opportunity to penetrate the region. On its own, the British Colonial Administration misinterpreted and regarded Olonana as being a hereditary "Chief" of the Maasai people and gave him the requisite support. He was thus elevated and assumed the administrative chief of the Maasai. It will be noted that "Oloiboni" was just a traditional medicine man and seer. He neither had administrative roles nor responsibilities. Indeed, as stated before, the Maasai had no central authority to which they answered. Hence, on 15th August 1904, the Maasai were cunningly induced to sign an agreement with the colonial administration. It is held that Olonana represented the Maasai State as a sovereign power and Governor Sir. Donald Stewart was acting on behalf of His Majesty the King and representing the British Colonial Administration. Under the terms and conditions of the Agreements, it is held that 'the Maasai decided of their own free will and that it was for our best interests to remove our people, flocks, and herds into definite reservations away from the railway line and away from any land that may be thrown open to European settlement under this agreement'.

According to Moijo Ole Keiwua (2002), the British came, saw, and coveted the land and disrupted communal land ownership. A hasty study of the Maasai was undertaken, with equally hasty conclusions made. The rights of the Maasai to own their land had been watered down to mere grazing rights:

> "Elliot could not, in fairness, call the Maasai wanderers. Between the Maasai on their land, and the British who had

wandered all the way from little England, who was a wanderer?" (Keiwua, 2002)

A common perspective that is held by the Maasai today is that the British manipulated and forced the Maasai into signing the agreements. According to Hughes (2006a), the Agreements between the Maasai and the British settlers were that the Maasai would keep the land in the reserves for as long as the Maasai existed as a race. Hughes (2006) argued that the agreements were not done in good faith, which led the Maasai to file a court case in 1913 challenging the legality of the agreements.

Emanating from the injustices of the above-stated treaties, certain elders led by Murket Ole Nchoko (whose name the British misspelt as being Ol Ole Njogo) felt aggrieved and decided to confront the injustice by filing a suit to challenge the move by the British Colonial Administration. The parties brought a suit for the breach of the 1904 agreement because the agreement was a civil contract, which was still subsisting, and the agreement of 1911 had not been made with Maasai elders capable of executing decisions that would be binding on the whole tribe. Damages were also claimed in tort for the wrongful confiscation of some of the herds of cattle. Comments made by the modern-day Maasai bear the bitterness that is embedded in Maasai narratives about the agreements. The study participants expressed their views through the following statements:

> "The Agreements all have to do with the Maasai ceding their land to give white settlers space in the fertile highlands to settle and establish modern agriculture and husbandry. Both agreements led to the loss of large swaths of land by the Maasai."

> "The agreements were treacherous and coined to bring down the Maasai supremacy and to dispose of the Maasai of their best pastures".

> "The Maasai describe the moves to the Southern Reserve as a deliberate move by the imperial regime to send them to 'Ngatet' to go and die from 'Oltikana' (East Coast Fever)."

> "The British colonial government decided to move certain sections of Maasai out of areas that were wanted for settlement by people (largely farmers) of European descent, including

Boers from South Africa. This began a long process of land alienation that continued through the 20th century, but in different forms at different times and was of varying severity."

"Maasai were moved from the Laikipia Highlands to Narok and Trans Mara (Cis Mara) after the settlers were allocated land along the railway line."

"My personal opinion is that the Maasai had come to the realization that the British were out to dispossess and disenfranchise them, and they (British) were not very good at keeping their word."

"The agreements ushered in a long period of untold suffering for the Maasai, which is still being felt to date."

The comments also note the breaking up of the Maasai territory, and the move from what the Maasai perceived as productive and fertile land to land of low quality. The participants also expressed their views on the legality of the agreements and held the view that the agreements were illegal and should be contested in courts both in Kenya and the United Kingdom.

"The 1911 agreement was illegal, null and void, and unacceptable to the Maasai people. Unlike the 1904 agreement, which might be said to have been ratified by an agreement, the 1911 Treaty never received the approval of the tribe and had to be implemented by means of government-orchestrated violence with the inevitable loss of human life and property. The losses in cattle, men, women, and children who died while en route to the Southern Reserve, escaping from Laikipia, were a gross violation of human rights; an act of genocide and a crime against humanity." (Saitabau Ole Kanchorry)

I agree with the claimants that this was not a treaty in the real sense, as there was no way the British Colonial Administration could enter into such an agreement with its subjects. Accordingly, Olonana's capacity as a medicine man was also questioned, as he had no authority to agree on behalf of the Maasai community. Additionally, I concur with the idea that the agreements were unilateral, as it was not possible for the Maasai elders, being illiterate in matters of British law, to possess the same bargaining power in an agreement of such magnitude with an enlightened British Governor. According to a memorandum submitted to the British High Commission by Maasai protesters in August

2004, the aggrieved parties claimed the 1911 agreement was void for the following five reasons:

1) The plaintiffs and other Maasai had never consented to it or authorized the Maasai defendants or anyone to agree to it on their behalf;

2) The defendants had no authority to alienate the interests of minors and unborn children of the Laikipia Maasai in Laikipia district;

3) It was not for the benefit of the Maasai generally nor of the Maasai of Laikipia;

4) The government was also in a fiduciary position to the Maasai (they were trustees, as a result of the 1904 agreement and later declarations of the Secretary of State) and had thereby gained financially; and,

5) The Maasai, particularly the signatories, had not been provided with independent legal advice before signing it.

According to Morgan (1960), the British forced Lenana (Olonana), a Maasai medicine man, to sign an agreement that was to move the Maasai from their land in the North of the Rift Valley to create room for what came to be called the White Highlands. In the real sense, this was not an agreement but a way to forcefully evict the Maasai (Hughes, 2006a). Demand for more land for new settlers in the new British protectorate further made the British abrogate the first agreement that had guaranteed the Maasai no further moves, and once again forced Lenana on his deathbed to sign another agreement in 1911. The Maasai contested the moves first by filing a case in 1913, which they lost on a technicality, and later in 1932 in a memorandum presented during the then Kenya Land Commission (Hughes, 2006b).

In relation to the Maasai agreements, I argue that the Maasai moves had psychological, social, and economic impacts on the general lives of the Maasai community. The Maasai lamented that the land they were to move to in the Southern Reserve was cold and infested with East Coast Fever, which killed thousands of their livestock. The death of the livestock rendered many families poor and dependent on the goodwill of the local Maasai who lived in the Reserve. The climate was cold, and many people died of pneumonia as they crossed the Mau ranges towards the warmer southern slopes of the Mau and the Loita plains (Ongata E-Loita), where most of the Purko settled. The community's social fabric, which provided a social support mechanism, was severed.

Traditional and religious rites that were collectively performed could no longer be held at the shrines. These moves from the pristine plains of Laikipia had a very negative impact on the Maasai people, demoralized them, and rendered them vulnerable. The Maasai, as well as other commentators, describe the moves to the Southern Reserve as a deliberate move by the Imperial regime to send them to Ngatet to go and die from *Oltikana* (East Coast Fever), *Olodua* (Rinderpest), and *Entidiyai* (Malaria). Lack of medical and veterinary services contributed to the loss of life among the Maasai population as well as their livestock and weakened the Maasai economy and strength to fight back or resist further European aggression. Other researchers have also described the numerous difficulties and negative outcomes faced by the Maasai and other pastoralist groups (Davis, D'Odorico & Rulli, 2014; Lawson, Muller, Gishelli, et al., 2014; Catley, Lind & Scoones, 2013; Mwang'ombe, Nyariki, & Thompson, 2009, and Sellen, 1996). Thus, losing ancestral land can carry with it a variety of economic, social, health, psychological, and cultural consequences.

I concur with a statement issued by Lucas Leperes Naikuni during the 2004 Maasai demonstrations that:

> "The irony of it all concerning Treaties', Agreements', and/ or 'Contracts' between the colonialists and their subjects was that the colonial authorities would enter (whenever it was convenient to them) into a 'treaty' with a particular tribe and when the situation arose, the agreement would be interpreted to mean that the colonialists executed the treaty not with a native tribe but between themselves on one hand, and with a foreign state on the other. Essentially, in such a situation, the breach of the agreement would only be determined by an appropriate jurisdiction, the International Court of Justice, so as to seek redress."(Lukas Naikuni, August 2004)

The net effects of these twin pacts were devastating in that they sounded the death knell for the Maasai by dismantling their land or space, which was a key foundation of their existence and reliance on pastoralism. The agreements also catalyzed a systematic reduction of Maasai herds, thereby exposing the same to threats such as droughts, famine, epidemics, and reduced pastures, minerals, and water, which characterized the Kajiado and Narok Reserves where the Maasai were moved to (Galaty, 2013; Nyariki, Mwang'gombe & Thompson, 2009).

There was reduced ability for the Maasai to produce and maintain large herds, which subjected people to hunger and despondency, thereby exposing them to threats related to hunger. The people were also confined to a small area that affected their movements, and subsequently, they faced the threats of overcrowding and the related social and health risks (Little, McPeak, Bareli, et al., 2011). The takeover of the land that they relied on for herbal medication subjected them to further ill health. To date, the Maasai, including the participants in the study, are lamenting about the effects of the agreements.

The Kenya Land Commission (Carter Commission) of 1933-1934

British colonial land policy in Kenya revolved around the Colonial Ordinance of 1902, which established the procedures under which land in the East African Protectorate would be alienated to European settlers (Coray, 1978). Rights, which the Africans had come to view as customary, were trampled upon by those that were seen to have developed under British hegemony. Once the Africans vacated the land, the land was privatized, and the title of the land became Crown Land. The land of Africans, hence, became European land. To address the increasing concerns about land by the Africans, Phillip Cunliffe-Lister, Secretary for Colonies, commissioned the services of Sir William Morris Carter, Captain Frank O'Brien Wilson, and Rupert William Hemsted to investigate African land grievances. The commission was to review the terms of the 1930 Native Lands Trust Ordinance and seek ways to serve Africans' interests in the land, as well as settle grievances from past transactions in the land. The trio produced a report titled the Kenya Land Commission Report, otherwise commonly referred to as the Carter Commission Report of 1932. The perspectives of the Maasai regarding the Commission were expressed as follows:

> "This was the first attempt to put a policy in place to justify rather than to correct the previous anomaly. It only served the purpose of legitimizing the appropriation of the Maasai territory. The process was neither representative nor participatory, nor consultative." (Daniel Salau).

It is worth noting that the Kenya Land Report, in its conclusion, underscored that the main fault in the traditional (Maasai pastoral) system is the combination of the communal range with unrestricted individual ownership. Neither the community nor the individual has regard for the effects of their actions on the land. This is contrary to reality, as nomadic and transhuman pastoralism is founded on sound ecological management and preservation of nature through intricate regulatory frameworks that have, for centuries, ensured the survival of nature and near-pristine conditions of the rangelands. The report failed to acknowledge the circumstances that noted effects on the environment were a direct consequence of reduced space as a result of dispossession by the colonial authorities to create space for the settler community.

Pastoralism is founded on three key pillars, i.e., land and natural resources, livestock herds, and traditional governance; when one of these pillars is threatened, then the whole pastoralism system becomes perilous. Therefore, whereas some of the observations were practical from a modern perspective, sight was lost on the causative aspects of land and ecological degradation, as well as the reduced space due to the takeover of the vital drought reserves by the colonial authorities.

The authorities crafted and introduced further laws on the assumption that problems in the reserves were due to overpopulation, bad land use, and defective tenure arrangements. The recommendations in the report included the intention to force the Maasai to lease out their land to other communities, especially the cultivators of land to bring tsetse-infested areas into cultivation" and to reduce overcrowding in densely populated areas. The report also recommended the replacement of African "native land tenure with private ownership of property (Kieya, 2007).

In my view, the British Government pretended to secure special protection for the Maasai to continue enjoying the same rights under the 1904/11 agreements, in respect of which the land they were removed from shall not be alienated to non-Maasai without their consent or that of their traditional institutions. The safeguard was in relation to land transfers and land acquisition and intended to be attained by some unalterable provision in the new constitution. I argue that the safeguard was missed in relation to land transfers because the control of land transactions was vested in the commission, whose chairperson was a government representative, with all other members being the appointees of the Government. Appeals from the Africans were sent to the Central Board, which was part of the Commission and presided over by a government official who was also not a representative of the people whose interest was supposed to be safeguarded. The promised safeguard in the form of controlled land transactions turned out to be the conduit by which a great deal of the land of the Maasai ended in the ownership of persons who were themselves not Maasai. When the Maasai appealed, Carter ruled against the Maasai (Kiereini, 2019). The British also established a tenure system that only recognized land rights secured by individual freehold titles. While ideal for securing the private estates of settlers, customary tenure involved a complex system of nested and overlapping individual and group rights derived from kinship relationships that did not lend itself to concepts of absolute individual ownership. As a result, most customary land was left unregistered and vulnerable to appropriation and transfer to settlers. This introduced titling and leasing of land to the settlers for periods of between 99 and 999 years.

The Million Acre Scheme

Towards the mid-1950s, the clamour for land by Africans through the Mau Mau uprising, the settler community, and the European administrators was put under intense pressure to address the issues about land (Sygga, 2011). By 1960, the European settlers occupied some 7.5 million acres (3 million hectares) of land held on leases and freehold tenure, which the Africans were demanding. To safeguard their interests in the event of a power transfer, the colonial government initiated a settlement plan for the Africanization of the White Highlands as well as an elaborate scheme of constitutional and statutory guarantees of property rights (Sygga, 2011). The plan was informed by the following:

a. A perceived need on the part of colonial authorities to entrench the settler community firmly in Kenya and maintain the rights they had to land, without having to give any land back to the natives.

b. The socialization of the new African elites into the colonial political, economic, and social patterns through the establishment of a multi-racial alliance of European settlers and African landowners to forestall independence and majority rule.

c. The process was geared towards preventing the mobilization of a nationalist base that would be opposed to the continuation of colonial policies after independence (Wasserman, 1976).

Thus, in 1960, a Land Development and Settlement Board (LDSB) was established to devise and administer resettlement schemes for some 20,000 families of all races. Through the facility amounting to 7.5 million sterling pounds from the World Bank, the scheme also offered credit facilities to Africans who wished to purchase farmland in the White Highlands. The Yeomen Programme, as it was called, envisaged buying 240,000 acres in the White Highlands to be subdivided into 100-acre parcels and distributed to a select group of Africans who would farm alongside the whites. In 1961, the programme was renamed the Assisted Farmers Scheme and formed part of the independence negotiations. The One Million Acre Scheme differed from the previous ones in that the one million-acre scheme was designed to accommodate masses of landless families; it was not designed for a relatively small number of carefully selected farmers. What such a scheme required, therefore, was huge financial support in terms of loans and grants. The World Bank, the British, and West German governments provided this assistance.

In 1962, the colonial administration negotiated the terms of the scheme on which 35,000 families of smallholders who were landless would be settled in more than one million acres of largely high-density settlement. This new scheme, established at a cost of twenty-five million sterling pounds, was more realiztic in its approach to the land question. It was meant to benefit both the landless and the prosperous Africans. Another remarkable feature of the scheme was its thrust into a highly populated settlement. About 5000 peasants were to be accommodated on 73,000 hectares. The initial plans provided for the sharing of this amount between the peasants and the Yeomen or assisted farmers. As noted above, the total cost of the scheme was about £25 million, of which £19.6 million was to support the high-density populated settlement. These were organized into separate units or schemes with scores of individual plots. When the Million-Acre Settlement Scheme ended in 1971, a total of 1.25 million acres had been used in resettlement, a comparatively small portion of the 7.5 million acres occupied by the Europeans at the time of independence.

The Million Acre scheme was infiltrated by the Kenya's elites who acquired land in the designated areas through an order by then President Jomo Kenyatta in 1964 that all colonial farmhouses together with 100 acres surrounding the farmhouses be reserved for "prominent people" alongside poor farmers in the settlement schemes in what came to be called the " Z" plots. The Z plots became an avenue for politicians and elites to settle their kin and kith and get choice land for themselves. The sale of these lands was so scandalous that the British government appointed a commission in July 1966 to investigate the Million-Acre Settlement Scheme and what went wrong. According to the British government, the identified farmers could have acquired land by private means without using the scheme funds (Kamau, 2009). The first benefactors of this process included the late Dr. Julius Kiano, who benefited from land in Dundori; Martin Shikuku, then MP for Butere, was allocated land in Kiminini Scheme; former President Moi (then a cabinet minister)was allocated Perkerra Scheme in Eldama Ravine; President Kenyatta, Minister Jackson Angaine, Assistant Minister Mwai Kibaki, and Permanent Secretary Robert Ouko, among others (Sygga, 2011). The ramifications of the land buying companies are now being experienced in the land conflicts in Namuncha, Kedong, Olmara, Narasha, Olchurai, and Natooli, where the Maasai, who historically owned and lived on the land, are being evicted to give room to land owners who have titles to land that they have no historical attachments to.

The Lancaster Independence Conference

The Lancaster House conferences were three meetings (1960, 1962, and 1963) in which Kenya's constitutional framework and independence were negotiated. The first conference was under the chairmanship of the Secretary of State for the Colonies, Iain Macleod, in January 1960. There was no agreement, and Macleod issued an interim constitution. The second conference commenced in February 1962, and a framework for self-governance was negotiated. Kenya's independent constitution of 1963 was a negotiated document that was expected to provide a framework capable of embodying the interests of all groups sustainably. These groups had emerged on racial lines and were involved in racial tensions, pitting, on the one hand, Africans who had been forcibly dispossessed of their land and displaced, and on the other side, the white settlers who had a mission of turning Kenya into a "White man's Country". The 1963 conference finalized constitutional arrangements for Kenya's independence as a dominion, marking the end of more than 70 years of colonial rule. Matters of land were key during the Lancaster deliberations, where the opposing parties, KANU and KADU, were all driven by land claims by communities that were dispossessed by the British. While KANU was a proponent of the agreement between the British settlers, the KADU team stood for returning the land to the original owners. The Maasai delegation fronted their demands for the land through KADU.

The Kenya Constitutional Conference in London during 1962, on the eve of Kenya's independence, ended in bitter failure (Hughes, 2006). The Kenyan delegation to the conference was made up of political parties, the Maasai (spelt Masai), and representatives from the then Northern Frontier District. The Maasai delegation was comprised of: Mr. J.K. Ole Sein; Mr. P. Ole Lemein; Dr. Likimani; Mr. Partasio Ole Nampaso; Mr. J. Ole Tameno; Mr. J.K. Ole Tipis; Mr. J. Keen; J.L.N. Ole Konchellah; Mr. J.L.N. Rurumban (Observer), and Mr. R.L. McEwen (who was the Legal Advisor).

During the deliberations for independence at the conference, the Maasai delegation demanded the following as a condition for their engagement:

a. They wanted the ownership of the land they vacated to be recognized and to have the first claim on the land when the Europeans left.

b. They wished to enjoy the security of tenure in the areas where they lived, then, in both the North and Southern Reserves.

c. They claimed that certain areas within their Reserves had been alienated in contravention of the Agreements;

d. They requested that some means be found to unite the Maasai with their kins who lived in the Northern and Southern Reserves (Colonial Office, 1963).

In response to the Maasai demands, the Secretary of State stated that:

> "The Imperial government had no obligation to ensure that the Maasai would continue the same rights as they did enjoy under the Agreements, but Maasai land will not be alienated to non-Maasai without their consent, and could not be taken away from them by the government, with an exception of when the land was intended for public use and mining. The Maasai delegation agreed that the Maasai should continue to enjoy the security of tenure in their reserves but did not accept that they had no claims in respect to the land that the Maasai had vacated within the Agreement." (Colonial Office, 1963, p.121)

The statement from the Colonial Office was not received well by the Maasai delegation, as reported by some of the attendees (John Keen and Ole Lemein). As a result, the Maasai protested by walking out of the conference. The walkout may have given other parties interested in land issues an opportunity at the expense of the Maasai. The results of the Lancaster Conference deliberation have elicited different opinions among the Maasai, especially those who have been involved in researching Maasai claims. Such differences were evident in comments from Maasai people who are conversant about the deliberation. Such are some of the views expressed by the Maasai about the Lancaster Conference deliberations.

> "The Maasai representatives should have never walked out of the deliberations. They should have been more tactful. Even among the Maasai traditions, you don't walk out in protest if your point of view is not taken. Their absence from the final recommendations may have cost the Maasai tracks of land. Having allowed the Lancaster Conference to conclude without their presence was short-sighted, and they should have stayed put and caused trouble within the discussion room, and delayed the conclusions of the meeting. The outcomes were therefore disastrous and allowed the post-colonization of the Maasai people and the taking over of their lands. This included the independent government, where the political elites, who were mostly not Maasai, took over the land that was supposed to be returned to the Maasai." (Nicholas Soikan)

The process of negotiation for independence at the Lancaster Conference was rife with conspiracy between the British and Kenya, where Kenyatta's main ambition was to access most of the land that was going to be left by the settlers, while that of the settlers was an assurance from the incoming president that the safety of the settlers would be guaranteed. While the Maasai demands were well articulated, the British and KANU delegation had already hatched a strategy where the Maasai claim would not be discussed, and that the British would announce that the incoming Kenyan government would be responsible for addressing the Maasai demands. This led to the Maasai delegation walking out of the deliberation, which in a way was a win for KANU because the Maasai agenda was off the table.

PART IV:
POST INDEPENDENCE GOVERNMENT REGIMES

Introduction

In the post-colonial African context, the construction of political identities must be understood because of the history of state formation. I contend that the formation of contemporary political identities often began in the colonial period, where the application of different forms of legal personhood was part of the construction of difference. First, in racial terms (between Europeans and Africans), then in ethnic terms (between African ethnic groups). I posit further that often the independence movement contributed to the perpetuation of the colonial legacy of ethnic division as new African leaders adopted the very same institutions of subordination and ethnic division first introduced by colonial rulers. In Kenya, this was perpetrated by the leaders through coalescing around ethnic grouping, especially to acquire the land that was then being either bought from the colonial settlers or being forcefully acquired by the political elites. This is further entrenched in the current political dispensation, where political parties are formed along tribal and regional alliances.

On the attainment of independence in 1963, colonial property laws and policies were entrenched in the law through the Registered Land Act (RLA) of 1963 (Wachira, 2008). As alluded to previously, the institutionalization and titling land laws were instituted in early 1930 with statutes that recognized only individual land tenure, to the frustration of groups, among them the Maasai, whose way of life was incompatible with this regime. Although the aim of individualization of land tenure was to spur economic growth, the policy ignored indigenous peoples' needs and the contribution they might have made to such. According to Moiko (2004), early government engagements with pastoralists in Kenya came as part of pacification processes aimed at "establishing" law, order, and security in the colony.

According to Boone, up to date, land politics and policy in Africa have been around the debate over whose rights are to be recognized by the state, and this has led to many disputes arising from the processes that the state has used to allocate land (Boone, 2012). In the regulation of land ownership and land use, governments employ law and policy instruments, which, when inappropriately enacted and implemented, have caused conflicts, discrimination, inequality, and poverty. Boone (2007) further argues that African governments have used laws, policies, and decrees to "consolidate the power of the central state, promote national integration, accelerate the expansion of commercial agriculture, and demobilize rural populations who entered the political arena at the time of the nationalist struggle" (p. 3).

The individual land tenure system sanctified by the Registered Land Act was favoured by the state on the basis that Kenya's largely agricultural economy was dependent on it (Wachira, 2008). The imposed process of individualization of land, especially among the pastoralists such as the Maasai, spurred more tension and dispossession within the community. The retention and entrenchment of the colonial laws and policies relative to land rights by the independent Kenyan government legitimized the dispossessions of the original owners of the lands (Koissaba, 2015). This argument was further supported by Wachira (2008), who stated that "The independent government justified the retention of colonial land laws on the grounds that the independent Constitution had provisions which tied the hands of the government (p.28).

Group Ranches (Representative) Act of 1968

Arising from the neo-classical economic theory prevailing at the time, and with the support of multi-lateral donors, the Kenyan Government advocated for the formation of Group Ranches through the enactment of the Group Ranches (Group Representative) Act of 1968. According to current narratives, the group ranch system, which later led to individualization of land, was alien to the Maasai and has contributed to continued land appropriation among the Maasai. Some of the comments by the study participants include:

> "The Group Representative Act was supposed to model the modern ranching enterprise, which was practised by the white ranchers.

The idea was noble, but it was lost to elite capture. The members of the groups, who were more educated and aware of the law, took advantage of the ignorant members to fleece them of their land and business of keeping livestock. In many of the groups, management is a big impediment to their development. Many of the officials are illiterate and cannot understand many technical issues concerning the running of the ranches as it was intended."

"The group ranch model was a system where a group of people jointly held title to land, maintained agreed herd sizes, owned livestock individually, but herded them together. Group Ranches was the idea of the World Bank and was implemented in collaboration with the Kenyan Government. The project aimed to regulate traditional pastoral practices of herding cattle across the arid land and to control herd sizes. In addition, the Government intended to ensure boundary maintenance, sensitize the Maasai to make them aware of the scarcity and value of land, and encourage them to make necessary investments to improve the land. In the development of group ranches, the principles applied in high-potential lands (highlands) were also applied to the rangelands, which flopped. The project was undertaken with the consultation of educated Maasai tied to the national political system. The government project brought about further loss of land and the traditional way of life of mobility and flexibility. In the process of subdividing land, some large pieces of land were set aside for individual Maasai leaders and government officials, and there was the migration of farming communities in areas with good climatic conditions for farming into Mau Narok, Enoosupukia, Nairagie Enkare, Melili, and many other high-potential areas in Narok. In my opinion, the idea of group ranches radically transformed the Maasai social and political organization and traditional livestock management strategies. The role of traditional leadership in managing natural resources was replaced by the group ranches committees, which had a new level of territorial administrative organization and a new method of decision making supported by law. This incapacitated the role of traditional leadership. In addition, the group ranches as a new model did not consider equity in the registration of the whole community.

The subdivision of group ranches started in Kajiado in the mid-1960s and later in Narok in the early 1970s. Arising from presidential declarations by President Moi about individualization of land in group ranches as a way to make landowners access loans for development, and the involvement of government officials, many group ranches started experiencing disillusionment.? The study participants gave examples of group ranches where subdivision had been going on for many years.

> "Elang'ata Wuas Group Ranch was dissolved by members in the 1990s, and the process of subdividing and allocating members' parcels of land has been going on for several years. An elected committee oversees this process. This process of land subdivision has not only been marred by illegal alienation, acquisition, and sale of individual and public land, land extortion, forceful relocation, and disinheritance, said the letter to the National Land Commission, but it goes against all laws of natural justice, the Constitution, and all International legal statutes on human rights. These malpractices, besides being illegal, have a profound, long-lasting, and disproportionate impact on vulnerable groups of our community, such as the poor, women, widows, orphans, and persons with disabilities. The documents also told the National Land Commission that the community's attempts to seek redress at the county level have failed to bear fruit. The role of government institutions at the county level has significantly perpetuated these land injustices by failing to honestly and adequately address them on several occasions, and according to the law. The residents are recommending that a thorough audit of the Elangata Wuas land subdivision be carried out and that all land sales in the area be stopped." (Ole Taiko, 2015)

This study also pointed out that the group ranch registration processes were discriminatory and neglected the interests of women, the youth, children, and poor members of the community who, because of their status, were not registered in many group ranches.

> "Only fathers and sons who were eighteen years and above were registered, excluding and discriminating against women and girls who are an integral part of the community." (Rahab Kenana date)

The sentiments of segregation of women and youth by the group ranch committees were also echoed by female study participants from both Narok and Kajiado, whose responses are captured below.

My children and I are landless because the committee refused to register me as a member of the group ranch. After all, I am a woman.

> My sons were not of age by the time the registration was going on, so they could not be registered. I do not know what happened to my late husband's share because he was a registered member. I did not know where to go for help because all the leaders, including the chief, did nothing to help me."(Widow from Kajiado).

Case Studies

For a better understanding of the magnitude of corruption and deception in the group ranches, I will use case studies from Iloodoariak and Elangata Wuas, both from Kajiado County.

Case Study 1: Iloodoariak Group Ranch

Iloodoariak (the Maasai word for a place of "red waters") is the land situated about 80 kilometres from the southern part of Nairobi in Kajiado County within the Rift Valley Province. It is approximately 146,682 hectares. Since time immemorial, land has been occupied and managed by over 6,000 indigenous Maasai inhabitants of the Keekonyokie clan, who are the ordinary residents of the area and practised traditional pastoralist activities centred on livestock. By Section 114 of the old Constitution of Kenya, the Iloodoariak was vested in Olkejuado County Council as a Trustee. The County Council was to hold the land in question for the benefit of the persons whose ordinary residents were thereon. By the declaration notice numbers LA/LDO/1/8 dated 22nd November 1978 and LND/MOS/56/4 dated 11th July 1986, the government declared Iloodoariak and Mosiro, respectively, land adjudication sections within the meaning of Section 5 of the Land Adjudication Act (Cap. 284). It was meant to ascertain, record, and register the pre-existing customary rights and interests of ordinary residents in the said area. Such residents were to be issued title deeds. As the primary users and occupiers of the land, the Maasai were entitled to expect significant consultation with the adjudication team and positive results from the whole process.

The process of adjudication at Iloodoariak proceeded until 1989 when it was pronounced complete. The adjudication register was published for inspection, and objections were invited within sixty (60) days of publication. Consequently, 159 objections were lodged and determined in 1990. Soon thereafter, those recorded as owners of the parcels of land in the section were registered as absolute proprietors of the land and hence issued with the title deeds in respect of the requirements of the provisions of the Registered Land Act (Cap. 300).

However, the adjudication process was marred with greed, abuse of office, acts of arbitrariness, and corruption exhibited by the officials from the Ministry of Land and Settlement who were ostensibly facilitating the adjudication process (MCSF 2005). During the alleged adjudication process, available evidence indicates that many of the government officials were recorded as the owners of the land in this area (MCSF 2005). Further, a great deal of the land was demarcated to people, friends, and relatives of these officials who were not ordinarily residents. This did not happen for free or by accident. The non-residents made hefty payments to these government officials and Land Adjudication Committee members. According to a report by Mainyioto Pastoralists Integrated Development Organization (MPIDO), a Non-profit from the local community, the outcome of land adjudication and subsequent subdivision had the following outcomes (MPIDO, 1998).

362 persons who were (still are) neither residents nor members of any of the existing group ranches of this area—were nonetheless recorded as owners of the land in the section. They were allotted land and issued with title deeds. A significant number of these non-residents were and still are highly placed politicians, adjudication officials, other senior government and local officials, and their relatives, friends, business people, and associates who had no connection with the area. These people were providing bribes in order to lubricate the process. The officials took advantage of the ignorance and the illiteracy level of the members of this community.

Over 2,000 legitimate and indigenous Maasai families and inhabitants were deliberately and, through fraudulent means, left out of the adjudication process and were declared to be squatters on the land allotted to other people (MCSF 2005). These residents were not aware of the demarcation and recording taking place. The community was not made aware of these matters. The same was never effectively communicated to them as required by section 14 of the Land Adjudication Act.

The Maasai residents of Iloodoariak from Kajiado District undoubtedly lived on this ancestral land for generations on end. Their case is to protect the land being taken away through unfair, arbitrary, and gross abuse of power perpetrated by government officials. The rightful and laid-down land adjudication procedures were not applied. There was neither publication nor any notices to this effect. These acts of omission and commission were deliberate with the intention of frustrating any efforts to lodge either appeal cases with the Minister of Lands and Settlement, or with the high court as required by the primary Land Adjudication Act[1] (MPIDO, 1998).

Case Study 2: Elangata Wuas Group Ranch

According to the participants, Elangata Wuas Group Ranch is a good example of how Group Ranches have been a conduit of Maasai land appropriation. Elangata Wuas Group Ranch lies in the jurisdiction of Kajiado County, Kajiado Central Division, and Iloodokilani Location in Kajiado West Constituency. The Group Ranch covers a total of 69,474 Ha with 489 registered members. The Group Ranch borders Torosei and Lolngosua Group Ranches to the South, Oldonyo Onyokie and Olkeri Group Ranches to the West, Kilonito Group Ranch to the North, and Ildamat, Nkoile, and Enkaroni Group Ranches to the East.

The dissolution of group ranches in Kajiado drove the members' request for the dissolution of their group ranch. The group ranch was dissolved by group ranch members through an Annual General Meeting resolution in the

---

1   Case study courtesy of Mainyioito Pastoralist Integrated Development Organization..

year 1990. Two group ranch subdivision committees have been in place since. According to a report submitted to the National Land Commission by the community, the current group ranch office bearers have broken all the rules and have illegally allocated land to non-members. They have allocated extra land parcels to themselves, relatives, and friends, sold public lands and allocated the same to individuals, and disinherited the poor, widows, and orphans. These officials have also turned out to be land brokers and are manipulating gullible group ranch members to sell their land to them at a price that is below market prices for onward sale to third parties for a premium (Taiko Lemayian et al., 2013).

An elected committee oversees this process. This process of land subdivision has not only been marred by illegal alienation, acquisition and sale of individual and public land, land extortion, forceful relocation, and disinheritance, said the letter to the National Land Commission, but it goes contrary to all laws of natural justices, the Constitution of Kenya (2010), and all International legal statutes on human rights (Ole Taiko et al., 2013). These malpractices, besides being illegal, have a profound, long-lasting, and disproportionate impact on vulnerable groups of our community, such as the poor, women, widows, orphans, and persons with disabilities. The documents also told the National Land Commission that the community's attempts to seek redress at the County level have failed to bear fruit (Ole Taiko et al., 2013). The role of government institutions at the county level has significantly perpetuated these land injustices by failing to address them honestly and adequately on several occasions and in accordance with the law.

The residents are recommending that a thorough audit of the Elangata Wuas land subdivision be carried out and that all land sales in the area be stopped. The members further suggested that a new group should be constituted from the Annual General Meeting under the supervision of the National Land Commission, and the County's authorized institutions (Ole Taiko et al., 2013). Their mandate, Terms of Reference (TOR), and timelines not exceeding one year should be drawn by the National Land Commission or any other delegated authority. Further recommendations from the aggrieved members were:

1. All Elangata Wuas land transactions should be stopped forthwith with immediate effect pending an audit of illegal land allocation and sales;

2. All public utility land issued to individuals should be nullified, while titles of the said lands should be transferred to the county government as dictated by law.

3. All land parcels allocated unprocedurally to non-members of the group ranch should be nullified.

4. All the extra land parcels that the group ranch Officials allocated to their relatives, cronies, and themselves should be nullified. If they have sold the extra parcels, then the ones in their custody automatically are forfeited;

5. All books of accounts for the committee should be audited by the relevant authorities to unearth all financial impropriety, and those found culpable should be held to account.

6. All direct transfers of land auctioned by the said committee to third parties parties unprocedurally be nullified;

7. All legitimate group ranch members who were maliciously denied parcels of land for both political reasons or who have been members of the previous committee should be identified and given their rightful parcel of land; and

8. All civil servants who collaborated with the group ranch officials in this land scam should be investigated, and necessary disciplinary measures instituted.

Narok County has also had its fair share of elite capture, in matters related to land, where those who are in political positions have had the opportunity to allocate themselves, relatives, and friends in group ranches and urban centres. In Narok, it has been reported that in the then Narok North Constituency, where "clashes" in October 1993 left over thirty-five dead, and at least thirty thousand displaced (ROK, 1995), the clamour for the growth of the Kikuyu vote by the then opposition was the only way to gain political mileage in the area. In response to that, the ruling party that was patronized in Narok by William Ole Ntimama had a genuine response to protect the Maasai land and political domination by immigrant communities, rallying the Maasai to reject any settlement of non-Maasai in Narok (Koissaba, 2013).

As it stands now in Narok, the principle of the tyranny of numbers will determine the nature of political dispensation that the Maasai will face for many general elections to come. Given the increase of immigrant communities in Narok County and the current political dispensation, the Maasai will face a herculean task of safeguarding their political clout in Narok. With the deliberate support of other communities with support from senior people in government to import voters from Bomet, which predominantly consists of the Kalenjin, the Kikuyu from Nakuru and other parts of Kenya and the increase in the number of the Kisii community, there is a great danger that if the Maasai go into the next election divided, they will lose their political leadership in Narok. Unfortunately, every time a Maasai leader in Narok raises the issue of land, the immigrant communities view it as ethnic antagonism and a recipe for conflict.

Numerous cases of legitimized land acquisitions have been experienced. The most glaring of such situations is the group ranches bordering the Mau Forest, the largest water tower that feeds the Mara River, whose waters flow to Lake Victoria, the largest lake in Africa. According to the Report of the Commission of Inquiry into the Illegal/Irregular Allocation of Public Land (ROK, 2004), the sizes of most of the group ranches allocated were inflated significantly, and the difference was sold to unsuspecting non-indigenous settlers. The report, whose recommendations were recently implemented, noted that the Nkaroni Group Ranch registered the initial size as 1,597.5 hectares and its current size is estimated at approximately 9,000 hectares. Others include the Enaikishomi Group Ranch and the Sisiyian Farm. The extension of the boundaries in the group ranches has created a cyclical conflict between the Maasai and the immigrant community, who bought the land through corrupt politicians and government Ministry of Lands officials (Kenta, 2015).

In total disregard of the law, the non-residents and illegal beneficiaries of the land were issued with land titles of the illegally acquired land by the Ministry of Lands. This rendered the indigenous and rightful owners of the land trespassers on their land of birth. Since the law recognizes the sanctity of the title, the titleholder is recognized as the legal owner of the land. Protracted legal battles ensued, but given the political clout of the illegal allotees and their positions in former and current governments, the courts have continuously ruled against the Maasai due to the prevailing laws on land that recognize the sanctity of the land titles, and not for indigenous land ownership (Koissaba,2014).

The legitimacy of "willing buyer, willing seller" seems paradoxical because most land transactions were often dubious. Group ranch officials and their assigned brokers often illegally approached prospective landholders and purchased the land at far lesser prices than market prices, or the direct transfer of the title deeds to third parties and buyers with or without the consent of the landowner. This not only alienates the land from the community members but also denies the government revenue. While the government has evicted people who settled in Mau to save the Mau Water Tower, it has degenerated into a conflict between the Kalenjin and the Maasai, and will be a contentious issue during the next general election scheduled for 2022.

In summary, the group ranches were an artificial creation that failed to consider the Maasai culture and way of life. Instead, the group ranches were created to support the government's plan for "development" with no input from the Maasai or any consideration of their needs. The disassembling of the land into group ranches also contradicted the forms of productive land-use systems that underpin Maasai pastoral mobility (Lesorogol, 2008). Furthermore, the creation of the ranches and issuance of individual title deeds introduced a new alien concept of land tenure as well as the perception of the land as a commodity to be bought and sold. From 1968 to 1990, most of the academic scholarship related to land was based on Hardin's (1968): *Tragedy of the Commons,* which portrays the users of a common-pool resource, such as a pasture open to all, as being trapped in a tragedy of overuse and destruction.

Many scholars and policy makers thought that all common-pool resources were 'owned' by no one. Thus, government officials had to impose new rules or policies, such as privatization of the land through titling, to prevent the destruction by users, mainly the pastoralist communities such as the Maasai, who could not do anything other than destroy the resources on which their future depended. For the most part, academic and policy debate on common property resources did not accept the view that, under certain conditions, groups of individuals could sustainably hold property. After the publication of Ostrom's (1990) *Governing the Commons,* that viewpoint changed. Ostrom's text describes how common property can be successfully managed by communities without the intervention of the state, and without having to privatize a common-pool resource. Since the publication of the book, extensive research has demonstrated that a group/community can successfully sustain long-term use of common-pool resources (Ostrom, 2009). For years, the Maasai demonstrated that they can self-organize as they modulated herd size and distribution in a way that prevented degradation of their pastures (Galaty, 2013). Unfortunately, to this day, the tragedy of the commons has polarised the policies and actions of Kenya's government. The Maasai perspective (and that of other pastoral communities) has yet to be accommodated within Kenya's mainstream development paradigm or in their thinking and policies.

The Trust Land (Amendment) Act of 1968

Trust Land was that land declared to be as defined in Section 114 of the old Constitution of Kenya. Under both the former Constitution and the Trust Land Act (Chapter 288 Laws of Kenya), neither the government nor the County Councils owned Trust Lands. The local County Councils simply held the lands on behalf of the local communities (ROK, 2009). The constitution defined the control of Trust Land as follows:

> "All trust land shall vest in the County Council within whose area of jurisdiction it is situated. (Constitution of Kenya, Section 115(1)). Each County Council shall hold the trust

land vested in it for the benefit of the persons ordinarily resident on that land and shall give effect to such rights, interests or other benefits in respect of the land as may, under the African customary law for the time being in force, and applicable thereto, be vested in any tribe, group, family or individual" (Constitution of Kenya, Section 115(2) (ROK, 1998).

This implied that if the land remained unadjudicated and unregistered, it belonged to the communities, groups, and families in the area in accordance with African Customary Law. The community ceased ownership of the land once the land was registered under any of the land registration statutes; hence, Trust Land was transferred into private land. Corruption at the then County Councils saw councillors use the right provided in the constitution to register land in either their names, friends, or other institutions to disfranchise communities of the land, hence dispossessing the Maasai. Through such deals, the Maasai community lost most of the land in urban centres, forest reserves, and livestock holding grounds (Koissaba, 2014).

The power to alienate Trust Land was with the Commissioner of Lands, who was a direct representative of the President. The total disregard for African Customary Law and the lack of recognition of pastoralism by the government and County Councils denied the community the right to be consulted. I conclude that this resulted in irregular alienation of Trust Land to individuals or companies with total disregard for the needs of residents. Indeed, no law required the government or state to take the local people's interests first or to give priority to residents if such land should be alienated. The process led to progressive land losses by the local communities. These allocations were done with total disregard for the rights of local communities in the process of planning ownership of land. Over time, such lands were offered to politically correct people or as rewards for engaging in pro-system projects aimed at entrenching the ruling powers. The then County Councils dished out land to their families and friends, while the Commissioner of Lands allocated various pieces of land to people at the behest of the president. In Kajiado, for instance, all government land around the then Ngong Administration offices was hived out and given to State House operatives, while some of it was given to politically correct individuals. Most of the land was subdivided into plots and dished out to supporters of the ruling party, KANU, and the then Member of Parliament, the late Professor George Saitoti. In both Kajiado and Narok, some livestock holding grounds were allocated to senior government officials, while government houses and plots were allocated to the political elites. In Kajiado, for instance, the Ilkaputiei lost all the land across the Nairobi-Mombasa Railway to Machakos County without any information on how the boundary was moved to its present location. Historically, the Kenya Meat Commission and the Goat farm were in Kajiado, but it was also annexed into Machakos County.

High Levels of Illiteracy

The high level of illiteracy among the majority of Maasai individual landowners was also another significant contributor to land sales among the Maasai in Narok and Kajiado. With a lack of formal employment, the large number of the Maasai population limited them from accessing employment. This has also contributed to poor animal husbandry skills in managing their livestock in the smaller parcels of land that they individually owned. In his argument, Galaty (1992) posits that:

> "Those without any education were three times as likely to sell land as those with education, while those without employment experience were twice as likely to sell land as those with such experience." (p. 32).

According to the study, lack of education and the understanding of the value and importance of land has deprived many Maasai of their decision-making ability on matters related to the land sale, who makes the decisions, how the decisions are made, and who implements the decisions. Here are some comments:

> "When you look at most people who have sold land in Kajiado and Narok, you will realize that almost all are illiterate and do not know the value of land, and therefore do not have the negotiating power. They do not have any control over the process, and the pricing is left to the land brokers."

"Most decisions are made in boardrooms by government officials and the land brokers. The Maasai are mostly spectators and only wait to be told the worth of their land according to the whims of the broker or buyers. The few Maasai who have known the value of the land have become co-perpetrators with the buyers and play a big role in fleecing the poor and illiterate majority."

"Since I did not go to school, I do not know the law and do not know where to go to seek help to be registered. My children, too, were young and were in primary school. The furthest I went was to the chief, who was not willing to help and kept on referring me back to the committee."

"With a lack of education and deficient business skills, many Maasai landowners were sweet-talked to sell their land by greedy prospecting buyers through local brokers."

The Maasai are mostly spectators and only wait to be told the worth of their land by the brokers or buyers. The few Maasai who knew the value of the land have become co-perpetrators with the prospecting buyers and formed cartels that are fleecing the poor and illiterate majority (Koissaba, 2014). While illiteracy has contributed to the loss of land by the Maasai, I argue that some individuals have sold their land and invested in education for their children. Others have sold some portions of their land to invest in other revenue-generating ventures that become a source of income for the families. There is some evidence of investment diversification by a few Maasai people who have disinvested in livestock and ventured into other revenue streams like real estate, agriculture, and tourism-related businesses (Koissaba, 2014). However, children in Maasai pastoralist households are the least likely to attend school, compared to neighbouring farmers and business owners (Hedges, Mulder, Gishelli, et al., 2014).

In summary, while the Maasai themselves, due to high levels of illiteracy and little knowledge of the cash economy, have voluntarily sold their land, corrupt government officials and land brokers played a big role in working as the go-between of potential land merchants and either individual landowners or group ranch representatives. Local politicians have also been accused of either abetting the vice of illegal land appropriation or not taking steps to stop it. Several people who engaged in this discourse equally expressed the need for the National Land Commission and the County Land Boards to work together to reduce the rampant corruption among government officials, Group Ranch committees, and the land brokers.

Land Sales

The phenomenon of rampant and indiscriminate land sales, both in Narok and Kajiado counties, featured most of the interactions among many Maasai narratives.

> "The uncontrolled sale of land in Kajiado and Narok has left many families destitute. There are no mechanisms to guide land sales once the land is subdivided into individual title ownership."

The above statement was supported by a study informant who lives in Kajiado County with her two co-wives, who emotionally narrated how her husband moved to Ngong Town, and all they could see were vehicles coming to plant beacons on their land in Saikeri. She stated that:

> "Our husband moved to Ngong town, and all we know of him is that he was always drunk in the company of other women in town. He used to send food home by taxi and occasionally would come with strangers to give them goats. These strangers would come and walk all over the land, planting land beacons on our land. It was not long before we started seeing strangers coming to build homes on our land. I did not know how big the land was, but all I have now is only two acres where I have my house. All the land was sold."

In some of their remarks about land sales, a participant in the study lamented that not only are individual parcels of land being sold. But also, according to one of the participants, group ranch committees are selling community land:

> "The Elangata Wuas Group Ranch committee has been selling and leasing community land without the consent of the members of the group ranch. Almost all the shopping centres have been sold out to non-Maasai."

According to the study participants, land sales in Maasai land have led to massive land loss and destitution, and were driven by several factors.

> "This was driven by several factors. One, there was a perception that individual land owners would be able to develop their land and improve their livelihoods, as was seen among the few Maasai who had individual ranches. Secondly, the money economy was introduced through loans that were advanced to the landowners by the Agricultural Finance Corporation (AFC) to buy steers. The third factor that led to massive land sales was the idea of 'Maendeleo' (meaning development). The Maasai wanted to live like the 'others', drive cars, build better houses, eat and drink like other communities."

The study participants also elaborated on the impact land sales have had on women and children, who are the most affected by land sales, and by men who are the only ones registered as title holders.

> "Since women are not allocated land, men neither consult women nor family members when they sell land. Many of them move to big towns, marry women in towns, and to support them, they sell land in total disregard of the families they have left back in the villages."

Study participants, who have participated over a long time in land-related issues and have witnessed how land sales have contributed to the massive loss of land by the Maasai in Narok and Kajiado Counties, expressed despair if the current trend is allowed to continue.

> "The Maasai are a dying people; they have sold all their land from Kitengela to Namanga in Kajiado, and now, after group ranches have been subdivided in Narok, all the land along Narok-Mulot road, as well as Narok-Maasai Mara road, is being sold like chicken. Soon, the Maasai will have nothing."

According to the participants, the precursor to the initial land sales in Kajiado and Narok was driven by loans that were advanced to individual landowners who used their titles to acquire loans to buy steers from the Agricultural Finance Corporation (AFC). Due to the diminishing grazing land, persistent drought, and reduced mobility of the livestock in search of pasture, many borrowers were not able to repay their loans. This prompted some to voluntarily sell their land to repay the loans, while others had their land sold by the Corporation to recover the loans.

Conservation and Tourism

Large tracks of Maasai land have been carved out and converted into game parks, game reserves, or forests. This has led to the reduction of pasture land and denied the Maasai access to dry-season grazing areas. The creation of conservancies around the Maasai Mara Game Reserve was also cited as an issue that has contributed to the loss of grazing land for local communities, since once the land is leased, there are restrictions on grazing. The current community conservancies in the Mara area are: Enoonkishu, Lemek, Mara Naboisho, Mara North, Mara Siana, Motorogi, Nashlai, Olkinyei, Olare Orok, Olarro, Olare Orok, Olchorro Oirowua, Olderkesi, Oloisukut, and Pardamat.

Study participants had this to say:

> "I was among the local Maasai elders who decided that the Maasai should conserve the Mau Forest as a dry-season grazing area as well as a source of water. I was also among the people who set up the Maasai Mara Game Reserve to act as a source of money to help the Maasai develop. All these that we set aside have now left us. Mau has been grabbed, and the Maasai no longer benefit from money coming from Maasai Mara."

> "Since Maasai Mara is considered the 8th Wonder of the World, many private conservancies have been established around the Game Reserve. The conservancies lease the land with very little money for periods of over fifteen years. During this period, the Maasai are not allowed to graze their livestock on the leased land. As the land for grazing continued to diminish, coupled with persistent droughts that decimated livestock, many Maasai found themselves dispersed, and the only commodity they had was land. In order to meet their daily needs, many families sold their land, albeit without knowing its value; hence, they were exploited by the buyers and the land brokers. The cash economy compelled many landowners to sell their land."

Residents from Narok raised the issue about the creation of private conservancies around Maasai Mara, which, according to them, has deprived many families of their livelihoods.

A conservancy is defined as "land designated by a community or private landowners, groups of owners, or a corporate body for purposes of wildlife conservation and other compatible land uses. The term conservancy also refers to an institution that is set up to manage such land (KWCA, 2016). Conservancies are classified into private, group conservancy, community conservancy, or proposed conservancy

> "This conservancy model approach involves the leasing of land from landowners around the Maasai Mara Game Reserve. Owners in the previous community-owned group ranches of Siana, Olkinyei, Koyiaki, Olchoro-Oirowua, and Lemek. Behind the creation of conservancies are local Maasai politicians and elites with connections to global eco-tourism organizations who use their connections to seek funding to support their ventures. While the land leases have slowed down the sale of land to outsiders and allowed for free movement of the wildlife within the conservancies, it has created direct competition with community livelihoods, especially pastoralism."

> "From what I am observing and hearing from the local communities in the Mara, conservancy leases have introduced regulations that exclude grazing, agriculture, fencing, and other livelihood activities, including permanent settlement by land owners within the designated conservancy area. I have observed internally displaced families."

According to Markakis (2004), concern about the preservation of forests, valuable species of flora and fauna, and wildlife has triggered another major intrusion into the Maasai and other pastoralist zones (Markakis, 2004). Under the National Parks Ordinance of 1945, the Kajiado Maasai lost access to two areas bordering Nairobi National Park and Tsavo National Park. This Ordinance also established a game reserve in Amboseli (3248 square kilometres), and game conservation areas at Kitengela (583 square kilometres) and West Chyulu (368 square kilometres), restricting the use of these areas by the Maasai (Grandin, 1986). Subsequent areas of Maasai Mara were also alienated. Beginning in a moderate way under colonialism, the designation of animal sanctuaries, controlled hunting areas, game parks, and reserves, nature reserves, protected forests, and 'wildlife corridors' spread significantly after independence (Markakis, 2004). Most of the land that was alienated from the seemingly 'idle' land was perceived by the policy makers who were ignorant of the pastoralist way of land use management practices.

Eco-tourism and conservation have been identified as some of the leading global land-grab processes (Zoomers, 2010). Recent studies indicate the emergence of a new conservation model in the Maasai Mara area in Narok County (Bedelian, 2012). This model conservancy involves leasing land from property owners around the Maasai Mara Game Reserve.

The conservancies have excluded women and youth who have not been allocated land within the conservancy area, thus negatively impacting average household incomes. According to Thomson et al. (2009), the average annual income for those who have leased land to the conservancies is $2,626, and they have no right to engage in any other livelihood activities within the leased parcels of land. Strict regulations with exorbitant fines are charged to any person found grazing within the designated conservancy areas, regardless of the circumstances (Thomson et al., 2009).

I believe that this has created conservation refugees, otherwise called internally displaced families, which has contributed negatively to aspects of infrastructure development, especially education, because of family mobility. Maasai Mara has the highest illiteracy rates in Narok County despite the lucrative business being carried out by both local and international tourist organizations (Thomson et al., 2009). The creation of conservancies has created displacements that have disproportionate effects on the pastoralists, the Maasai, and especially women and children due to the loss of livelihoods and family roles.

The displacement of people to provide room for conservancies has exposed women and girls to high risks of exploitation, such as sexual violence, high school dropout, and prostitution (Thomson et al., 2009). The loss of access to resources and livelihoods has increased vulnerability and resulted in greater insecurity (Thomson et al., 2009). The zoning of the land has increased pressure on the remaining land, which has resulted in overgrazing, and human-wildlife conflicts have become a common phenomenon (Thomson et al., 2009). Neo-conservation also brought in an opaque system of accountability where local communities that leased their land to Conservancies are not privy to the annual incomes made by the projects. It appears that the conservancies are running their businesses in a non-transparent manner, and their accounts have continually shown that the conservancies are running at a loss. I believe this is a deliberate way of exploiting the Maasai by the management of the Conservancies by taking advantage of the high illiteracy level of the local communities.

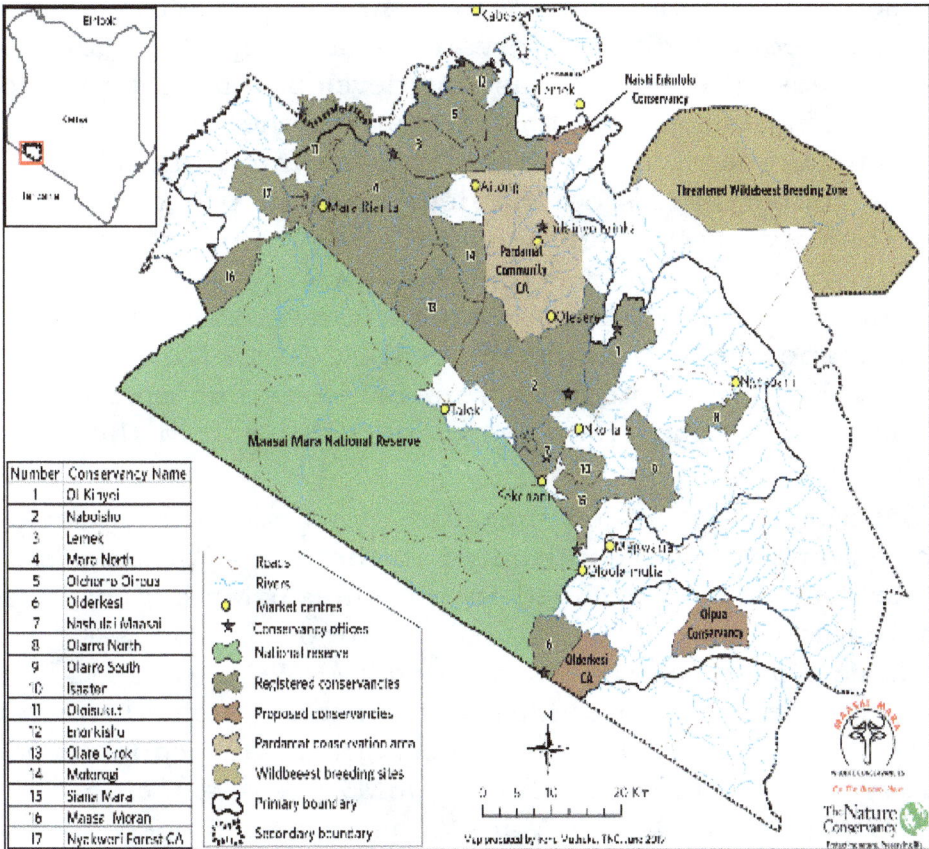

Figure 2: Maasai Mara National Game Reserve and Conservancy Areas
Source: Maasai Mara Wildlife Conservancies Association

While the case presented above points to a gloomy situation, I also posit that despite the losses of land to conservation, there are enormous benefits, and a few individual Maasai have benefited from wildlife tourism revenues from the protected areas. Despite varied views about whether the Maasai benefit from the existing conservancies, there is evidence of a considerable number of Maasai who have gained socio-economically from the creation of conservation efforts being carried out on their land. Such benefits include employment and business ventures in tourism-related enterprises. It is also important to note that the creation of Conservancies in the Maasai Mara has contributed to the restriction of land sales in the areas where land has been leased out for conservation. In summary, while the current model of community conservancies has helped in reducing land sales, the model has not developed a best practice for benefit sharing and has no plan for the development of required infrastructure within the local communities. Despite some conservancies having helped to put up schools and community health facilities, there is no uniform, agreed-upon strategic initiative that may provide services to the communities. Due to the creation of awareness about the importance of land made by local NGOs in the area, and the realization of incomes from conservation, community conservancies may help stop land sales within the areas that have conservancies.

Contrary to previous negative perceptions about how conservancies have contributed to the loss of grazing land, a new model has emerged in the Maasai Mara Ecosystem in Narok County. The establishment of the Maasai Mara Wildlife Conservancies Association (MMWCA) in 2013 was to conserve the greater Maasai Mara Ecosystem through a network of protected areas (conservancies and conservation areas) for the prosperity of all. MMWCA is a membership organization of all the Mara conservancies, open to any existing or upcoming wildlife conservancies whose land is part of or integral to the greater Maasai Mara ecosystem. The Wildlife Conservation and Management Act of 2013 envisaged community conservation as the instrument for protecting and managing wildlife outside designated protected areas, hence reducing human-wildlife conflicts.

This model has shown an exponential growth of conservancies, an increase in local earnings by members of the conservancies, and employment creation. This exponential growth is attributed to the conservancy's administrative structure, which includes all stakeholders.

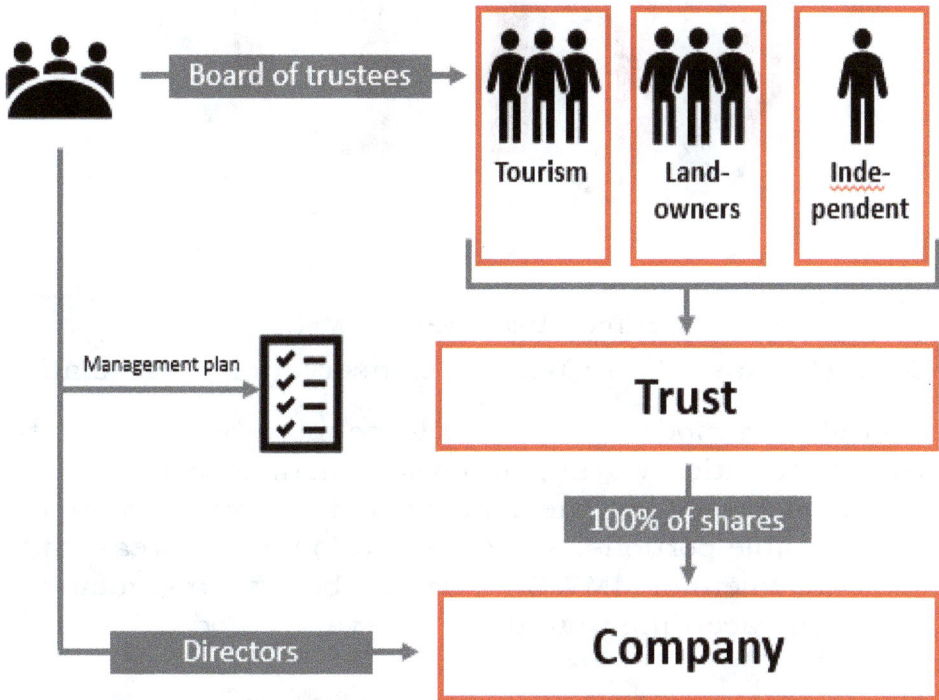

Figure 3: MMWCA Conservancies Administrative Structure Source: Maasai Mara Wildlife Conservancies Association

Data provided by MMWCA indicates that the number of conservancies increased from 11 to 16 between 2015 and 2016, the size of the conservancy area increased from 9,000 acres to 14,000 acres, the number of landowners increased from 4,000 to 14,000, and the number of rangers employed by the conservancies increased from 200 to 550 within the same period. The annual incomes of the landowners increased to Ksh. 7.5 million. The figure below indicates the trends in growth within the MMWCA-managed conservancy area.

Total Area under Conservation

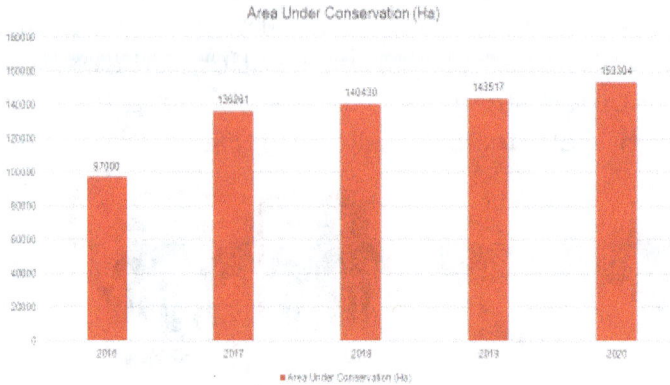

Area Under Conservation (Ha)

Fig.4: Total Area Under the MMWCA

Source: Maasai Mara Wildlife Conservancies Association

Overall, this model has proved to be more beneficial to the local communities who are landowners in diverse dimensions, as well as protecting the land from sale, subdivision into unsustainable portions, and conservation of the areas under the management of MMWCA. Figure 4 below is a summary of the benefits accruing from the conservancy model.

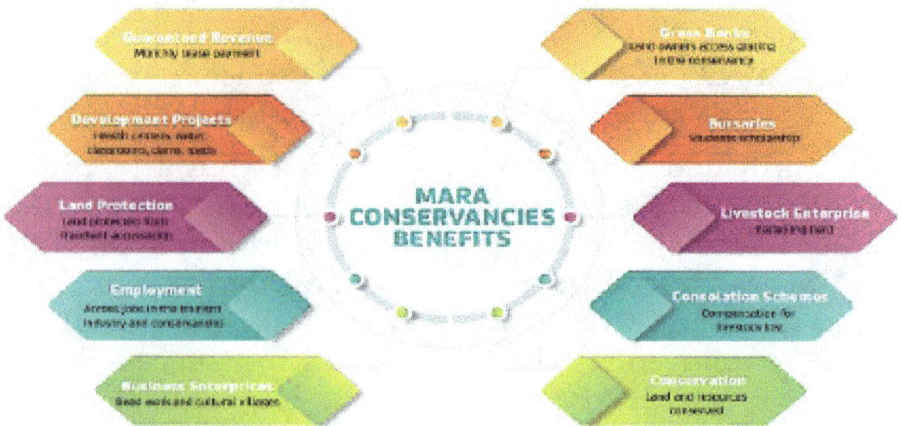

Figure 5: Summary of Benefits Accruing from the Conservancy Model.

Source: Maasai Mara Wildlife Conservancies Association

Legitimized Corruption and Impunity

Based on the results of our study, the legitimacy of national laws is seen by the participants from the context of how the laws have ultimately subordinated the law of morality. This is in such a way that they have been used to disenfranchise communities of their natural rights to ownership and control of their land. Legitimacy is used to describe both what is perceived to be the rights of governments to make legally binding decisions on behalf of the citizens according to the inherent national legal statutes, and the degree to which such decisions conform to recognized natural principles or accepted rules and standards of natural justice.

It is my view that the rules and regulations are perceived as legal rules and standards that everyone ought to follow, whether they reflected cultural and traditional practices, the law of the cosmos, or the will of God, or they were democratically approved or simply enacted according to established procedures. Based on this, I argue that legitimacy is subjective and found in the beliefs and perceptions of individuals and groups towards the actions and behaviours of others (Habermas, 1996). I further argue that the laws and other legal instruments used to appropriate Maasai land created a legitimization crisis, in that there now exists evidence of a decline in the confidence of administrative functions, institutions, or leadership by the Maasai, who view local legal instruments as instruments of dispossession.

According to Habermas (1996), it is assumed that any legal system has a higher level of legitimacy over and above individual legal norms. This was the force that drove Kenyan policy processes, where laws were enacted to create and facilitate nationhood. In reference to the works of Ralf Drier, Habermas states that:

> "First, the legal system must, by and large, be socially effective and, second, by and large, ethically justified. The legal validity of individual norms requires that they be enacted in accordance with a constitution satisfying the criteria mentioned above. In addition, norms individually

display first, a minimum ethical justification or the potential for such (Habermas, 1996, p. 30)."

Kenya's political system has used the 'tyranny of numbers'[2] both in Parliament and in the Senate, and in the name of democracy to legitimize their existence and land appropriation, even where freedom of choice is infringed, and the rights of all citizens are not protected. In my arguments, I posit that the use of quasi-democratic systems for choosing and replacing the government and passing laws has variously been manipulated to favour certain communities by virtue of their numbers. Others argue that the country is led based on 'consensus of the elite' such that even when they use their ethnic bases to get elected, leaders deliver very little to the people who elect them, in the end, those that benefit from the system are those associated with the elite or, in one way or the other, feature in the elite's client-patron networks.

Regarding the use of national legislation, I argue that the laws disregarded the interests of the Maasai. The laws are morally and legally illegitimate from the Maasai context, for they lacked adequate consultation and were deliberately enacted with the primary goal of appropriating Maasai land. Such laws derive their legitimacy from legislative processes based on state sovereignty. However, their inability to secure the rights and political autonomy of citizens (subjects) denies the laws the legitimacy as they deprived individuals as well as whole communities of the rights to own land and practice traditionally accepted land-use systems.

I contend that despite the illegality and corruption inherent in the Ministry of Lands, the fact is that land grabbers who are known to have acquired land in Narok and Kajiado have not been prosecuted, and the land titles have not been nullified. This is an indication that the law has legitimized the ownership of land that was acquired through corrupt and illegal means. From the perspective of the Maasai, the failure to take legal action against the perpetrators of such acts legitimizes corruption and impunity.

---

2   Tyrany of numbers is a term used to express a political situation where the majority or more numerous communities' subject others to their rule through the use of numbers in a democratic environment.

Global Focus on how much land was taken away from the Maasai to cater to globalization.

Globalization is a human historical process where competing ideologies form the basis for global economic and political systems to compete for dominance in resource ownership, access, and control (Groody, 2007). Globalization, both as a political and economic system, has had its fair share of both positive and negative impacts on the lives and livelihoods of pastoralist communities in East Africa, and especially the Maasai. Land alienation through forceful acquisition, treaties, and legislation introduced privatization of land, which was alien to the Maasai and occasioned massive dispossession of land and other natural resources without creating an enabling environment for the community.

The impact of globalization was first felt by the pastoralists after the Berlin Conference of 1884-1885, when the African continent was partitioned by the European colonial powers of France, Germany, Great Britain, and Portugal. These colonial powers superimposed their domains on the African continent by drawing arbitrary boundaries that resulted in dividing some African communities into several countries under different European masters (Muler & Blij, 2003). This was the case for the Maasai of East Africa, who were placed under the British in Kenya and under the Germans in Tanzania. Sindiga (1984) agreed with most observers that before the advent of the colonial government, the lifestyle of most pastoral groups was spatially designed to provide a stable ecological foundation for their economy.

People I have interacted with regarding their perspectives about globalization have repeatedly mentioned how the Maasai, as a tribe, were placed in Kenya and Tanzania, as well as further reclassified as different people groups in Kenya. The study participants and the general Maa speakers have variously expressed their concerns about why the Samburu and the Ilchamus are not classified as Maasai, yet they share the same language and many cultural practices. According to the study participants, globalization has had an enormous impact on their daily lives. These are some of the comments from the study participants:

"Globalization has influenced everything in Kenya."

"Recent shift by the Kenyan government to increase power projection as a result of economic growth and foreign investments is driving land appropriation in Naivasha. The World Bank is funding Ken Gen's geothermal power in Naivasha, and China is funding a new railway line from Mombasa, which is displacing hundreds of people."

"Globalization has brought in new dynamics and characteristics, and with the influence of the so-called development partners like organized religions, development initiatives aimed at establishing schools, and donor-driven interventions aimed at modernizing the Maasai, the Maasai model has since started to collapse due to the influence of the modernizing society and the emergence of new structures that are not in tandem with the Maasai settlement patterns and hence their culture."

"These big companies should consult the local people and compensate them adequately for any land lost."

"Globalization has influenced everything in Kenya, especially China's construction of the standard gauge railway across Kajiado. This has implications on land loss, compensation, and subsequent dispensations."

"Multinationals are working with governments that alienate indigenous people from their land. However, multilaterals like the WB have tight safeguards that protect Indigenous Peoples from being relocated, unlike other countries like China, Qatar, and many others that do not have any safeguards, and their due diligence is weak or non-existent. Governments, therefore, find it easier to borrow from these countries like China and not the WB anymore, as they do not have safeguard policies. Loans by the World Bank are 'safer for Indigenous People' as they come with safeguards than loans from China, which have no human rights-based approaches or safeguards. It is basically "large-scale, neo-colonial land appropriation, through perceived development."

Western culture, in the guise of globalization, has continued to negatively impact other global cultures. Since the advent of colonization of Africa in the early 19th century, globalization forces in the name of modernization and development have gradually affected the social structure of the Maasai and their culture, beliefs, values, and family structure. According to Mittelmann (2000), globalization is characterised by economism (a tendency to over-emphasize material factors to the neglect of the political and cultural aspects of globalization), state-centricity (tendency to focus more on nation-states at the expense of individual cultures within the state), and over-emphasis within area studies on particularities and detailed descriptions about the transformations in a given locale without also grasping the linkages to evolving global structures.

According to Rozman (2005), modernity is connected to the idea of modernization. Modernization suggests updating something or bringing something into line with what is seen as present-day fashions and needs (Rozman, 2005). The end of the Second World War was followed by decolonization in Asia, Africa, and the Middle East. The underdeveloped nations began to adopt the notion of development to be like the (technologically) developed countries of the West (Rozman, 2005). This process was identified with economic growth. However, this process did not involve only economic growth; it also carried many other phenomena, such as social, cultural, and political change (Gandolfo, 2009). It was a complicated process of change that influenced a wide scope of life, both individuals and society (Nyangira, 1975). This development led to the establishment of institutions in the underdeveloped countries that were meant to propel modernity (Nyangira, 1975). Modernization theories regarded cultures of non-industrialized societies in the South as obstacles to development. This is because of their kinship institutions that, according to the modernists, seem to hinder individual enterprise and capitalism. They were perceived to be traditional and barbaric, and as something to be discarded to realize development (Ntuli, 2002).

Structural Adjustment Programmes (SAPs) emphasized free trade liberalization and investment as well as high-interest rates to attract foreign investment. The privatization of government-held enterprises led to the proliferation of private sector conservation entities increasingly recognized as an important form of governance for protected areas, which continued to attract donor support, like the Global Environment Facility's funding for private sector initiatives. Such initiatives reached areas in Maasai land that were deemed to have high potential for conservation and tourism. The outcome of such projects has had both positive and negative impacts among the Maasai people in Kajiado and Narok, where tourism and conservation are the leading income earners (Thomson et al., 2009).

According to Bedelian (2012); Oxfam (2012); Thomson (2009) Galaty (1999); and Grandin (1986), the Maasai, just like the rest of the communities in Africa, were introduced to modern institutions such as schools, large-scale agriculture, Western medicine, business, formal employment and a wage-based economy, and in the recent past, advanced tele- communications and cyberspace. With such institutions, modernity has profoundly penetrated the Maasai community and presented the modern values of life, which have become the ultimate ideals of 'civilized' society. The colonial and post-independence governments propagated these ideals and exerted pressure on the conservative communities like the Maasai to let go of their 'primitive' traditions and instead embrace modernity. It is, therefore, my contention that globalization has contributed to the erosion of the Maasai culture and resulted in changes within community structures, hence impacting family life.

According to Robinson and Green (2011), globalization has restructured economic, political, and social relationships at the local level. They argued that technological and social changes have ushered in new avenues for sharing collective interests. The Maasai culture that thrived on collective responsibility, ownership, and control of resources was eroded as individual land owners could sell their land willingly without consulting other members of the community. I posit that private investments in agriculture meant to alleviate poverty and food insecurity failed to deliver benefits to the local communities. Large tracks of land leased to multi-nationals for commercial agricultural purposes in Narok reduced the grazing areas for the pastoralists, but the land was not sold or leased for its full value (Oxfam, 2012). Most of the crops produced were mainly sold to big millers through middlemen, and the highly mechanized operations provided minimal work opportunities for the local community. There are increased poverty levels that arose from the capital flight, which has created food deserts for local communities, making them travel long distances for food and other basic requirements.

I argue that unintended consequences arising from such ventures are health hazards ranging from aerial pesticide sprays used to control weeds and diseases in the farms, land degradation, decreased household incomes, human-wildlife conflicts, and decreased pasture for livestock. While no research has been done to confirm the impacts of the chemicals on the health of communities and their livestock, narratives from the local communities indicate high levels of upper respiratory tract infections in humans, and stillbirths in their livestock during planting seasons (Koissaba, 2014). The clearing of the land for cultivation has also created indiscriminate destruction of ground cover, which has increased incidences of soil erosion and destruction of vital genetic species that local communities use for medicinal purposes.

One glaring example is the extraction of soda ash in Lake Magadi. Tata Chemicals, formerly the Magadi Soda Company, which is now part of the giant Tata Group after the franchise was acquired from Brunner Mond Group of the United Kingdom, is Africa's leading soda ash company and presumably the lowest cost producer in the world (Hughes, 2008). The Magadi concession area covers about 206 square miles and has a history dating back to 1911, when the Maasai agreements and treaties were enacted. The Magadi Concession area was carved out of land traditionally occupied by the Maasai and has since been out of bounds for the indigenous communities. This has denied the local community access to pasture, watering points, and salt licks for their livestock. Despite massive opportunities for employment creation, the local communities have obtained few jobs in this industry due to their low levels of education and nepotism. Protests by the Maasai started in earnest in 1950 and subsequently in 1962 during the Lancaster independence conference. Later, in 2003, hundreds of Maasai were arrested for blocking the railway line used to transport the soda ash. These protests have not yielded any meaningful results (Tiampati, 2005). Below is a map of the Magadi Concession area and the adjacent Maasai group ranches where the land was alienated.

Comments about how the Maasai in Kajiado are dissatisfied with the exploitation of salt in Magadi are rightly expressed by the Kajiado Governor. According to Governor Ole Lenku, "Cooperation between the county government and Investors should not only benefit these parties but also the people of Kajiado. It's unfair for the investors to sack locals, yet they rely on their resources to benefit themselves. We just can't take any more of this marginalization in our motherland" (Governor Ole Lenku's Facebook page, 7/14/2021).

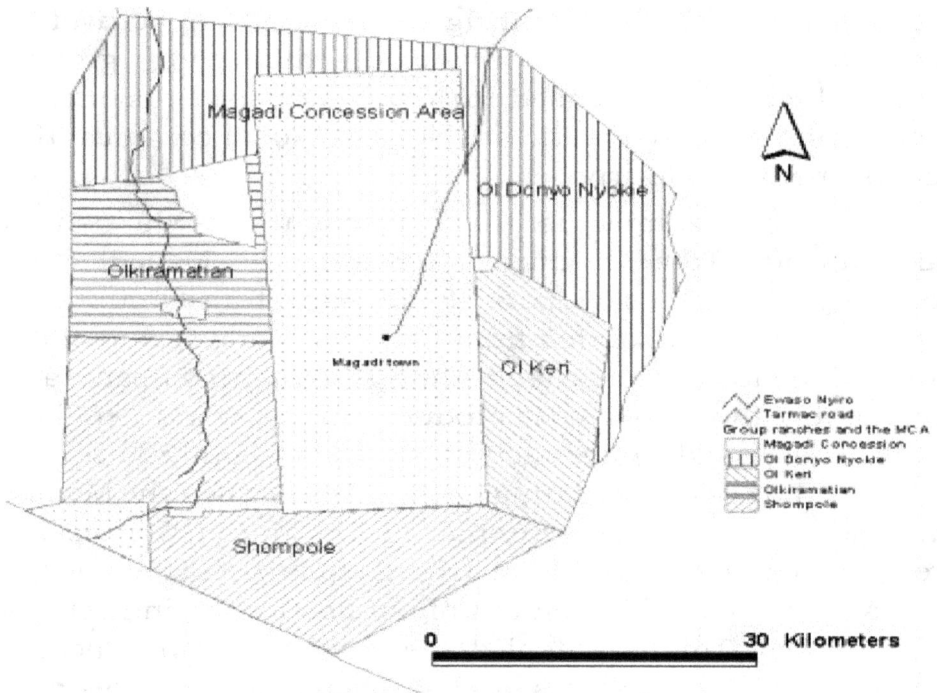

Figure 6. Magadi Concession Area and adjacent Group Ranches. (Source: Department of International Development; DFID East Africa.)

The current discoveries of vast amounts of geothermal and potential oil exploration in Narok and Kajiado, where multinationals are seeking to obtain concessions from the government without the consultation of the local communities, are a further threat to the loss of land by the Maasai. According to Koissaba (2015), the government has adopted a system of seeking international aid in the name of development grants, prospecting rights to local and international companies, and subsequently giving concession rights for exploitation of the natural resources without prior and informed consent of the local communities.

With globalization came urbarnization and the establishment of local business centres in the heart of Maasai land. Because the Maasai were not very keen on running businesses, other non-Maasai communities established strong economic bases in Narok and Kajiado. The population of these migrant communities increased drastically in areas closer to Nairobi and along the Namanga-Nairobi highway, with several small business centres established. Equally, in Narok, the migrant community, mostly made up of agriculturalists, leased land to grow crops. Later, they established small shopping centres to sell their commodities to the local Maasai, who were predominantly pastoralists. As time went by, many local Maasai ended up selling their land to the immigrant businesspeople. I believe that due to their friendly nature and welcoming attitude, many Maasai adopted some immigrant communities, where to date you will hear them being referred to as *"Olkokoyoi lai or Olkisii lai"* (meaning my Kikuyu or my Kisii, respectively).

Leadership and Land Appropriation

In this section, I look at Maasai leaders from their political point of view regarding Maasai land-related issues and the roles they played. In discussing leadership, I am biased in speaking mainly of those leaders who voiced their concerns about the loss of land by the Maasai and those who have played certain roles in abetting the loss of land. However, before I delve into that, I wish to express my own opinion about land, identity, culture, and self-preservation of the Maasai. According to the Constitution of Kenya, every Kenyan has a right to live, invest, and vie for any political position or other position in the Republic of Kenya. It is my position that there is a need to consider the interests of the local communities regarding their representation and economic development to forestall situations of being dominated by others. This is the case with the Maasai, where immigrant communities have outnumbered them in certain areas. Since political representation determines other factors of development, I suggest that the protection of the Maasai land is key to preserving not only the culture but the existence of the Maasai as a people.

Regarding leadership and land appropriation among the Maasai, it is important to note that there is no leader without land for his people, a vibrant economy, strength, and power that can stand to be called a leader. As far as land is concerned, if one is not a landlord or land owner, they are at best tenants, squatters, and at worst vagabonds. Losing land is the fastest way to be engulfed, assimilated, trodden upon, and utterly dominated. This is the case for the Maasai in Laikipia, Baringo, Nakuru, and some parts of Narok and Kajiado, where, despite the land having been historically theirs, they have been rendered a minority and have no political and economic voice. In today's Kenya, politicians, landowners, and prospectors don't use bows and arrows, spears, and guns to acquire Maasai land; they use economic, political, and numerical power to acquire Maasai land. Land goes away with leadership, language, ambitions, renewable riches, and identity, among other important values and life factors.

The immigrant land owners are skilled and very strategic in the use of economic power to acquire the single most important commodity that makes a people who they are; that is, land. They are skilled in turning the same land into highly productive land and in exploiting the locked-in resources into gold. What they produce from it and the local communities buy will give them the profit to buy even more of it. The worst thing about this disaster is when your own people are the spies, the brains, the hands, the legs used to entice their own people, to fraudently sell their land, protect the interests of others, or even lobby for other communities for political favours.

As discussed previously, traditionally, the Maasai leadership was structured around their sub-tribes and age groups. This structure was dismantled during the arrival of the Europeans. The new structure that was introduced by the colonialists was the indirect rule that the British instituted in their colonies and protectorates as a means of limiting resistance to their rule. However, the enforcer was 'one of our own' but acting in the interests of the colonizer. The new structure did not augur well with how the Maasai made their decisions. First, the colonialists appointed Olonana as a leader, yet his role was that of a medicine man and a seer. They went further to create a position of a headman in every sub-tribe or elevated some of the traditional leaders and opinion leaders to the positions of headsmen or chiefs. The headsmen became the spokespersons for the Europeans and later on for the Kenyan government and wielded a lot of power. They were used to collect taxes and give instructions on what the government of the day needed to be done.

In traditional Maasai society, there were also no elective positions since the leaders were secretly selected and chosen by elders from Olpiron (the age-set that stirs the fire to begin a new age set). The first Maasai to be selected to the government was the late Dr. John Ole Tameno, who was the representative of the Rift Valley in the Legislative Council (LegCo); he was first nominated for the position in 1952. Contrary to the writings of Andrew Morton in the autobiography of the late president Daniel Moi titled *"Moi: The Making of of an African Stateman"*, where Morton wrote that Ole Tameno was recalled because he was a drunkard and replaced by the late president Daniel Arap Moi who was a tea totler, Ole Tameno was seen to be a threat by the colonialists. This narrative was refuted by Dr. Tameno through a letter to the publishers of the book, Michael O'Mara Books Limited, which was written by his lawyer, Sankale Ole Kantai, dated 15th June 1999.

Dr. John Moroyian Ole Tameno resigned from his political position in protest because of how the colonialists were treating the Maasai. His anger arose from the inauguration of Queen Elizabeth on 6 February 1952, whereupon, being inaugurated, a Maasai chief from Ilkaputiei gave Ngong Hills as a gift to the new Queen. Ole Tameno protested the gifting of the Ngong Hills, which did not go down well with the colonial government. Further, Ole Tameno protested the burial of the colonial era Narok District Commissioner Hugh Murray Grant, who was speared to death by a Maasai warrior named Karampu Ole Senteu at Morijo Loita. In his protest, Ole Tameno moved to live next to the grave to ensure that the land would not be taken by the colonial government. The colonialists also did not trust Ole Tameno because he was suspected of being a sympathizer of the Mau Mau freedom fighters, as his home was close to the detention camp in Ngong, commonly referred to as "Gichagi"[3]. Dr. Tameno later became part of the Maasai delegation to the Lancaster independence conference.

Another Maasai who rose to a political position was Joseph Ole Morompi (spelt Murumbi). Kenyatta had known Murumbi's organizational skills since the Second Lancaster talks in London, when he managed all the delegates' appointments and did all the typing required. In January 1963, Mr. Kenyatta appointed Joseph Murumbi as KANU national treasurer and asked him to reorganize the headquarters, which was torn between the Tom Mboya and the Oginga Odinga camps. He was later appointed to the position of Minister of Foreign Affairs of the Republic of Kenya from 1964 to 1966, and the second Vice-President between May and December 1966, when he resigned from the position due to his dissatisfaction with Kenyatta's dealings with matters of land. Joseph Murumbi later started the African Heritage and owned land in Kilgoris.

According to reliable information, the late Murumbi defaulted on an Agricultural Finance Loan of 8.9 million, and the corporation proceeded to buy a parcel in 1998 for Sh 28 million. In December 2015, five family members, three of whom are now deceased, sought the intervention of the Chief Justice to repay the loan and be allowed to retain the land that their brother owned, but they were turned down in unclear circumstances. The Trusted Society of Human Rights questioned the land acquisition, four years ago, of the Intona Ranch land in Trans Mara West sub-county by the Deputy President, Dr. William Samoei Ruto, after paying

---

3   Notes from Dr. Tameno's daughter Mary Tameno.

off a loan owed to the Agricultural Finance Corporation (AFC) by the late Murumbi. The land was bought through North Mogor Holdings (Sayagie, 2019)[4].

Leadership among the Maasai has been seen to have contributed to major divisions and a lack of a united front for the Maa speakers in Kenya. This began immediately after the Lancaster independence conference, where some of the members of the Maasai delegation felt that some of their members were compromised on issues related to land. Further after independence, superiority battles ensued with key politicians like John Keen and Oloitipitip, who engaged in disagreements on various issues about the Maasai. The differences between the two were further exacerbated when John Keen, who was the Secretary-General of the Maasai United Front (MUF), joined the Kenya African National Union (KANU). This action angered Stanley Shapashina Oloitiptip, who was the chairman of Maasai United Front. Oloitiptip, in his disagreement with John Keen, decided to rally the Maasai against John Keen and pass a vote of no confidence against the latter. The introduction of political parties, as well as the politics of elections, distorted the Maasai leadership because some of the elected leaders do not owe their allegiance to the Maasai but to the political party barons.

John Keen, who was then serving in the East African Legislative Assembly (EALA), did not have a smooth ride in KANU for challenging President Jomo Kenya and had to be detained. In 1967, John Keen became the first person to be detained in independent Kenya. He was put behind bars by the administration after he accused Kenyatta, Tanzania's Julius Nyerere, and Uganda's Milton Obote of being the main obstacles towards the formation of the East African Community. This was a cover-up because John Keen stood against Jomo Kenyatta regarding the settlement of non-Maasai in some of the land that was earmarked for settlement schemes. Kikuyu land buying companies were formed and funded through the Settlement Land Trustee, which excluded the Maasai, who were the ancestral owners

---

4   Daily Nation, October 2nd, 2019. Ruto sucked into controversy over purchase of 900 acres.https://www.nation.co.ke/kenya/news/ruto-sucked-into-   controversy-over-purchase-of-900-acres-209586.

of the land, mainly in Nakuru, Naivasha, and parts of Mau. Such lands are still embroiled in court cases, and the Maasai are being displaced in Kedong, Narasha, Olchurrai, and many others.

Keen's other name could as well have been 'Mr. Rebellion'. While in Form Two at Alliance High School in 1946, he annoyed Carey Francis, the famous headmaster, by repainting the map of Africa fully in black and not in the five colours that represented the colonizing powers: Britain, France, Belgium, Germany, Italy, Spain, and Portugal. Angered by the act, the headmaster called Keen to his office and asked, "Young man, what do you mean by re-painting the map of Africa in black?" Without batting an eyelid, the student responded, "I did that because Africa belongs to black people! (Ngotho, 2017)"[5] Although outspoken and fearless, Keen was blamed by his constituency residents for not bringing home the development they wanted. John Keen viewed the development of roads and other infrastructure as a way of opening up Maasai land to intruders and non-Maasai communities. On his part, he accused the local Maasai of still wearing the traditional dress and keeping to traditional ways of life, including *moranism* (warriorhood). He urged them to send their children to school and to modernise. His rival, Oloitiptip, by contrast, defended traditional Maasai customs and worked hard as an assistant minister to bring development to the benefit of his family and friends in his home area.

John Keen stood his ground about the incursion into Maasai land by other tribes until Moi developed a scheme to get him out of parliament. Being a student of the colonial regime, Moi created a position called 'Paramount Chief' and appointed Maura Ole Loolpisia in Kajiado and Lerionka Ole Ntutu in Narok. Moi's main intention was to use these people to make inroads in Narok and Kajiado. In Kajiado, during the 1983 elections, they settled on supporting Phillip Odupoy against John Keen. Odupoy was seen to be non-combative and easily manipulated. The other

---

5 Kamau Ngotho, 2017, Daily Nation, Sunday, January 1, 2017.

contestant was Earnest Ole Mpaayei, who had challenged John Keen in previous elections. During this time, the main interest was the then Kajiado North Constituency because of its proximity to Nairobi. Moi used the Paramount Chief Maura Ole Lolpisia to whip the Maasai opinion leaders to support the idea. Moi also used friends among the Kikuyu community to vote out John Keen. To entrench his clout in Maasai land, Moi found Odupoy inadequate and hatched a plan to handpick the late Professor George Saitoti to be the Member of Parliament for Kajiado North. In the 1988 elections, the then Kajiado district was divided into three constituencies: North, Central, and South. To entrench their interests, John Keen was re-embraced by Moi, who was using the harmless Saitoti in readiness for the coming elections. In the North, Saitoti, backed by Keen, was returned unopposed. Keen himself became a nominated MP and was appointed assistant minister in the Office of the President.

To ensure Saitoti's election, the incumbent MP's life was made difficult (e.g., Philip Odupoy was charged with holding illegal meetings[6] , and so was the late Oliver Seki)[7]. On his part, Saitoti used his position to influence rich political friends to invest in buying land in many parts of the then Kajiado North by organizing loans for many of his political followers. In the end, many of these defaulted and either sold the land themselves or the land was auctioned by the banks. Saitoti's tenure as a Member of Parliament for Kajiado North ushered in a new era where massive land sales were experienced among the Ilkeekonyokie through agents who were themselves Maasai to solicit and purchase land on behalf of the then Kenyan United Insurance Company.

In Saikeri, between Ewuaso, Iloodoariak, and Mosiro, many people have sold land through agents representing the United Insurance Company, which was a Kikuyu-based company, aimed at usurping Maasai lands in increments in order to resell the same to the Kikuyu who wanted to purchase land in Maasai land at a profit. The Company was also said to have

---

6   Daily Nation 14/01/88
7   Daily Nation 10/02/88

raised funds internationally to resettle internally displaced Kikuyu communities. Another buyer of Maasai land was Nyakio General Contractors. While Nyakio bought land within the interior of the Maasai land, he was used as a conduit to expropriate Trust Land within Ngong Town. The company was allocated land between the then-District Officer's office and Ngong town, and along Ngong Kiserian road. Then the land was either sold or given to politically correct individuals. Most Maasai from Intashat, Ewuaso, Oldepe, and Ilkesumeti lost vast land to these two companies. Due to high levels of illiteracy, many land sellers were duped into handing over their land titles after receiving partial payments in order to take them to the Land Control Board, but the titles were never returned.

The Land Control Board was then chaired by the Ngong District Officers, who established special land boards to sanction the land transfers without the consent of the landowners. During this time, young educated Maasai people raised concerns about the land, especially among the Keekonyokie, which was being sold out to individuals and companies. It is important to note that several people interviewed during this study expressed their experiences that indicated that the rivalry and competition for political space facilitated the loss of land in Kajiado. One such expression was:

> "It is very unfortunate that our political leaders have sought political leadership positions by giving away the best land in Narok and Kajiado. I can remember how the then Member of Parliament for Kajiado, Stanley Oloitiptip, had given away Amboseli National Park, and the boundary between Kajiado, Nairobi, and Machakos, which was traditionally the Mombasa-Nairobi railway, was changed. The Ilkaputiei lost Maboko and the Kenya Meat Commission land, including the former Livestock Marketing ground adjacent to Kitengela. The Maasai lost a lot of land that is still in contention and a cause for conflict between Machakos, Makueni, and Kajiado Counties."

All is not lost for Kajiado County. During the tenure of the first governor, Dr. David Nkedienye, Kajiado County developed a land policy document and made declarations that were criticized by land brokers and prospectors but lauded by the Maasai by banning land sales. The current governor, Joseph Ole Lenku, has also become a vocal proponent of Maasai land-related issues. He strongly supported evictions in the Mau and put the Tata Chemicals Magadi on the spot regarding land rates, access to water, and other resources by the local communities. Ole Lenku is also being lauded for the recovery of the Oldonyio-onyokie Group Ranch Title Deed, which the committee had used to secure loans. Below are some of his comments regarding issues affecting the Maasai:

> "The Mosiro community is bleeding from the diversion of the Kisamis River by Tata Chemicals Magadi Ltd, which has destroyed their land. I demand the removal of the dikes they built, which have caused flooding and left deep ravines in people's farms. It is the company's role to handle siltation, not the communities. Their solution to siltation cannot be to the detriment of local community livelihoods. People's farms are now flooded by the diverted water[8] (Governor Ole Lenku's Facebook Page).

Governor Ole Lenku has also not shied away from leading from the front in issues related to the general Maasai fraternity. Together with other Maasai leaders, he condemned the forceful evictions of the Maasai in Kedong to give room for a dry port and other infrastructure.

> "Together with other Maa leaders, we have today called on the National Government to hold dialogue with our people over the controversial Kedong' ranch land that is earmarked for the dry port. This land runs across Kajiado and Narok Counties. We oppose the harassment of the Maa community over land and reject the eviction notice issued recently. The land is enough for all of us. We support the government's dry port project, and at the same time, the local community's rights should be upheld. There is a solution to this dispute. Let all the concerned be brought on board for talks to solve the stalemate"[9].

---

8   Joseph Ole Lenku's comments about diversion of a river by Tata Chemicals Magadi
9   Governor Joseph Ole Lenku with other Maasai leaders addressing press regarding the displacement of the Maasai in Kedong.

Fig 7. Kajiado County Governor Joseph Ole Lenku, with other Maasai leaders, addressed the press regarding the displacement of the Maasai in Kedong on November 12th, 2019.

Source: Governor Joseph Ole Lenku's Facebook page.

In the then Narok District, one of the leaders who fronted for Maasai land rights during the colonial and post-colonial times was the late Justus Kantet Ole Tipis. Ole Tipis was born in Narok in 1919. He later trained as a veterinarian and was employed in the Livestock Department in 1937. When the Second World War broke out, Ole Tipis was enlisted in the Army and rose to the rank of a colonial Colonel in 1946. After the war, Ole Tipis joined the Provincial administration and was deployed to work at Olenkuruone in the present-day Nakuru County. Ole Tipis ventured into politics in 1957 and was elected to the Legislative Council as a representative of the Central Rift Valley. Ole Tipis ventured into politics to fight for the return of all Maasai land that was taken away by the colonialists.

Ole Tipis became part of the Maasai team that went to the Lancaster Constitutional Conference to demand the return of the land. Due to the land-related intrigues between KANU and KADU, and the conspiracy between KANU and the British, the Maasai demand was not discussed, forcing the Maasai delegation to protest and walk out of the deliberation. Upon attainment of independence, Tipis was elected as a member of parliament between 1960 and 1969. During the 1969 general election, when Narok was divided into Narok North and Narok South, Tipis lost to Moses Ole Marima. In the 1974 General Election, Tipis trounced Ole Marima and continued to be elected until 1988, when he lost to William Ole Ntimama, who garnered 14,240 against Ole Tipis's 12,369[10].

William Ole Ntimama rose to political prominence as the Chairman of the defunct Narok County Council between 1974 and 1984. During his tenure, he represented Inkareta Ward, whose boundaries extended to the current Narok Town. Contrary to common perceptions about Ntimama being a tribalist, during his time as the Chairman of Narok County Council, Ntimama allocated plots in Narok town to several non-Maasai to establish businesses. During his long political career, Ntimama distinguished himself as a great agitator and defender of Maasai rights. As a result, he gained unrivalled popularity in the community and became one of the most influential Maasai leaders. At the height of politically instigated ethic clashes of the 1990s, the late Ntimama warned members of a certain community living in his constituency to "lie low like an envelope."

Due to the high agricultural production, Narok saw an influx of immigrants who came to lease land and carry out business in Narok. As the immigrant population increased, so did land prospectors who took advantage of the illiteracy of the Maasai to draw leases and sale agreements that disposed of the Maasai off their land. Corrupt land officials facilitated the fraudulent land deals, which angered Ntimama and other pro-Maasai land rights advocates. Ntimama was instrumental in securing several water catchment areas like Enoosupukia and the Mau forest from encroachment by immigrant communities in Narok, as well as supporting other Maasai communities in Laikipia, Samburu, Baringo, and Nakuru.

---

10 Weekly Review 31/01/97.

Ntimama was known to be the voice of the Maasai in Parliament, where he raised issues that touched Maasai land rights. Some of the occasions where Ntimama will be remembered were when Ntinaai Ole Moyiare was shot in Laikipia. Ntimama mobilized the Maasai to attend the funeral, where he was the main speaker. He was also instrumental in the funerals of Ole Kipuri and Ole Kunkuru, who were shot by Kenya Police helicopter gunships in Kedong under the direction of the late John Michuki and the supervision of the Naivasha Member of Parliament, Jane Kihara. While Ntimama was hailed as a hero, he was also viewed as a proponent of the Ilpurko, who are numerically superior in Narok's expansionist strategy against smaller sub-clans such as Iloitai, Ildamat, and Ilkeekonyokie. This raised conflicts where lives were lost in Ntulele, between Ilpurko, Ilkeekonyokie, Ildamat, and Endarkalal. The Iloitai have also had several conflicts in Ongata E Loita and Osupuko Oirobi.

During his political career, Ntimama was faced with several political opponents in Narok North. One perennial opponent was Harun Lempaka of the small Ildamat section, John Tiampati also from Purko, and Doctor Kaiseyie Ole Punyua from Ilkeekonyokie. Ntimama had such influence among the Maasai in Narok that he was able to influence who got elected as members of Parliament and councillors in Narok and sometimes Kajiado. Ntimama's political history was crushed after his defeat by a lawyer, Moitalel Ole Kenta, who also hails from Ilpurko, crossing swords with Ntimama's numerically powerful Purko Maasai in 2013.

Unfortunately, after the promulgation of the Constitution of Kenya 2010, tables were turned against the Ilpurko when Samwel Ole Tunai was elected the Governor with massive support from Kalenjin immigrants, and the Kikuyu who were in the Jubilee Party. Ole Tunai, having worked in the government as a spy in the National Intelligence Service, perfected the art of divide and rule. His leadership portrayed the Ilpurko as the aggressors, appointed a Kalenjin as his deputy, and rallied around the call of small Maasai clans against the Ilpurko. Ole Tunai mobilized Ilkeekonyokie, Ildamat, and Iloitai to marginalize Ilpurko and used the Kalenjin numbers with the support of the senior government officials to entrench himself. To weaken the Ilpurko, Ole Tunai took upon himself to give contracts for revenue collections to companies associated with some senior politicians[11] (Daily Nation, January 13th, 2015).

In Narok, for instance, it was impossible to set up a County Land Management Board (CLMB) due to political divisions. In 2014, the County Assembly rejected two out of the seven members nominated by the National Land Commission (NLC). Most of the nominees were from the majority Ilpurko clan of the Maasai, but the Governor mobilized the minority clans led by his own Isiria to shoot down the appointments in the pretext that minority clans were not represented. Isiria filed a case in 2015 challenging the process of setting up the board on the grounds that it lacked transparency and was not substantially representative of the people of Narok. This placed the Narok CLMB in a stalemate until the NLC appointed a secretary. It is believed that the stalemate has created a window for illegal land transactions under the political bigwigs in Narok[12] (Interview with Hassan Ole Kamwaro in Oklahoma City).

The regime introduced a new revenue collection that made the Maasai lose 19% of the revenue that used to be distributed to each ward for development, centralized all financial services, and only those close to him were alleged to have benefited. Revenues were being collected by a firm in Nairobi, and only his right-hand men would benefit. He maximized his connection with Vice President William Ruto, who is a Kalenjin, to propel the Kalenjin agenda in Narok County to a point where it is alleged that there are more Kalenjin speakers in the County Government than the Ilpurko, who are more numerous than any other Maa community in Narok County. It has been a small clan vis-à-vis Ilpurko. This worked for him because during Ntimama's Ilkeekonyokie, Ildamat and Iloitai were subjected to the dispossession of land as the Ilpurko expanded their land occupation, which resulted in clashes over the expansionist drive fronted by Ole Ntimama.

---

11   Daily Nation, January 13th, 2015. Money and politics: How 2013 poll tsunami has come to haunt Narok. https://www.nation.co.ke/kenya/news/politics/money-and-politics-how-2013-poll-tsunami-has-come-to-haunt-narok-1064768.

12   Interview with Hassan Ole Kamwaro, May 23rd, 2019, Oklahoma City.

The above sentiments were supported by people interviewed during this study. As indicated in their comments below, leadership among the Maasai played a role in abetting land losses. Such comments include:

"The current leadership dispensation in Narok and Kajiado Counties is a tragedy for the Maasai. The political leaders have been compromised to the point that the Maasai have no political bargaining power. See what happened, a Kikuyu constituency has been hived off Kajiado North in Kajiado, and one for the Kalenjin in Narok. Unfortunately, given the current political dispensation, the Kikuyu and Kalenjin are sponsoring electoral candidates in both Counties to front their agenda, not the Maasai Agenda."

"It is unfortunate that when the rest of the Maasai are standing up to support the evictions in the Mau Forest, some Maasai political leaders in Narok, such as the Governor Ole Tunai, the Women Representative Soipan Tuya, MPs Korei Ole Lemein, and Gabriel Ole Tongoyo, are supporting the Governor, who is against the evictions."

Despite all the political platform outlook in Narok, the Narok North Member of Parliament, Moitalel Ole Kenta, has come out to be the voice of reason regarding the Maasai grievances on land. Ole Kenta became very vocal about the excision of the Mau Forest to settle people who were illegally issued with title deeds for pieces of land in the forest. The Senator, Ledama Ole Kina, has also come out as a lead proponent of the just concluded evictions of the settlers in Mau and has also warned that subdivision of agricultural land into small uneconomical parcels will not be approved by the County Land Control Board. If this is implemented, it may lead to the reduction of immigrants who buy small parcels of land and secure community livelihoods, and reduce the chances of political dominance by immigrant communities, who are mainly the Kalenjin and Kikuyu.

Fig 8: Environment and Forestry Cabinet Secretary Keriako Tobiko, Narok North MP Moitalel Ole Kenta, and Maasai leaders appreciating the efforts made to preserve the Maasai Mau Forest. Source: Keriako Tobiko Facebook page

In summary, at the global scale, land is becoming a scarce resource. Addressing global land availability is made even more complex by the process of economic globalization. The flow of transnational capital into Kenya from such places as China, the World Bank, and other bilateral financiers has led to the new displacement of the Maasai. These displacements have sometimes led to significant social impacts. It is also not surprising that the land grabbers associated with economic globalization have benefited the Kenyan government, local elites, and businesses.

Given the above about how land matters have been handled in Kenya, there is a need to consider that the appropriation of land, or land grabbing, should not just be an examination of the specific acts of land grabbing, but should instead examine many processes, including globalization, that are associated with it. Economic globalization, combined with the looming global land scarcity and the complexity of future pathways of land-use change, needs to be guided in addressing land-related matters. Since healing requires that all stakeholders are truthful about events that have contributed to land-related conflicts, the government needs to own up to the fact that the government, through proxies of government officials, has been involved in malicious, illegal, and corrupt processes that have contributed to the dispossession of many communities in Kenya. Further, since matters of land have created wounds in various communities, the government needs to be objective in implementing various land-related commission reports that were meant to address land-related issues. Such reports include the Njonjo Commission Report, the Ndungu Commission Report, and the Truth, Justice, and Reconciliation Report.

The role of the Kenyan government needs to be more closely studied because, as noted, state officials often collaborated with partners in land deals and acted in ways that maximized their returns on what they considered marginal lands or marginal communities. Again, as noted in this study, actors within Kenya exploited others whenever they could and acted against each other to engage in land appropriation. Economic globalization seems to be providing additional incentives to obtain land for profiteering purposes.

Land Appropriation as an Affront to Human Rights

In this section, I discuss land rights from an experiential perspective. Having worked as an advocate for Maasai land rights for over 20 years, I developed personal opinions, perceptions, and convictions that land rights are discussed in exclusion of other human rights, and when discussed, they are not discussed within the context of the affected communities. According to the United Nations Human Rights, land rights are not typically perceived to be a human rights issue (United Nations Human Rights, [UNHR] 2015). These rights broadly refer to the rights to use, control, and transfer of land. They include rights to occupy, enjoy, and use land and its resources; restrict or exclude others from the land; transfer, sell, purchase, grant, or loan; inherit and bequeath; develop or improve; rent or sublet; and benefit from improved land values or rental income. Legally, land rights usually fall within the categories of land laws, land tenure agreements, or planning regulations, but they are rarely associated with human rights law. Internationally, no treaty or declaration specifically refers to a human right to land. Strictly speaking, there is no human right to land under international law. However, behind this façade, land rights are a key to human rights issues. Land rights constitute the basis for access to food, housing, and development, and without access to the land, many people would find themselves in a situation of great economic insecurity.

Land is not a mere commodity, but an essential element for the realization of many human rights (UNHR, 2015). Land is a cross-cutting issue that directly impacts the enjoyment of several human rights. To many people, land is a source of livelihood and is central to economic rights. Land is also often linked to people's identities, and so it is tied to social and cultural rights. Land disputes are frequently the cause of violent conflict and place obstacles to restoring sustainable peace. In short, the human rights aspects of land affect a range of issues, including poverty reduction and development, peace building, humanitarian assistance, disaster prevention and recovery, and urban and rural planning, to name a few. Emerging global issues, such as food insecurity, climate change, and rapid urbanization, have also refocused attention on how land is being used, controlled, and managed by states and private actors.

An increasing number of people are forcibly evicted or displaced from their land to make way for large-scale development or business projects, such as dams, mines, oil, geothermal, wind energy, and gas installations or ports. In many countries, the shift to large-scale farming has also led to forced evictions, displacements, and local food insecurity, which in turn has contributed to an increase in rural to urban migration and consequently further pressure on access to urban land and housing. A considerable portion of this displacement is carried out in a manner that violates the human rights of the affected communities, thus further aggravating their already precarious situation. In Kenya, such project includes the geothermal projects where massive forceful evictions of the Maasai from their land have been witnessed, the Lake Turkana Wind Power Project, the Lamu Port-South Sudan-Ethiopia- Transport (LAPSSET), the Corridor project, among others.

Urban development projects have led to socio-economic polarisation in cities owing to escalating costs of land and housing and depletion of low-income housing. Measures taken to protect the environment are also at times in conflict with the interests and human rights of populations that depend on land for subsistence and survival. Failure to effectively prevent and mitigate environmental degradation and the negative impact of climate change could drastically reduce access to land, especially for marginalized groups. Land remains a crucial element in conflict and post-conflict contexts.

In the discourse about land, the land should be considered a human right. Human rights are indivisible, interrelated, and interdependent, and the land is a cross-cutting issue. While access to land most obviously affects the underlying rights to housing, food, and water, there are additional rights within the international framework that are impacted[13]. For the Maasai people of Kenya, land is much more than an economic asset; it serves as a foundation that provides social status throughout the community as well as a cultural and religious identity. Here are some comments from the study group:

> "Successive regimes have continually trampled on the human rights of the Maasai regarding land. The appropriation of land from the Maasai, first by the European colonialists to make room for white settlers, and then by the independent Kenyan government, through culturally insensitive laws and land policies, raises tremendous issues of social injustice."

> "The Maasai have been treated as second-class citizens when it comes to issues of land. They have been deprived of their pastureland, salt licks for their livestock, which is a violation of human rights."

> "The laws in Kenya are selective; the Maasai are not protected by the law when it comes to matters related to land. The law is

---

13 Committee on Economic Social and Cultural Rights (CESCR), General Comment 14, The right to the highest attainable standard of health (Art. 12), 27 (Nov. 8, 2000).

used to deprive the Maasai of their land, which in my view is an infringement of human rights."

In conclusion, land appropriation as a human rights issue has gained global attention, thanks to the Human Rights Council of the United Nations. In 2009, the Special Rapporteur on the rights to food issued a set of Minimum Principles and Measures to Address the Human Rights Challenges of large-scale land acquisition (DeSchutter, 2009). The Minimum Principles are grounded in the right to self-determination; the rights to development, and the right to food. These principles also insist that any sale or transfer of land be a transparent process that includes the full participation of the potentially affected local communities. As noted by the participants in this study, the process of Maasai land appropriation has not been transparent, and the local Maasai communities have not been included. The problem of the right to food, as directly associated with land appropriation, was noted earlier.

A graph showing the changes in household land ownership and income over the different periods would demonstrate the dispossession. Arguably, land rights are inherently contentious, as land is such an important source of wealth, culture, and social life. The distribution and access to land are not politically neutral, and land rights affect the overall economic and social basis of societies. Additionally, the different economic, social, and cultural facets of land rights create tensions between different interests, notably the need to protect the land while also providing rights to the landless. Finally, land rights are an essential element of economic growth and, as such, involve a range of stakeholders that includes powerful foreign investors. While land rights are never absolute and subject to constraints that society puts on them, provided there is consensus, transparency in the manner in which land is transacted and used should be guided by the primary land use practices of the community.

Metaphors

The goal of this study was, in part, to identify overarching metaphors that reflect the central themes of the text and that further explain the relationships among the themes associated with each research question. Two overarching metaphors were identified: disassembling and loss.

Disassembling

The comments from the study participants indicated that Maasai land appropriation had been an issue since the colonial period. From their comments, it was clear that their conception of land was an integral component of their identity, their way of life, and their sense of sovereignty. The Maasai were an entity located within a territory at the advent of colonial rule. The appropriation of their land led to the disassembling of their land, their system of land tenure, their way of life, their rituals, their families, their culture, and their patterns of governance.

The land is understood by the Maasai to connote ancestral heritage. The understanding of land, as described by the study participants, is situated within their worldview, where land, water, and other aspects of nature are intertwined. These were described as not just economic resources, but as a part of life in toto. The participants described an interwoven triad of the Maasai world, the natural world, and the spiritual world. This interwoven understanding of land by the Maasai influences their actions and relationships with nature, generally, and their land. Their worldview of land is that of a communal property given to them by God to be used wisely and held in trust for future generations.

The appropriation of Maasai land disassembled the Maasai worldview by removing them from their ancestral lands. In the process, it also disassembled clans, families, and villages, as well as their way of life, culture, and governing structure. It also created structural holes, and thus, the processes of unity within the Maasai nation were disassembled. The disassembling of the Maasai land led to multiple diverse spatio-temporal groupings of the Maasai in new settings that were not part of their ancestral lands. The concept of disassembling captures the visual impression of a landscape that was once continuous and whole and is now broken apart. In a broader context, it reflects a picture of ancestral pastoral lands that were disassembled through acts of government appropriation and progressive encroachment of farmers or other outside interests, as well as through the privatization of land.

Loss

Closely related to the metaphor of disassembling is the metaphor of loss. Land is a critical resource that underpins the lives of the Maasai. The land acts as a symbolic, economic, and political resource, which the study noted forms an important part of their daily lives and those of their communities. The participants of this study commented on numerous ways in which the Maasai's lives had been disrupted by the loss of their land. This left them both sad and upset since the appropriated land reflected the life they once had, which was now lost. One example of this loss was pastoralism, which is a key part of Maasai culture, economy, and way of life. The cultural tenet of social connectedness among the Maasai is associated with their pastoral way of life. While pastoralism was the Maasai way of life, changing trends will definitely affect the way and manner in which the Maasai adapt to changes that will make pastoralism a national economic system that not only affects their economy but also the national economic system in Kenya.

When the land is lost, communal management of livestock by men and the emotional bonds between women and children living in close quarters in the *inkangitie* (homesteads) end. The results are reduced social connectedness. Quite evident in the participants' comments was their strong sense of distinct Maasai culture and their strong identity with ancestral homelands. They viewed their land as a substance endowed with sacred meanings that defined their existence and identity.

The study also noted that losing their land affected the capacity of the Maasai to raise their livestock, feed their families, maintain their connection with wildlife, and engage in meaningful economic activities that evolve from having their land and not being relegated to smaller areas of poor-quality land. Thus, they lost the ability to maintain a decent standard of living. The traditional social roles of men and women were also disrupted. Several of the participants also noted that the loss of their lands was associated with the loss of water that was essential for their livestock. Livestock production is a major component of the Maasai economy, and several of the participants described the link between the land and livestock loss. Livestock is the living bank for the Maasai, as they provide direct cash income. Livestock is also closely linked to the social and cultural lives of the Maasai community. The loss of livestock means the loss of varying degrees of sustainable production and the stability of their domestic economy.

Closely associated with the loss of livestock is food security, agricultural production, and the ability to meet social/cultural obligations. The loss, as expressed in the study, also displayed a sense of desperation, hopelessness, and uncertainty. Since land supports livestock, which is their main source of livelihood, the smaller the land, the fewer the livestock, and hence the increase in family vulnerability. According to the study, the composition of the herd is closely linked to production and reproduction potential; hence, the more females one has in a herd, the more long-term security a herd owner and his family have because they provide milk and future calves. This, according to the study, has been disrupted due to land loss and limited movement of the livestock in search of pasture. Without enough land, the cattle will die, and subsequently, the Maasai culture will die as well.

According to my observations, the implication of Maasai land appropriation has drawn a lesson that can be used to address global land grabs. The participants expressed that since most of the lands being appropriated are mostly for urban development, large-scale agriculture, tourism, and conservation, which is a global phenomenon, governments and investors should avoid situations where land appropriation infringes the rights of local communities.

PART V:

THE EMERGENCE OF THE MAA CIVIL SOCIETY

Introduction

The Maa speakers of East Africa are known to have had no historical engagement in civil activities. I suppose one of the reasons has been the autonomous structure of their social set-up. Each Maa section (*Olosho*) was independent and had its leadership structure, and only the other sections were consulted as needs arose through their traditional leaders. There were instances where two or more sections came together, mainly either to protect each other from aggression or war against other Maasai sections or other communities. A good example is when several Maa sections combined their armies, fought and defeated Ilaikipiak, and when the Ildamat fought Ilkeekonyokie, and the Illpurko organized their warriors to fight off Ildamat in support of Ikeekonyokie. The most recent of such cases is when the Ildamat and Ikeekonyokie combined their forces to fight off Ilpurko at Ntulele in Narok over land in the mid-1990s. While this is the case, there is evidence that some Maasai who had access to basic schooling in the early 1900s attempted to coalesce around their affiliation with early missionaries to advocate for the Maa rights. To better understand this process, I will start by revisiting such narratives of the Maasai individuals who got involved in trying to voice the Maasai concerns.

Among the earliest Maasai to seek to unite the Maasai to address their land rights were Ole Nakulto (spelt Nakuldu), Molonket Olokorinya Ole Sempele, Oloibaosioki Ole Kindi, all from Ilkeekonyokie, and Ole Gilisho, and Ole Masikonte from Ilpurko. According to King (1971), one by the name 'Professor' Nakulto (referred to as Nakuldu) of Ilkeekonyokie was said to have accompanied Count Teleki in his travels to Lake Rudolf in the 1880s and got his name because of his ability to learn English quickly. Others included Molonket Olokorinya Ole Sempele, who was also Keekonyokie, who worked with the Church Missionary Society and was said to be the first Kenyan to travel overseas. Molonket was the first Kenyan to study abroad. He enrolled in the Boydton Academic and Bible Institute in Virginia in 1909. Molonket returned home in 1912 but could not secure gainful employment besides a brief conscription to the Career Corps during the outbreak of World War I in 1914. Due to their exposure, Ole Nakulto and Ole Sempele attempted to create a Maasai movement to help protect Maasai land. This never bore any fruit because of mistrust by community traditional leaders who thought that since they lived with white men, they were probably spies.

Others were Oloibaosioki Ole Kindi and Ole Gilisho, who also attempted to mobilize the Maasai to resist the Colonial moves (King, 1971). While these early Maasai pioneers attempted to bring the Maa speakers together to agitate for Maasai concerns about land and other issues that affected the Maasai, their efforts were not successful because they were isolated from the traditional Maasai leadership structure. While Ole Kindi attempted to mobilize Ilkeekonyokie around land rights, he was not able to get collective support from the community. Ole Gilisho, on his part, had some degree of success in litigating the Maasai land rights when he and other warriors like Ole Masikode filed the famous Maasai case of 1913, which was meant to reverse the Maasai agreements of 1904 and 1911.

Later in the mid-1900s, the Maasai attempted to organize themselves by forming the Maasai Association, which was formed in 1930. The Association was an attempt to unite the Maasai, just like other tribes in Kenya, which were creating tribal groups. In 1945, another group, calling itself the Group of the Educated Maasai, was created to decide what could be done to develop Maasai land. The Association was the first Maasai political organization, and its members prepared and presented the Maasai memoranda on land grievances to the Kenya Land Commission. Unfortunately, the organization broke down in 1955, but some of its members went on to organize and start another outfit called the Masai United Front (MUF), which became the first-ever Maasai political party in 1960. The MUF brought Kenyan and Tanzanian (then Tanganyika) Maasai together, and their objective was to declare Maasailand an independent state from Kenya and Tanganyika. This did not happen since there was no adequate mobilization, and the British could not allow such to happen at a time when negotiations for independence for Kenya were on the table. The British were fearful of how an independent Maasai state would affect the Europeans who had settled on land previously owned by the Maasai.

Since then, the Maasai did not have any strong social movement to front their grievances or agitate for any political rights until 2004, when the Maa Civil Society (MCSF) was formed by Maasai NGOs, Community Based organizations (CBOs), Faith-Based Organizations (FBOs), and like-minded individuals. The society was created to seek redress for land lost to the British and subsequent post-independence regimes. MCSF did not last long because of conflicts of interest among the founder members, fear from sitting politicians who saw it as a threat to their political survival, intimidation, and threats from the government. Later, in late 2017, another outfit called Maa Unity Agenda came into being. The main agenda of the group is to seek opportunities to unite the Maa speakers. The group is more of an online forum with frequent interventions when issues arise, but it has failed to build a strong base in the grassroots. The group has yet to achieve tangible results in uniting the Maasai due to its structure, outreach, and suspicion that it is yet another platform that its founders are using for personal political mileage.

Maa Civil Society Forum

The Maasai land claims have become a major political issue in Kenya since August 2004, when representatives of the Maa Civil Society Forum (MCSF) organized a public demonstration in Nairobi, Nakuru, Laikipia, Narok, Samburu, and Kajiado. Through this mobilization, the representatives declared the community's intention to pursue a claim with respect to the land that the community had been dispossessed of one hundred years earlier through the so-called Maasai Agreement signed on 15th August 1904 and in 1911[1]. The Maasai land claims were premised on the fact that some of the 99-year leases that were created in favour of colonial settlers following

---

1   The date for signing of the 1911 agreement is contested because it is said either Lenana signed it on his deathbed, his fingerprints were used after his death or his son Supeet signed.

the Agreement of 1904 and 1911 were expiring on 15th August 2004. The Maasai also demanded that the land that was occupied, or being used by the government, be returned to the Maasai. Such lands that the Maasai are laying claim to include land that was formerly under the Agricultural Development Corporation, Livestock Marketing Division, and other government organs[2]. Most of the land that the Maasai lay claim to is in Kajiado (Kibiko holding ground, Ngong Veterinary Farm, and the Goat and Sheep), Nakuru (Entapipi, Natooli, Kedong, Namuncha), Samburu (Land under the National Youth Service), and Laikipia (Mutara Ranch and other land tracks that were not occupied). In addition to the return of their land, the community had indicated that they wished to pursue compensation for death and injuries as well as the loss of property occasioned by the mass movement of the Maasai from their traditional land to the reserves in what is now Narok and Kajiado counties, and the northern reserve in Samburu and Laikipia. In order to achieve the goals, there was a need to have an all-inclusive Maa outfit to be tasked with the leadership of the quest. This was the basis of the formation of the MCSF.

MCSF was a conglomeration of civil societies, religious and faith-based organizations, and individuals from all the then districts, now counties that were inhabited by the Maa speakers in Kenya. I got fully involved with advocacy work in 2004 when the MCSF was formed, and I was made the National Coordinator. My first task was to mobilize Maa speakers to commemorate 100 years of the signing of the Maasai Agreements of 1904 between Olonana and the British colonialists[3]. MCSF was formed out of the Maasai's need to seek opportunities to redress historical and contemporary injustices on land, natural resources, and intellectual property rights. The forum was able to organize several meetings with political and religious leaders and members of the civil society to prepare for the countrywide procession to demand the redress of historical land injustices. As a result of the

2   There hae been disagreements and misinterpretations about whether the actual Agreements were leases which had an expiration time, or the leases were done after the Agreements between the then landowners who were awarded the land by the Crown Ordinance.

3   These Agreements have variously been referred to as Anglo Maasai Agreements.

tasks ahead, Mainyioto Pastoralist Integrated Development Organisation (MPIDO) and other collaborators supported a strategic planning workshop to lay down a strategy to carry out all the activities that would facilitate the processes required.

Although not everyone who should have attended the strategic planning workshop was present, the overall attendance represented a diversity of the Maasai community from different districts in Kenya (See table 1). The participants, while acknowledging that they could not purport to represent the entire Maasai community, nevertheless took up the challenge of developing a structured process for the pursuit of the land claims. They agreed that once the strategic plan was ready, it would be presented to the community through stakeholder consultations at which even more representatives would be invited. Nevertheless, it was appreciated that the process of mobilization and consensus-building had to be ongoing, over a period, before all the Maasai of Kenya would properly own this initiative.

Within the Maasai community, it was intended to engage all the social and political structures, including traditional leaders, women, and key traditional institutions and systems on the claim. Outside the community, key supporters were identified, and their support was mobilized, while efforts were made to provide information through different means, including print and electronic media. Special efforts were made to network with like-minded organizations locally, regionally, and internationally to share their experiences and benefit from their links. Specific opportunities from global frameworks that address human rights violations as well as indigenous peoples' rights were explored, and linkages made with them in order to place the initiative on the global advocacy agenda and framework.

Table 2. Participating organization during the M.C.S.F. Strategic Planning Workshop

District	Organization
Samburu	• RETO Women Association • Samburu Women Advocacy Network
Laikipia	• IMPACT • OSILIGI
Nakuru	• Municipal Council of Naivasha • Keekonyokie Pastoralism Council (KEPACO) • Oloserian Welfare Society
Narok	• Touch of Love Integrated Development Project (TOLIDP) • Narok Environment and Sustainable Development Network • Narok Human Rights Network • Maasai Pastors Association
Kajiado	• Simba Maasai Outreach Organization (SIMOO) • MPIDO • Olmaa Pastoralists Development Project
Transmara	• NARAMAT • Transmara Wildlife Forum
Isiolo	• Ndugu Zangu Christian Community

Additional problems for the claims arose from the situation that much of the land from which the Maasai were evicted more than one hundred years ago is now occupied by local Kenyans whose right to the land is not traceable to the Maasai Agreement, but rather to policy interventions of governments of independent Kenya and individual property transactions. This, in part, explained the high-handed reaction of the Kenyan government towards the Maasai claims, as it sought to reassure such settlers. These circumstances and reactions to the Maasai land claims reaffirmed the need for a more structured and well-thought-out process for pursuing the claims. It had become clear that a lot more would have to be done to make out a strong case for the claims, to identify the specific claims and persons or institutions against whom they had to be made, and to mobilize both intellectual and financial resources for what came to prove to be a long and tedious exercise. The Maasai community also had to engage in a meaningful way with other communities and institutions to build confidence and mobilize support for the claims; hence, there was a need for more structured thinking around the claims and for the development of a strategic plan.

MCSF Overall Goal

The overall goal of the Maasai land claims initiative was to redress historical injustices and wrongs perpetrated against the Maasai as a community, particularly concerning their land rights. While the goal was set in mid-2004, the Maasai still have the view that the goal then is still the goal to date. The historical wrongs and injustices are traceable to the establishment of European settlement in the territory that is now Kenya. These were first perpetrated by the colonial administration, and later compounded by the policies of the independence government. It was important to emphasize from the outset that the claims by the Maasai are primarily against the state, both colonial and post-colonial, even if portions of the lands they claim may presently be occupied by specific individuals.

The Maasai Agreements of 1904 and 1911 are important as marking major thresholds in the history of the Maasai community and their engagement with external forces that culminated in the dispossession of their lands. The agreements marked key milestones in the dispossession and alienation of the community from their traditional lands, but they were by no means the only basis of the community's claims. Instead, the claims traverse the entire history of Kenya, right from the commencement of colonial settlement to the present.

Specific Objectives

To realize the overall objective stated above, the Maasai land claims initiative was to pursue the following three specific objectives:

1. To claim for restitution of Maasai ancestral land appropriated by the British colonial government and/or the Kenyan government, as well as adequate compensation for the use of those lands to date;

2. To claim damages in compensation against the British government for the loss of lives, injuries, and loss of livestock and property occasioned by the mass eviction of the Maasai from their ancestral land as a result of the 1904 and 1911 Agreements; and

3. To claim from the Kenyan government compensation as well as the right to share in benefits derived from the use of ancestral land and natural resources situated in those ancestral lands

Restitution and Compensation for Ancestral Land

That the Maasai Agreements of 1904 and 1911 were, at best, quasi-legal mechanisms aimed at duping the Maasai out of their land and, at worst, a fraudulent abuse of power and advantage by the colonial administration against an indigenous population cannot be gainsaid (Okoth-Ogendo, 1996). That the agreements were not worth the paper they were written on was made manifest when the colonial administration moved the Maasai for a second time in 1911 under yet another agreement, despite the provision that the first agreement would endure "so long as the Maasai as a race shall exist, and...Europeans and their settlers shall not be allowed to take up land" anywhere in the reserved area.

Many questions have been raised about the nature of the Maasai Agreements, the extent to which they were true 'agreements', and contracts between two competent parties acting on their own free will and in their best mutual interest. The Maasai went to court to contest the agreements based on these very questions in the case of Ole Njogo & Others, Attorney-General of the East African Protectorate (EALR, 1914). The case was thrown out when the court upheld a preliminary objection that argued that the local courts had no jurisdiction over the matter, given that the pact giving rise to the dispute was not a contract within the meaning of municipal law, but a treaty between two sovereigns over which no municipal court had jurisdiction.

The legal basis for the decision was at best tenuous. The Maasai argue that they were wrongfully dispossessed of their land and that this was done in circumstances that led to a lot of suffering and pain. The dispossession and the way it was done have adversely impacted their life and the destiny of the Maasai as a community. Over the years, the Maasai have voiced the need for restitution and compensation for their ancestral land, but even the independent government has done nothing to address their claims. Instances where the Maasai have expressed their grievances about land are the Ole Nchoko Case of 1913, the Kenya Land Commission of 1932, and the Lancaster independence conference of 1963. Instead, at independence, the new government confirmed the *status quo* left behind by the colonialists and took further steps to entrench the sanctity of private property in the Constitution. This constitutional provision has come to define the basis for validating the property regime borne out of the dispossession of the Maasai and other communities of their land by the colonialists.

What is more, the independent government itself has appropriated portions of Maasai land to declare protected areas or to use for other public purposes without any consultation with the community or payment of any compensation. Such areas include the Maasai Mara Game Reserve, the Amboseli National Park, Nakuru National Park, Hell's Gate National Park, and Nairobi National Park. The claim under this heading is for restitution to the community of those portions of their land that are still identifiable as such, and compensation, whether by the allocation of other land or by payment of the value thereof, for those portions that it is no longer possible to identify or return.

Compensation for Death, Injuries, and Loss of Property

The claim under this heading is against the British government in respect to loss of life and property, as well as personal injuries that were occasioned by the acts of its colonial agents in the implementation of the mass displacement of the Maasai from their ancestral land, first from Laikipia and thereafter further south to what subsequently became Narok and Kajiado. It is estimated that, both during the movement itself and because of it, many Maasai lost their lives, suffered personal injuries, and lost livestock as well as other property. The process itself was executed with extreme violence as a military force was employed against the community. No plans were made for food provisions and medicines, and many lives were lost in transit due to sleeping sickness, anthrax, the whims of the weather, and lack of food, water, and shelter.

Thousands of cattle are said to have died from East Coast fever, pleuro-pneumonia, and rinderpest, while many young men and women died from the flu, malaria, and pneumonia. It is estimated that up to 98,000 cattle and 300,000 sheep were lost in the process of relocation, leading to a substantial depreciation of the Maasai stock. There are no known estimates of people lost, but it is said that the elderly, the sick, and children succumbed to harsh climatic conditions. More losses were suffered once the community settled, as it got its bearings in the new locality. The first movement was followed shortly thereafter by a second movement, which exacerbated the living conditions and worsened the situation of the community. The community shall assess the total loss under this heading and claim compensation from the British government.

Claims Against the Kenyan Government for Benefit-Sharing

It is acknowledged that the Maasai and other pastoral communities in Kenya bear the greatest burden of the costs related to the support of nature-based tourism. The bulk of the wildlife conservation areas that are the backbone of the sector are situated within their lands. The world-renowned Maasai Mara Game Reserve, the Amboseli National Park, Nakuru National Park, Hells Gate National Park, and even the Nairobi National Park are situated in lands that were traditionally occupied and used by the Maasai. The establishment of these protected areas in these lands has denied the Maasai what used to be essential pastures for their livestock, with serious consequences for their livelihood opportunities[4].

Moreover, it is estimated that about 70% of the wildlife population in Kenya is found outside the protected areas on private land[5]. Most of that land belongs to and is used by the Maasai and other pastoral communities for the care of their livestock. Indeed, the Maasai and other pastoral communities have a long history of living with wildlife. In the process, they bear an inordinate cost for the protection of wildlife. Recent debates about human-wildlife conflicts in Kenya have underscored this fact[6].

Apart from the costs arising from day to day losses suffered by the Maasai and other pastoral communities as wildlife kill members of their families as well as their livestock, injure and maim others and destroy crops and other property, the Maasai claim under this heading was grounded on the principle that the conversion of parts of their land into protected areas was never a participatory process and the communities involved were excluded. It was done without reference to them and any regard to their specific interests as communities. The Maasai claim compensation for the conversion of their ancestral lands into protected areas and a share of the benefits over and above what the rest of the country derives from the income generated by these protected areas by way of tax income. In addition to the claims under this heading related to wildlife and protected areas, the Maasai will lodge claims with respect to other natural resources within their ancestral land that have been exploited without any benefits to them and in total disregard of their rights. These include minerals like soda ash being exploited by Magadi Soda Company in Kajiado.

---

4   it is estimated that 29% of the land occupied by protected areas in Kenya forms part of the Arid and Semi-Arid Lands (ASALs) that are occupied by pastoral communities (Kenya Land Alliance, 'Fact Sheets on Human Wildlife Conflict in Kenya', Fact Sheet 1)

5   Patricia Kameri-Mbote, 2002: *Property Rights and Biodiversity Management in Kenya: The Case of Land Tenure and Wildlife*. Nairobi: ACTS Press, p. 86

6   A Kenya Human Wildlife Conflict Network has been formed to advocate for the protection of community interests against the destruction caused by wildlife, and in January 2005, Kenya Land Alliance launched Fact Sheets on this problem as part of its campaign for an appropriate land policy.

MCSF Key Strategic Issues

For these claims to be pursued in a meaningful manner, members of MCSF who were the proponents of the claims had to address some key strategic issues, among them the following five: (a) generation of information and resources, (b) supporting the emergence of a social movement, (c) engaging legal and political processes, (d) securing the land and natural resource rights, and (e) ongoing review and monitoring.

Generation of information and resources to pursue the claims. Information was essential for the pursuit of these claims, especially because the claims were historical and were based on facts that are therefore subject to different interpretations by different protagonists. The proper collection and collation of information, as well as its verification and organization, would, in large measure, determine the fate of the claims. For this and other purposes of the claim, there was a need for resources, which also must be generated, an inadequate measure if the claims were to be sustained and processed successfully.

Supporting the emergence of a social movement of the Maasai and other communities in Kenya around the issue of redress of historical injustices and wrongs was important for the necessary critical mass that would create social and political pressure needed for these injustices and wrongs to be addressed. Foremost, it was important that the Maasai, as a community, agree about the importance of this initiative and support it wholeheartedly, and secondly, that the initiative was situated within the wider context of redress of injustices and wrongs suffered by different communities in Kenya. Because the claim had such serious and long-term political implications, it was likely to be as long and hard as it was potentially politically divisive. Those opposed to the initiative sought to divide the Maasai community on the issue as well as isolate the community so that this appeared to be an agenda of a single community against the rest of Kenya, hence there was a need for a social movement that cuts across the Maasai community and includes other communities of Kenya that were similarly impacted.

Engaging legal and political processes to advance the cause of redressing historical injustices and wrongs was essential. This involved having recourse to mainstream legal and political processes at the national, regional, and global levels by filing cases before appropriate courts and tribunals as well as pursuing targeted advocacy on such institutions as Parliament, the East African Community, the Inter-governmental Authority on Development (IGAD), and the African Union. This again required substantial groundwork to optimize the benefits of these approaches and was likely to be protracted and costly.

Securing the land and natural resource rights of the Maasai on an ongoing basis had to be a key strategic concern. This meant that even as this initiative was pursued, the Maasai must not lose sight of the need to participate effectively in ongoing reform processes with a view to securing their rights to land and natural resources. Reforms in the governance sector, the land sector, and the natural resources sector generally have serious implications for the security of Maasai livelihood opportunities. However, for the benefits to be realized, there was a need for a concerted, structured, and informed participation by the Maasai alongside other pastoral communities.

Ongoing review and monitoring to take advantage of emerging opportunities and address emerging problems and challenges were core to tracking progress made, and feedback was necessary to ensure the initiative remains on course. The nature of this initiative was such that it would be too optimistic to imagine that it could all be planned and executed in one time. Once the implementation starts, many new opportunities are likely to emerge, even as new challenges and problems are identified. A key strategic concern, therefore, was to ensure the initiative is backed by an ongoing review and monitoring process that would enable those involved in it to keep track of these emerging trends and respond to them as appropriate.

Strategies and Activities

The strategic issues identified above were addressed through different strategies and are discussed in this section. The strategies that were to be employed included research, resource mobilization, networking and consensus building, lobbying and advocacy, negotiation, litigation, monitoring, and evaluation.

Research

The essence of information generation has been emphasized in the previous section. Research became the key strategy for the generation of information in support of the claims. Decisions about the use of the identified strategies were based on the outcome of the research, and changes were made where research suggested that it was appropriate to make such changes. The research was conducted by volunteer Maasai anthropologists and lawyers. It involved a review of the historical records and archival material both in Kenya and in the United Kingdom on the process of colonial land alienation, generally, and the dispossession of the Maasai, in particular.

United Kingdom government records on the circumstances surrounding the signing of the two Maasai Agreements were critical for the claims, as were the records of the colonial settlement reached between the British and the incoming independence government on the land question. In Kenya, research was undertaken on the alienation of portions of Maasai land over the years to support wildlife conservation and other governmental activities, and an assessment was made of the losses incurred by the community over the years to determine what should be claimed from the government. Similarly, research was undertaken on the income generated by the respective projects on the Maasai ancestral land to quantify the claims to be made in this respect. Other areas of research related to the cases to be filed in local and international courts against the British and Kenyan governments, as well as other relevant authorities and parties. This area of research included an investigation into comparative experiences relating to such claims from other parts of the world. The anthropological team was able to collect data that was used to draw working drafts for MCSF.

Resource mobilization

Resources were mobilized within the Maasai community and from other supporters, both locally and abroad. Enough resources need to be mobilized to support the pursuit of these claims sustainably. Thus, resource mobilization was backed by a well-thought-out strategy that was informed by a clear appreciation of the magnitude of the work, both in terms of what was to be done and the length of time it would likely take. Examples of other claims for the redress of historical injustices in New Zealand, Australia, Canada, and the United States clearly show that this initiative was enormous and would have to be pursued consistently over a long period.

Participants at the strategic planning workshop appreciated that there will be a need for substantial support from donors, but they emphasized that the Maasai community must own and be ready to contribute to the process if it is to be sustained. It was therefore envisaged that internal resource mobilization within the Maasai community would be integral to the success of the initiative and would, therefore, be a key component of the resource mobilization strategy.

To raise adequate resources, the secretariat reached out to the Maa politicians and professionals for support. Despite the fears that many had about intimidation by the government, MCSF was able to meet the politicians and professionals who provided support in-kind and financial. A team led by the late John Keen and the late Ole Ntimama convened several meetings in Karen, where several fundraisers were held to support the movement. MPIDO, which was housing MCSF, provided statistical supplementary support by developing proposals related to advocacy, which other Maa NGOs that provided resources included Ndugu Zangu of Isiolo, OLPADEP, and SIMOO.

Networking and Consensus-Building

The success of this initiative depended, to a large extent, on its capacity to mobilize a critical mass of sympathizers both within the Maasai community and outside it. As such, the mobilization of support, consensus-building, and networking was a key strategy in pursuing the claim. The initial mobilization was within the Maasai community itself.

This required that a strategic planning meeting be held to put strategies into place. Indeed, while the strategic planning workshop was itself a key event in this process of mobilizing the Maasai community, this process of mobilization started much earlier and was evident in the demonstrations held by the Maasai on the 15th August 2004 and subsequently to make the demands for the redress of their land claims. There was, therefore, a sense in which the strategic planning workshop and the need to develop the strategic plan were a response to the emerging challenges in the mobilization process. MCSF was able to build local networks at different levels to address both historical and contemporary issues affecting the Maasai.

Lobbying and Advocacy

Different tools and means were employed in lobbying and advocacy, including the use of media, negotiation, and litigation. There was a very active press presence in Kenya, and the Maasai land claims had already elicited substantial support in the media. Serious efforts were made to make use of the print and electronic media to argue the case for the land claims and to mobilize public opinion and support. In this connection, it was also recognized that there was a danger that the press reporting may fail to deal with the real issues and focus on exciting and headline-grabbing news unless there was a structured approach to the media. The initiative explored opportunities for a negotiated settlement of these claims with the relevant parties and reserved the right to file an action in courts and tribunals both locally and abroad if the efforts for negotiated settlements were not reciprocated.

Periodic monitoring and evaluation

It has already been indicated that the purpose of monitoring and evaluation was to both assess the progress being made in the pursuit of the claims and to track emerging opportunities as well as challenges so that they are addressed as they arise. To this end, a monitoring and evaluation plan was developed that included periodic meetings and consultations between and with key stakeholders. MCSF was able to carry out periodic monitoring and evaluation activities using its member organizations in each district.

The members were assigned responsibility to track down activities within their jurisdictions and report back to the national coordinator, who, through the media team, shared the information with the rest of the members. Such information was also shared through other Maa institutions like the Maa Pastors Association and the Maa Council of Elders. Informal interactions at the community level facilitated the sharing of all information that needed to be relayed to the respective constituencies.

Table 3: Summary of Strategies and Activities

Strategy	Activities	Outputs
Research	• review of literature, policy, and law • interviews with community members who have memories of the injustices and wrongs • Review of government records in the UK and Kenya • review of relevant cases and case law, both locally and globally	Research reports, legal and policy opinions
Resource Mobilization	• develop a resource mobilization strategy • identify and engage potential supporters and partners, both locally and abroad • mobilize community contributions	Material and financial resources

Networking and Consensus Building	• engage all social and political structures of the Maasai • engage key stakeholders • publish newsletters, develop a website, and engage the media	Consensus within the Maasai and among other communities in Kenya to pursue redress of historical injustices and wrongs
Lobby and Advocacy	• place a claim on the agenda of ongoing policy and legal reforms • place the issue on the agenda of the 2007 elections • Explore opportunities for negotiations with respondents to the claims • litigation in local and international courts and tribunals as appropriate	Lobby and advocacy agenda, court cases filed
Monitoring and Evaluation	• develop a monitoring and evaluation plan • Organise regular meetings to review progress and evaluate approaches	Monitoring and evaluation plan in place

Implementation Plan

The implementation of this strategic plan was expected to take a long time and required a constant review based on experience on the ground. Substantial and far-reaching consultations had to be made in order to ensure that members of the Maasai community had adequate ownership and commitment to the pursuit of the claims. At the same time, efforts had to be made to ensure buy-in by other communities and key human rights advocacy groups in Kenya, as well as potential supporters internationally.

The participants at the strategic planning workshop agreed that a proper implementation plan would be agreed upon after they convened to discuss, provide feedback, and validate the strategic plan. However, they also agreed that it was important to sequence the activities in broad terms, even as they await agreement on the details. The table below provides this broad sequence, which was further developed in subsequent consultations. In this connection, it was also envisaged that the different organizations involved in the initiative would undertake different activities derived from the strategic plan so that whatever framework was agreed for managing the process would work mainly as a clearinghouse and coordination.

Table 4: Implementation Plan

Strategies/Activities	Year 1	Year 2	Year 3
Research			
• review of literature, policy, and law	✓	✓	✓
• interviews with community members who have memories of the injustices and wrongs	✓		
• Review of government records in the UK and Kenya			
• review of relevant cases and case law			

Resource Mobilization			
• develop a resource mobilization strategy	✓	✓	
• identify and engage potential supporters and partners, both locally and abroad	✓		
• mobilize community contributions			
Networking and Consensus Building			✓
			✓
• engage all social and political structures of the Maasai	✓	✓	
• engage key stakeholders	✓	✓	
• publish newsletters, develop a website, and engage the media			
Lobby and Advocacy			
• place a claim on the agenda of ongoing policy and legal reforms	✓	✓	✓
• place the issue on the agenda of the 2007 elections	✓	✓	✓
• explore opportunities for negotiations with respondents to the claims	✓	✓	✓
• litigation in local and international courts and tribunals as appropriate			

Monitoring and Evaluation			
• develop a monitoring and evaluation plan	✓		
• Organize regular meetings to review progress and evaluate approaches			

Source: Michael Odhiambo, RECONCILE, Kenya.

Institutional Framework

The institutional framework for the pursuit of this claim was important and had serious implications on how the process would develop over time. The intricate nature of the claims required that there be a full-fledged secretariat to coordinate them over a long time. The claim could not be pursued meaningfully if the responsibility were merely an 'add-on' to the responsibilities of individuals and groups that have their own mainstream agenda. Those who had provided leadership for the process had exhibited a lot of commitment and had made sacrifices, but they could be expected to continue doing this as they had their other full-time engagements. In order to achieve its accomplishments, MCSF created specialized teams which were assigned specific areas that were of importance to the forum and the Maasai in general. The first team was the Legal Team, which was comprised of Maasai lawyers whose role was to research issues of a legal nature, including researching the opportunities to file cases in Kenya and the United Kingdom. The team, which comprised the late Moijo Ole Keiwua, provided leadership to the legal team, which comprised Keriako Ole Tobiko, Lukas Ole Naikuni, Saitabao Ole Kanchorry, Soipan Tuya, and many others. The other team was that of Media Liaison under the leadership of Michael Ole Tiampati. The Anthropological Team had the responsibility to carry out research and document issues that were perceived to help build the Maasai case. This team was comprised of organizations that founded the forum, including SIMOO, MPIDO, OSILIGI, and Ndugu Zangu. The last team was the Political Team. This team was made up of Maasai politicians who were friendly to the forum and identified with the Maasai quest to seek historical land injustices. Members of the team included the late William Ole Ntimama, the late John Keen, the late Joseph Nkaiserry, and councillors from Kajiado, Narok, Baringo, Laikipia, and Samburu. All the teams were coordinated by the National Chairman (Ben Ole Koissaba) and the Vice Chairman (Mathew Lempurkel), who coordinated activities in Laikipia and Samburu.

Challenges and Accomplishments

The Maa Civil Society was mandated to take a lead in all major events associated with historical injustices that were outlined in the strategic plan. While some activities ran concurrently, some had to be undertaken on specific dates, and others had to be undertaken in response to issues that arose. MCSF was able to achieve the following:

Commemorating the 1904/1911 Agreements

In August 2004, members of the Maasai community in Kenya launched a campaign for the return of land allegedly stolen from them during the colonial era. The campaign was launched on 13th August 2004, a date coinciding roughly with the centenary of the signing of the first Maasai Agreement. It was planned as a series of demonstrations that would culminate in the presentation of a petition to the Kenyan and British governments demanding the return of lands stolen from the Maasai during the colonial era, and financial compensation for the trauma of land loss and the resultant 'under-development' of the Maasai community. While the campaign's broad objective was land restitution, the initial focus was on the return of Laikipia, the two-million-acre site of the former northern Maasai Reserve and now home to a handful of ranches largely in the hands of the remnant white settler community and Kenyan political elites. The demonstration of 2004 was the fourth time over the past century that the Maasai had challenged the loss of Laikipia and other lands. All three previous attempts – the 1913 court case, a 1932 petition to the Kenya Land Commission of 1933–34, and a plea made at the Kenya Constitutional Conference in London during 1962 on the eve of Kenya's independence had failed.

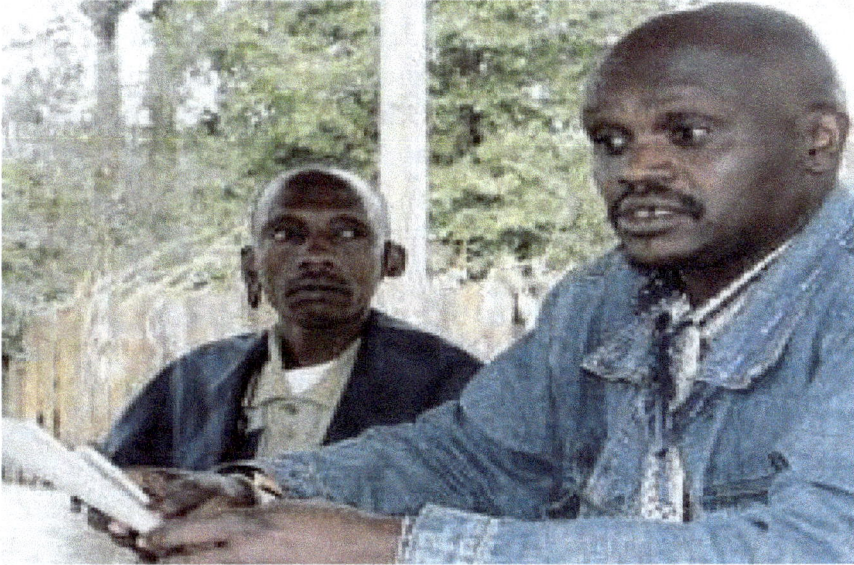

Fig. 9: The author leads a discussion about how the demonstrations by the Maasai will be conducted. © Michael Santeto Ole Tiampati

National Maasai Land Processions

August 15, 2004, was exactly one hundred years after the signing of the controversial agreement between the British Government and the Maasai, which allowed British settlers to allocate land to themselves in Kenya at the expense of the Maasai. Claiming that the 99 leases that were signed after agreements had expired, the Maasai demonstrated across the Rift Valley and in the capital of Kenya, Nairobi. Processions were also in Nakuru, Laikipia, Kajiado, Samburu, and Narok. The Demonstrators in Nairobi marched through Harambee Avenue to present the memorandum to the Office of the President. At the Office of the President, the protesters presented their memorandum to Danson Mungatana, who was the last public official the Maasai demonstrators would have any contact with, either on that first day of the demonstrations or at any other point during the campaign. The procession left the city centre and snaked one and a half kilometres up to Community Hill to the Ministry of Lands. Then Minister, Amos Kimunya, was not in his office, but the group was informed. The demonstrators further marched across the street to the British High Commission. Since it was a Friday, the High Commissioner Edward Clay was not in the office. As the demonstrations in Nairobi took place, other demonstrations were going on concurrently in Kajiado, Narok, Nakuru, Laikipia, and Samburu, where the protesters delivered the memoranda to the District Commissioners.

Unfortunately, during the same period, there was a bad drought in the country, and the Maasai in Laikipia were forced by hunger to invade private ranches, which are owned by white settlers and Kenyan political elites. In Laikipia District, 38 settlers whose ancestors came to Kenya during colonial times hold over one million acres, leaving almost nothing to well over 40,000 Maasai. The invasion created an impression that the Maasai wanted to forcefully reclaim the land, hence making the situation a national security threat. The situation was so dire that the late John Keen stated that:

> "It is criminal and immoral to let their [Maasai] cows die by denying them access to ancestral land taken away by colonial cheats" ([John Keen], Ndaskoi, nd).

William Ole Ntimama, who was the Minister in the Office of the President of Kenya in charge of Public Service, was also accused of inciting his community to invade private land.[7] The then Minister for Lands, Mr. Kimunya, requested Dr. Chris Murungaru, National Security Minister, to convene a meeting to pacify the Maasai.

The meeting called to discuss ways of settling the Maasai demand for land was held in the 10th-floor conference room of Harambee House, Nairobi, on September 07, 2004. It was chaired by Dr. Chris Murungaru, the National Security Minister, to ask Maasai and Samburu leaders to pacify those of their people who had started to invade lavish settler arms in Laikipia. Others who took part in the meeting were William ole Ntimama, the then Education Minister George Saitoti (Kajiado North), Assistant Ministers Gideon Konchellah (Kilgoris), Simeon Lesirma (Samburu West), and Mwangi Kiunjuri (Laikipia East), and MPs Joseph ole

---

7   The East African August 30, 2004.

Nkaiserry (Kajiado Central), G.G. Kariuki (Laikipia West), and National Assembly Speaker Francis ole Kaparo. They concluded that the Maasai do indeed 'have outstanding issues that require attention'. In the eyes of pastoralists in Kenya, 'the few commercial ranchers, regardless of their ethnic background or when they acquired the land, represent the forces of dispossession that date back 100 years ago'[8]. Participants suggested that Kshs 10 billion as a possible compensation figure for the land the Maasai lost in Laikipia District alone. Ntimama, it is reported, stood up straight and said:

> "...the battle for lost land would not end until the Maasai were given compensation...The Maasai were not demanding that they should be allowed to go back to their lost farms, but instead should be compensated for their land". ([Hon William Ole Ntimama], Ndaskoi, nd)

Figure 10: Maasai protesters marching along the Nakuru-Nairobi highway in Maai Mahiu demanding the return of Maasai land.

© Michael Santeto Ole Tiampati

---

8   Daily Nation August 25, 2004

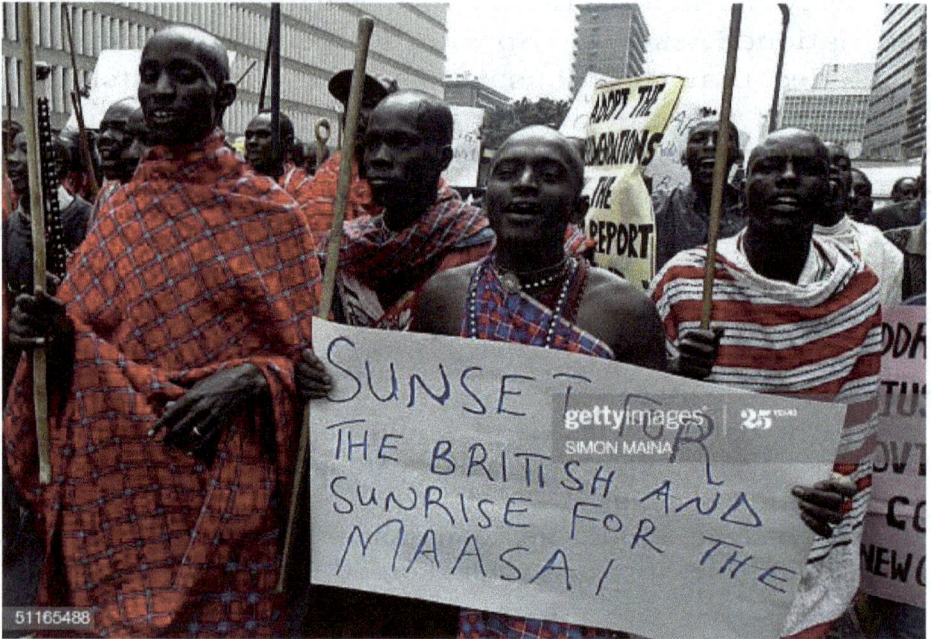

Figure 11: Maasai demonstrate in the streets of Nairobi demanding back their land. Picture by Simon Maina, Getty Images

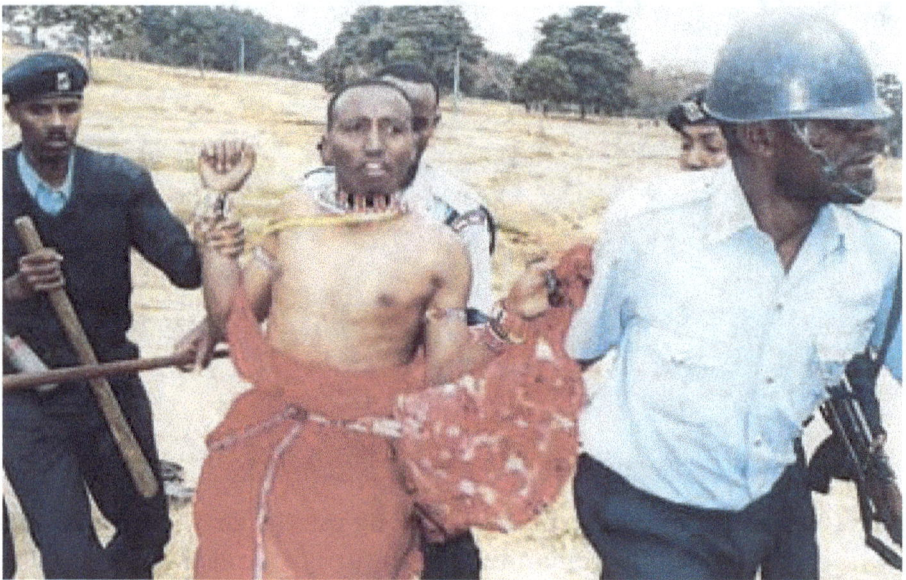

Figure 12: Thirteen people were arrested during the Nairobi demonstrations and arraigned in court. Picture courtesy of Mathew Lempurkel

Support for Funerals of People Killed by the Police

After the demonstrations, and due to severe drought in Laikipia, the Maasai invaded White ranchers for grass and water. In the ensuing security operation, the Maasai got the first fatal casualty in the name of Ntinaai Ole Moyiare, who was shot from behind by the police in the name of keeping Laikipia safe for the White settlers. This led to a major operation in Laikipia, which involved rounding up any Maasai seen in the streets of Nanyuki. School children were harassed while some schools were closed. Cases of rape, stealing, and actual brutality were meted out upon the Laikipia Maasai. Ntinaai Ole Moyiare's death created a hegemony between the Maasai and the government because the government wanted to cover up. MCSF was able to mobilize Maa speakers to facilitate the funeral plans because the government had placed a curfew for the Maasai in Laikipia. We were blessed enough to have had the support of the late Hon. William Ole Ntimama, who not only attended the burial but also provided financial support to mobilize people to attend the funeral.

There were a lot of challenges because the government learned that the Maasai from all over Kenya would attend the funeral. The government wanted to take over the funeral arrangements and used Ole Kaparo to try to sneak the body out of the Nanyuki mortuary for burial. Francis Kaparo was seen by the other Maasai as pro-settler and had, on various occasions, accused the other Maasai leaders of inciting the Maasai in Laikipia. There was a government scheme led by Ole Kaparo to take and bury the body in private without the participation of the Maasai community. MCSF mobilized its members to keep vigil and filed a case in court to stop any other parties, other than the family and the Maasai, from removing the body from the Nanyuki mortuary. MCSF and the family had to seek legal intervention to stop their plan. On the eve of the funeral, the government imposed a curfew in Nanyuki town, and police and National Youth Service personnel were on patrol the whole night.

Figure 13: The funeral of the late Ntinaai ole Moiyiare, who was shot dead in Laikipia, was attended by the late Hon Ole Ntimama

© Michael Santeto Ole Tiampati

Laikipia Plateau, estimated to be about 10,000 sq km or 2.5 million acres, has the biggest number of white land owners. It stretches from Mt Kenya in the east to the Rift Valley in the west. The Laikipia Maasai, who number approximately 35,000, are squashed on different patches of land, which measure about 1100 sq km, or an equivalent of 281,587 acres of land. On the other hand, foreigners, comprising mostly the British and American 'aristocratic' class and a few influential local, politically well-connected barons, occupy thousands of acres of land on an individual basis. Only twenty own 74 per cent of the total land in Laikipia County. In the Laikipia Plateau, private ranches range from 'small' concerns of 5,000 acres to endless horizons of massive land properties that are over 100,000 acres. There are approximately 36 estates. Two of the 18 estates are owned by multi-millionaire Hollywood A-list types who entertain tourist guests on the ranches. Many of the private farms and ranches are being converted to wildlife sanctuaries.

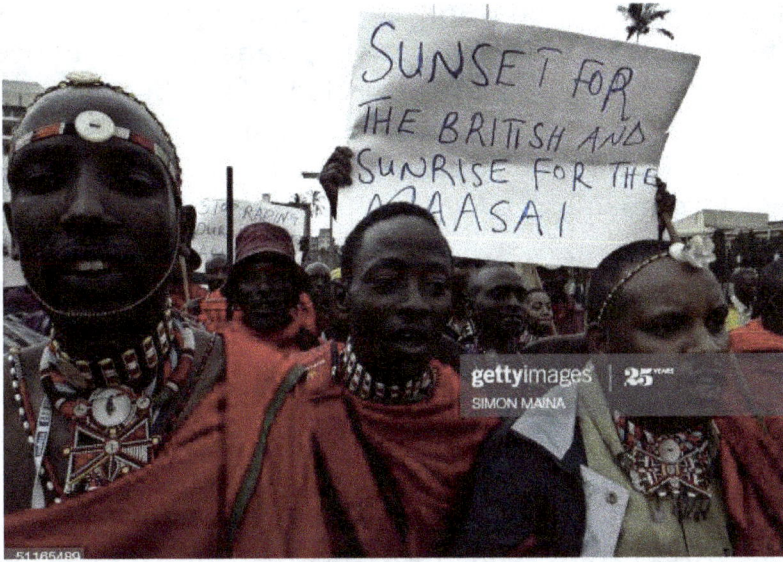

Figure 14: Mathew Lempurkel leading Laikipia Maasai during the Maasai demonstration in Nairobi © Simon Maina – Associated Press

In Nakuru County, there were simmering conflicts between the Kikuyu and the Maasai in Mai Mahiu because of the blockage of the Ewuaso River, where one of the Kikuyu farmers built a dam. The dam blocked the flow of the Ewuaso stream downstream, leaving the Maasai and their livestock without water. The Maasai took it upon themselves to break the dam. In response, the Kikuyus in Mai Mahiu took revenge and attacked a local chief, Ole Kibelekenya. This resulted in violent conflict where the Kikuyus blocked the Narok-Mai Mahiu road and ejected Maasai passengers from matatus to Narok. Seven Maasais were hacked to death (IRIN, 2005)[9].

The Maasai responded with brutal force that resulted in hundreds of Kikuyu homes being burnt down and tens of Kikuyus being killed, with their livestock taken by the Maasai. The clashes between the Maasai and the Kikuyu extended to Longonot Station. In the name of restoring peace, the government dispatched helicopter gunships to unleash terror on the Maasai (IRIN, 2005). A security operation was ordered by the then Minister for Internal Security, the late John Michuki,

---

9   See https://reliefweb.int/report/kenya/kenya-least-14-killed-clashes-over- water

47 Maasai herdsmen were arrested, several homesteads were burnt down, and a curfew for the Maasai was imposed. The operation was supervised by the local Member of Parliament, Jane Kihara. Two herdsmen, Kimasisa Ole Kunkuru and Saisa Ole Kipuri, were killed (Unrepresented Nations and Peoples Organization [UNPO], 2005).

The government banned the Maasai from burying their bodies in Oloonongot. MCSF, with the support of the late Hon Ole Ntimama and the late Hon Nkaiserry, mobilized the community to plan the funerals. With assistance from the Independent Medico-Legal Unit (IMLU), the post-mortems on the bodies of the deceased were done and a report submitted to the government for investigations, but the government declined. There was tension between the Maasai and Kikuyu regarding the burial site for the deceased because the Kikuyus claimed ownership of the land, and they filed an injunction with the Provincial Administration. Using local communities from Kedong and Oloonongot, MCSF mobilized the community and informed the late Ole Ntimama, who accompanied the people to Naivasha mortuary, to take the bodies for burial. The bodies were buried at Oloonongot with the presence of Maasai political and religious leaders in attendance.

The Maa Prayer Day at Oloonongot

Following all the foregoing activities and due to pressure and threats from the government through the police and the Provincial Administration, MCSF was denied permits to hold meetings nationwide, and was branded a national security risk by state apparatus between 2004 and 2006. MCSF changed strategy and facilitated the formation of the Maasai Pastors Association. This was meant to use prayer meetings to mobilize the community as well as raise awareness about the Maasai claims. This proved to be a very good and effective strategy. The first Maasai prayer meeting was held on 11 September 2004 at Oloonongot and attended by Maa speakers from Kajiado, Narok, Trans Mara, Baringo, Samburu, Isiolo, Nakuru, Marsabit, as well as Tanzania, where they declared a union of purpose to pursue the return of the land taken by the British and the Kenyan regimes. The prayers were led by

Rev Peter Mankura of the Dominion Chapel Church. Reverent Mankura said, quoting the Bible, that "what had been taken away must be returned. The prayers were also attended by the late General Joseph Ole Nkaissery, who, together with MCSF leadership, urged the Maa-speaking people in East Africa to unite as one and defend their land and natural resources.

Figure 15: The Maasai prayer day at Oloonongot. The Maasai from East Africa converged together to seek divine intervention for restoration and return of their stolen land © Michael Santeto ole Tiampati.

Maasai Suswa Declaration

MCSF engaged several national policy formulation processes. One key process was the Kenya Constitution-making process, where several individual and organizational members participated. Member organizations participated both as participants at the Bomas Conference between 2004 and 2005, and in the sensitization of the Maasai communities in their respective counties. Several workshops were held to analyze the draft, and upon the analysis, the Maasai were dissatisfied with clauses in the draft constitution that were related to land. It is with that regard that the Maasai, through MCSF, decided to hold a rally to reject the draft constitution. In June 2005, they convened a rally at Suswa to make their declaration. Members from each district were mandated to mobilize resources to transport people to Suswa, feed the participants, and make all other required logistical arrangements. Religious leaders used their churches, politicians used their political clout, and traditional leaders used their cultural authority to mobilize people to attend the meeting.

Suswa is known by the Maasai for its history. It is said that it was the place where the Maasai had their last feast before a combined force of several Maasai Iloshon (sub-clans) had their last warrior camp that defeated the Laikipia Maasai. It is also known to be the cradle of Maasai rituals, which were done at Oldonyo Onyokie. *Empaash,* which means the passage in Maa, is the name of the place due to its geographical location between Mount Longonot (Oloonongot) and Mount Suswa (Oldonyio Onyokie).

MCSF led the Maasai to use the occasion to make a declaration that became a national rallying call for the then-proposed Kenya constitution, called the Wako Draft. Maa speakers from all over Kenya attended the meeting. The meeting issued what has come to be known as Suswa Declaration One. After that meeting, Suswa has become the place for the Maasai in Kenya to make their political pronouncements.

The Ilchamus Constitutional Reference Case

In 2004, the Maa speaking community of Ilchamus filed a Constitutional Reference Case seeking to either have one of their persons nominated as a Member of Parliament or be given their Constituency. The Application was brought by the four Applicants led by Rangan Lemeiguran and others against the Attorney-General (on behalf of the Government of Kenya as its principal legal adviser) and the Electoral Commission of Kenya (the body charged with the creation and distribution of Constituencies under the Constitution). In a case that has come to be branded 'A victory, in Theory, Loss in Practice', they made several applications. These included the fundamental right of representation in the National Assembly of the Republic of Kenya under the provision of Section 1A of the Constitution of Kenya has been effectively denied to

152

the Ilchamus Community; the Electoral Commission of Kenya in the performance of its duties under Section 33(5), Constitution of Kenya, in respect to the Eighth Parliament has failed to ensure any or adequate observance of the primary principle of the representation of special interests which Section 33 (1), Constitution of Kenya, mandatorily provides for. The Ilchamus needed the support from all Maa-speaking communities to rally behind them. While the court ruling was seen to be a victory for the Ilchamus and other minorities who lack representation in political spaces in Kenya, it was rendered moot once the process of establishing the current new constitution was promulgated in 2010.

The Maasai saw this as an achievement that signalled possibly an opportunity for other historical land-related cases to be addressed, and decided to celebrate with the Ilchamus. In support of the initiative, MCSF and the Maasai Council of Elders mobilized Maa speakers to celebrate the victory, which was held in Ngambo in January 2007 and attended by several political, religious, traditional leaders, and civil society groups from Narok, Kajiado, Laikipia, and Samburu. Unfortunately, like many other court rulings in Kenya in favour of communities, the decision was never implemented as directed by the court.

Figure 16: The Ilchamus community celebrating the ruling in favour of their case in Ngambo, Baringo County © Michael Ole Tiampati

Networking and Consensus Building

The forum was also able to achieve significant success in addressing historical injustices on land and natural resources, building consensus among various Maasai institutions, and representing the Maa Community at various United Nations Permanent Forum for Indigenous Peoples' Issues in New York, and other indigenous peoples' related meetings globally. Key among the activities planned during the strategic planning meeting was networking and consensus-building.

As indicated previously, the first task was to seek consensus among the Maasai politicians to rally their support for the Maasai cause. The MCSF team visited each former and sitting Member of Parliament to inform them about the movement and its goals. While some members were positive, some thought mistakenly that the forum's goal was to prepare some of the members for political gains. The forum also reached out to traditional and opinion leaders. This led to the formation of the Maasai Council of Elders. Another key group that the team reached out to was the religious leaders. Several meetings were held in Narok and Kajiado to educate the church leaders of the important role they could play in unifying the Maasai. After several meetings, the church leaders formed the Maasai Pastors Association. This was very important, and it facilitated the forum in reaching out to the community since the government had denied the forum permits to hold any meetings.

At the national level, the forum partnered with Kenya Land Alliance (KLA), which became a key ally in the Kenya National Land Policy Formulation Process. The partnership enabled MCSF to reach out to other communities that had land grievances in Kenya. Such groups included the squatter communities in the Coastal and North Rift regions. Members of the forum participated in several demonstrations and meetings across the country to support ongoing national land-related processes. The networks also enabled the Maasai land agenda to be included during the World Social Forum in Nairobi in 2007, where MCSF partnered with global civil society groups to advocate for social, economic, cultural, spiritual, and gender rights globally under the banner, 'Another World is Possible'.

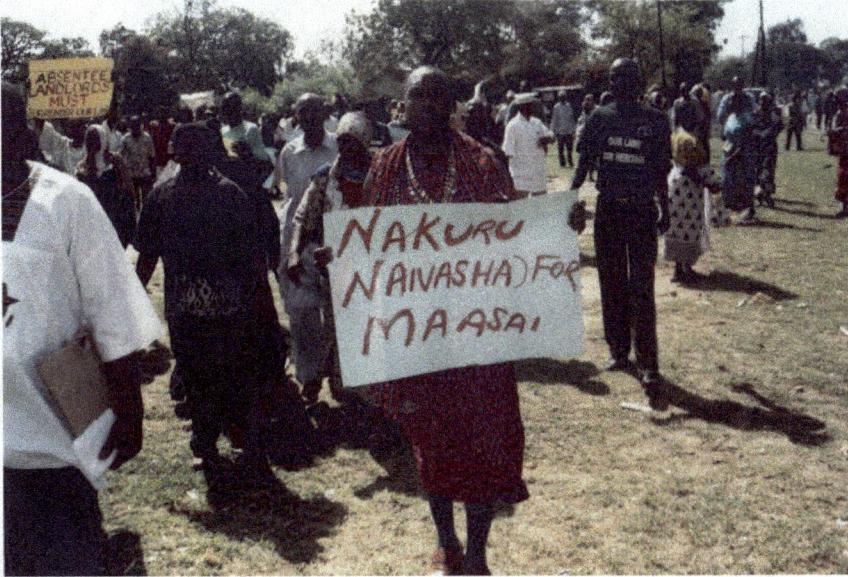

Figure 17: Joseph Mutaka Ole Kishau, a member of Namuncha Maasai Community, joining a procession of squatters from the Kenyan coast historical land injustices © Ben Ole Koissaba, 2007

During that period, there was the Kenyan Constitutional Process. MCSF was able to partner with the Centre for Minority Rights Development (CEMIRIDE) and the Pastoralist Development Network of Kenya (PDNK) to form an umbrella body called Minorities Reforms Consortium (MRC), whose objective was to engage in lobbying for the inclusion of ethnic, religious, and indigenous communities in the reference group of the Constitution Review Process. The lobby was able to press for representation, submitted a memorandum, and presented its views to the Constitution of Kenya Review Commission (CKRC), which was formed through the enactment of the Constitution of Kenya Review Commission (Amendment) Act of 2001.

After the 2007 post-election violence, the Maasai civil society members were intimidated and harassed by the state organs, but this did not stop the team from engaging with the peace-building processes. Such intimidation included the attack of Godftrey Ole Ntapayia in Keitenglela by armed people who attempted to break into his house, I together with Saina Sena (a lawyer who was representing several Maasai who were arrested in Narok) were forced to go into hiding but were later arraigned in the Narok Court but bonded by the court to keep the peace because there was no adequate evidence for a conviction. The MSCF team initiated a process of engaging the Panel of Eminent African Personalities, chaired by the former UN Secretary-General Kofi Annan, who led the forty-one-day peace-making process. This culminated in the Agreement on the Principles of Partnership of the Coalition Government, which was signed by President Mwai Kibaki and the Honourable Raila Odinga on February 28th, 2008, putting an end to the crisis which had engulfed the nation and taken the world by surprise.

The mediation process began on January 22nd, 2008, three weeks after the post-election violence erupted across Kenya. The Panel was charged with helping the parties get through the conflict to ensure that an escalation of the crisis was avoided and that the opportunity to bring about sustainable peace was seized as soon as possible. The main agenda for MCSF to engage in that process was Agenda 4, which addressed historical injustices on land. MCSF was able to hold a meeting with the late Kofi Annan team and delivered their letter of grievances to the Committee of Eminent Persons about Agenda 4, which related to land. In the letter to Kofi Annan, MCSF also raised the issue of intimidation, harassment, and deregistration of Maasai NGOs and threats to members and leaders of the forum.

Members of the forum were also able to collaborate with both national and international human rights organizations. In Kenya, MCSF developed links with the Kenya Human Rights Commission (KHRC) and the Kenya National Commission on Human Rights (KNCHR). The collaboration was mainly to protect Maasai human rights defenders who were constantly under threat of arrest by the government. Through the initiative, MCSF members were able to receive representation in courts and safe housing for some members during the 2007 post-election violence, mainly in Narok, where there were bloody conflicts between the Maasai and the Kikuyus. The Kenya National Commission on Human Rights supported the forum in reporting about the killings in Samburu by government forces after the Isampur (Samburu) retaliated against the Turkana who raided them, killed and maimed people, and took hundreds of livestock.

MCSF also engaged the United Nations Office of the High Commissioner on Human Rights. This facilitated the support of MCSF members in attending several meetings and conferences globally. The meetings placed the Maasai agenda on the international human rights agenda. Through such collaboration, MCSF was privileged to host the then United Nations Special Rapporteur on the Rights of Indigenous Peoples in December 2006. Stavenhagen, Rodolfo, paid a visit to several Maasai districts to hear from the communities about human rights issues affecting the Maasai. During his visits, Rodolfo was presented with memoranda by several Maasai groups and other indigenous people.

Figure 18: The then United Nations Special Rapporteur on the Rights of Indigenous Peoples, Stavenhagen, Rodolfo, addressing a Maasai community in Sekenani, Maasai Mara in Narok. © Ben Ole Koissaba, December 18th, 2006

The collaboration with the UN agencies also benefited the Maasai in other ways. In 2008, Ole Tinkoi and Ole Kaunga from the Maasai community of Laikipia in Kenya were trained in documenting and archiving their cultural heritage through a new project launched by the United Nations World Intellectual Property Organization (WIPO). The presence of the Maasai in such forums enabled the members of the MCSF to link up with other international organizations that have continually supported Maasai organizations in advocacy. This brought visibility in the international arena. Many of the MCSF representatives now have strong relationships with international organizations that are advocating for key global issues like climate change. These opportunities also made it possible for the Maasai to hold leadership positions in global forums like the United Nations Permanent Forum on Indigenous Peoples.

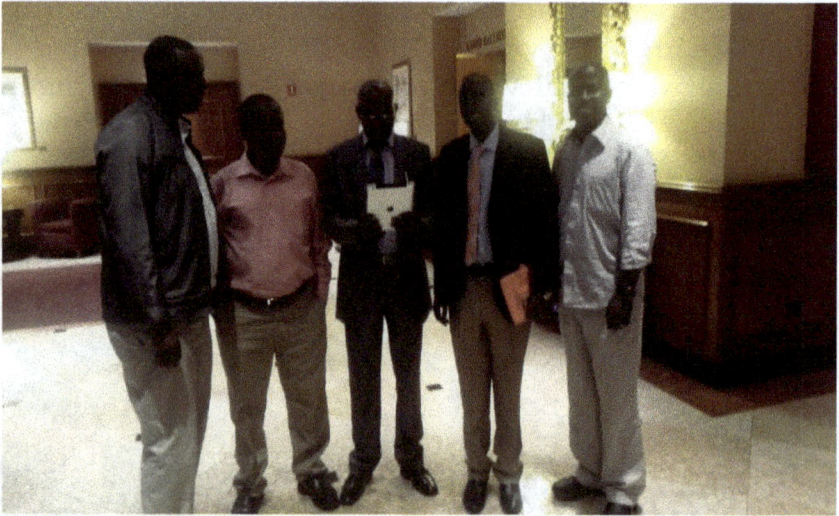

Figure 19: Maasai representatives at a United Nations Conference in New York, 2012, representing the interests of the Maasai. In the picture are the late Dan Ole Sapit, Kanyinge Sena, Ben Ole Koissaba, Hon. Ken Aramat (Member of Parliament, Narok East), and Kimaren Ole Riamit

The Government's response to MCSF

The reaction of the Kenyan government to the Maasai land claims was rather high-handed. Maasai demonstrators were violently dispersed, beaten up, arrested, and arraigned in courts on charges of incitement. The Minister for Lands and

Settlement asserted that the leases in question were not for 99 years but for 999 years and that they have therefore not expired. The minister, then Kimunya, suggested that the Maasai should wait for another 899 years before they can lodge their claims (BBC News, 16 August 2004)[10]. The British government, on its part, had asserted that any claims relating to the Maasai Agreements of 1904 and 1911 lie, because of state succession, with the government of Kenya and not the government of the United Kingdom. White farmers occupying some of the lands in question, especially in Laikipia, asserted that their rights to the land they hold derived not from the Maasai Agreements or any other actions of the British colonial government, but from titles issued by the independent Kenyan government. They sought the protection of their titles and property rights in accordance with the provisions of the Constitution of Kenya relating to the sanctity of private property. According to observations by members of the forum from Laikipia, when the Maasai protested, the government resorted to using uncalled force and enforcing curfew in the whole of Laikipia.

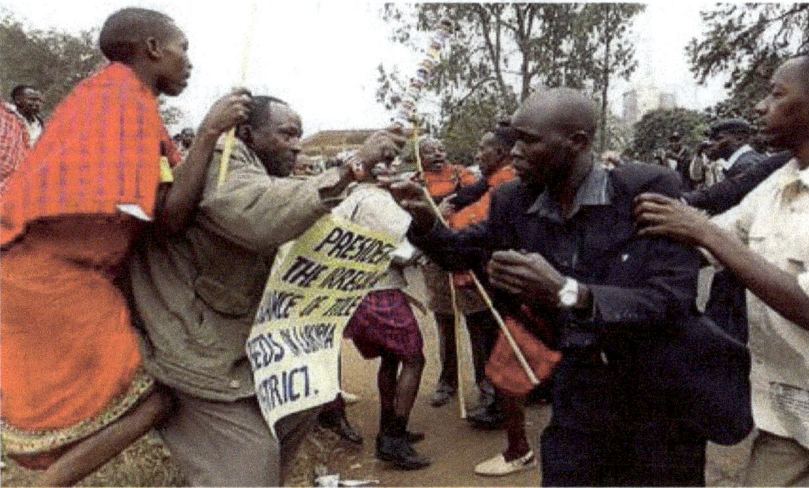

Figure 20: Kenya police confront peaceful Maasai demonstrators during the processions at Uhuru Park, Nairobi, © Ben Ole Koissaba August 13th, 2004

---

10   See Kenya Maasai land claims rejected BBC News Monday, 16 August, 2004 http://news.bbc.co.uk/2/hi/africa/3570656.stm

While the campaign's broad objective was land restitution, the initial focus was on the return of Laikipia, the two-million-acre site of the former northern Maasai Reserve and now home to a handful of ranches largely in the hands of the remnant white settler community and senior politicians. There was also clamour for some land in Nakuru County that the Maasai lay claim to. The government issued a statement citing incitement by Maasai Indigenous Civil Society Organizations and instructed that the Maasai be dealt with mercilessly (Kantai, 2007). When members of MCSF filed their claims about threats and intimidation by members of the Provincial Administration, the government responded by arresting 267 men, women, and children in Laikipia and arraigning them in courts in Nanyuki, Nyeri, and Nyahururu on fictitious charges (MCSF, 2005). Testimonies from the arrested people narrated incidents of overcrowding in police cells, denial of food and water, and physical body injuries. The offences committed were trespassing and malicious property damage, which usually attract court fines between Kshs. 2,000 to Kshs. 5,000, the Maasai were denied bail, and when the bails were granted, they were charged bonds of up to Ksh. 100,000.

A second procession to deliver the memorandum to the British High Commission on August 24th, 2004, was violently dispersed by the Police, terming the march illegal (Kantai, 2007). Thirteen men were arrested, several were injured, and personal effects were lost during the forceful dispersion of the Maasai by the Police. The first procession took the Government by surprise, and the memoranda were delivered to some government offices without any intimidation. This coincided with the time the Maasai were experiencing severe drought, which forced them to seek pasture in areas that had grass. These happened to be in historical Maasai territories, but are now owned by white settlers. This threat was real in that the government had introduced the NGO Coordinating Act (1990), which was meant to control the activities of Community Service Organizations (CSOs) that did not subscribe to the aspirations of the ruling elites.

Later, the government could not sustain the cases, and all the arrested were set free (MCSF, 2005).

Also, there were clashes between the Maasai and communities living on the lands that the Maasai claimed. Within one year, as the Maasai kept the momentum of demanding restitution with respect to the land, several people were killed by the police or unknown persons. The key murders were those of Marima ole Sempeta, who was a leading lawyer in researching the Maasai historical claims. As mentioned in the previous sections, the hostilities between the Maasai and the Kikuyus in Mai Mahiu were also experienced between the Maasai and the Kikuyus in Narok.

In Narok, the Maasai, under the leadership of the late Moses Ole Mpoe, were fighting to get back land that was taken by the family of the late Minister Mbiyu Koinage in Mau Narok. Mr. Moses Ole Mpoe was shot in cold blood on December 3, 2010, at the Njoro turn-off, four kilometres away from Nakuru town, sparking off protests among leaders of the Maasai who immediately pegged the death to a political motive. The killers are yet to be brought to book. Even though some suspects were arrested, the case has dragged on for more than 10 years. Mr. Mpoe's death raised suspicions due to his role in the ongoing campaign by Maasai leaders to have some of the ancestral land they say was taken away by the colonial government returned.

Fig. 21: The late Moses Ole Mpoe addresses fellow Maasai community members from Mau Narok who are against the buying of 2400 acres of land by the government to resettle post-election violence victims, a week before he was shot dead at the Njoro Nakuru Junction. Photo Courtesy of George Sayagie, Daily Nation, October 28th, 2013.

PART VI

CONTESTATION OF MAASAI LAND APPROPRIATION

Introduction

To understand the impact of land appropriation in Kenya, it is important to review the literature about how such appropriation has been challenged by affected communities and the opportunities that may be available for them to use in seeking redress. Atuahene (2009) noted that seeking redress for past land theft has always been a volatile political issue. This is evident in Kenya in the way the reports by the Njonjo Commission Report, the Ndungu Commission Report, and the Truth, Justice and Reconciliation Commission (TJRC), which the government has been reluctant to implement. Since the completion of the TJRC report and subsequent submission to the President, the government of Kenya has given conflicting signals about whether it will be made public as it was drafted or make changes to accommodate the interests of the political elites who were adversely mentioned by the report (Koissaba, 2014).

Seeking legal redress for land dispossession, evictions, and human rights violations in Kenya is not easy, given the political issues that are involved, more so because law has long influenced the development of Kenya's common law from other common-law jurisdictions (Wachira, 2008). It is a known fact that the Maasai were the first Kenyan indigenous community to use legal processes to challenge the British colonial regime (East African Protectorate, 1914). Given the outcomes of the case, it is evident that without an independent judicial system that is free from political influence, the Maasai case will have several challenges.

As was expected, the Maasai did not resist the violent moves of 1904 and 1911. However, with the advice from European sympathizers and as discussed previously, the Maasai filed a legal challenge in the High Court of British East Africa in 1913 in a landmark case often referred to as the Maasai case, the Ole Njogo Case of 1913, where the Maasai lost on a technicality (Hughes, 2006). And as presented previously, other recorded instances where the Maasai attempted to seek legal redress of the rights to their land were during their

presentation at the Kenya Land Commission Evidence and
Memoranda 1934 (Kenya Land Commission Report, 1934)
and during the Lancaster Independence (Colonial Office,
1963).

Again, as discussed previously, the Maasai were presented
with yet another opportunity to seek legal redress for the
injustices by the outgoing British colonial government,
during the second Lancaster conference convened to
deliberate the independence of Kenya held from February
14th to April 16th, 1962, in London. That was the basis for
the formation of MCSF, whose main role was to research,
document, and disseminate information on how best to
respond to the losses that occurred during the Lancaster
independence conference. The MCSF, in consultation
with legal experts, political leaders, and other people of
goodwill, had the intention of litigating the case locally
and internationally. Many believe that getting the land
back may be a tall order and that restitution (e.g., monetary
compensation) may be a manageable option. Such unbelief
was expressed by Lotte Hughes in her commentary about
the presentation to the Building Bridges Initiative[1]. There
are such examples of reparations being done in the world.
In a landmark decision on 13th March 2019, the Australian
High Court ordered the Government of the Northern Territory
to pay $2.53 million (1.78 million USD) in compensation
to the Ngaliwurru and Nungali people for the loss of Native
Title in the town of Timber Creek (IWGIA, 2019). Many case
laws may be used by the Maasai to lay claims to the lost
land. This can be accomplished through local, regional,
and international mechanisms. Like many indigenous
communities in the world who lost their lands far beyond
three hundred years, if the Maasai can articulate their
case even without living witnesses, there is a possibility
of winning restitution. Moreover, the government, through
various land commission reports, has conceded that the
Maasai have rightful claims, which are also supported by
the Truth, Justice and Reconciliation Commission report
(TJRC, 2018).

---

[1]   See Why Maasai's BBI demands are unworkable, especially on land. Daily Nation
    THURSDAY FEBRUARY 27th, 2020.

New Legal Regimes Related to Land in Kenya

According to Wachira (2008), the current Kenyan legal framework can potentially redress the Maasai land claims if it is progressively interpreted in keeping with international standards. The promulgation of the Kenyan Constitution in 2010 is regarded as the most significant achievement in Kenya's governance since independence in 1963. However, the full implementation of the letter and spirit of the Constitution is crucial to realize the promise of a democratically stable and prosperous future for all Kenyans. The Constitution makes provisions for rights whose enjoyment demands recognizing and protecting group rights. The new Kenya Constitution (Section 67) gives the National Land Commission the mandate to manage public land on behalf of national and county governments, among other functions of the Constitution (ROK, 2010).

The incorporation of the National Land Policy into the Constitution and the enactment of laws on land by Parliament is an opportunity that would eradicate legal roadblocks that have hindered the implementation of recommendations made by the Njonjo Land Commission (ROK, 2002) and the Ndungu Report (ROK, 2004). These commissions were formed to investigate issues related to the legal structure of land laws and historical injustices related to land appropriation.

Another constitutional provision that allows the Maasai to seek redress is the Land and Environmental Court enshrined in the Constitution (ROK, 2010). The Land and Environmental Court is expected to adjudicate cases related to land disputes arising from claims filed by the communities with land ownership grievances. Since the new constitution took effect in 2010, the Maasai community has filed several cases in various courts in Kenya. Case laws about similar cases adjudicated in favour of indigenous people in Kenya, like the Ogiek and the Endorois, can be used by the Maasai to seek redress for their ancestral lands.

Deep-seated interests still threaten or challenge the implementation of the Constitution (Koissaba, 2014). Key challenges are evident in how some political elites want to maintain the *status quo*, reverse gains, and manipulate the pace and nature of changes recommended in the new constitutional order (Koissaba, 2014). As is evident by recent actions and decisions by the President and Parliament, there seems to be a reversal of gains in human rights, freedom of expression, and freedom of association (Koissaba, 2014). The Kenyan parliamentarians are working on amendments to muzzle the freedom of the press and the conduct of non-profit organizations (Ogemba, 2013). This is a challenge to the Maasai quest for justice and rights to their land because most of the lands they lay claim to were acquired mainly by Kenyan political elites.

Grievances of continued loss of land by the Maasai were vividly expressed in a memorandum submitted to the Truth, Justice and Reconciliation Commission by the Maa-speaking pastoralists in Kenya in January 2011 (MPIDO, 2011). This outlined how land in Iloodoariak and Mosiro group ranches was illegally allocated to ineligible and non-residents of the said areas through illegal transactions by officials of the Ministry of Lands in collaboration with the Group Ranch Committees (MPIDO 2011).

The challenge to contested land appropriation lies in the historical legitimatization of dispossessions through the retention and entrenchment of colonial land laws and policies in Kenya (Koissaba, 2014). According to Wachira (2008), this betrayed the people who fought for independence and those who had hoped to get back the whole or parts of their land that were appropriated by the colonial regime. It is considered that various Maasai groups and individuals from Nakuru, Laikipia, Isiolo, Kajiado, and Narok have filed numerous court cases in different tribunals.

There have been mixed outcomes of the cases arising from the challenges of interpreting the laws governing private property and the sanctity of land titles (MCSF, 2005). Other challenges in pursuing the cases are the inhibitive high cost of litigation and the time it takes to adjudicate the cases in Kenyan courts. A unified approach by the Maasai has also contributed to a slow process that has often resulted in conflicts between the Maasai political leaders, opposing groups, and those in civil society who have been fronting for the cases. Such cases as the Maasai community at Satellite/Oloonongot, Kedong, Entapipi, Narasha, Namuncha, and Natooli have led to significant losses by the Maasai because of their internal conflicts.

The unfriendly political climate had also put the Maasai human rights activists in a confrontation with the government, resulting in intimidation, incarceration, and the death of some of the MCSF members (MCSF, 2007). Another phenomenon that has caused problems is the commodification of the process by some Maasai non-profit outfits, who have used the Maasai predicament as a cash cow to raise funds that, in many instances, have not been directed to the Maasai cause. Since land is a vital aspect of the global human rights movement, some Maasai NGOs and individuals, mainly from Kajiado, have taken advantage of the desperate need of the Maasai to reclaim their lost land to solicit funding from local communities and international donors in the name of fighting for Maasai land rights. Some individuals have also used the same to ascend to political positions or gain prominence as a result of that.

Regional Instruments for Contesting Maasai Land Appropriation

The East African Court of Justice (EACJ)

The East African Court of Justice (EACJ) is a treaty-based judicial body of the East African Community tasked to ensure adherence to the law in the interpretation and application of and compliance with the East African Community Treaty of 1999. The Court comprises a First Instance Division and an Appellate Division. The Court has jurisdiction over the interpretation and application of the Treaty and may have other appellate, human rights, or other jurisdiction upon conclusion of a protocol to realize such an extended jurisdiction. Reference to the court may be made by Legal and Natural Persons, the Partner States, and the Secretary-General of the community (EACJ, 2001).

Given that the court does not require that litigants exhaust local mechanisms before filing claims, the Maasai can leverage its existence where the Kenyan courts have failed to address their claims. Attempts by Maasai non-governmental organizations affiliated to MCSF to use the EACJ have not achieved any real results due to a lack of a united approach, and the dilemma the Maasai sections had with the overall mandate to represent the Maasai in any land-related case (MCSF, 2005).

African Commission on Human Rights (ACHPR)

The African Union has instruments for addressing human rights issues in Africa, commonly called the African Charter. The African Charter established the African Commission on Human and Peoples' Rights and was inaugurated in 1987. The African Commission on Human and Peoples' Rights is a quasi-judicial body that monitors the implementation of the African Charter on Human and Peoples' Rights (ACHPR 1986). Depending on who files a suit, the court has mandatory jurisdiction, which every state automatically acknowledges on ratification of the Protocol. It also has discretionary authority, for which a corresponding additional declaration of recognition of jurisdiction is required.

Kenya is among the fifty states that have ratified the Protocol. In addition to performing any other tasks that may be entrusted to it by the Assembly of Heads of State and Governments, the Commission is officially charged with three primary functions namely: 1) the protection of human and people' rights, 2) the promotion of human and people' rights, and, 3) the interpretation of the African Charter on Human and People' Rights.

The African Commission on Human and People' Rights has already set a precedent in the ruling of the Endorois case that was approved by the African Union in January 2010 (Minority Rights Group [MRG], 2010)[2], and the recent case filed by the Ogiek People Development Programme that was heard in Addis Ababa on November 27th and 28th 2014 (MRG, 2017)[3]. While the Kenyan government has yet to implement the decisions of the African Court regarding the two cases, the implications for the Maasai are that the cases can be used as case laws to file their cases. Despite having had

2   See https://www.refworld.org/pdfid/4ca571e42.pdf
3   See https://minorityrights.org/2017/05/26/huge-victory-kenyas-ogiek- african-court-sets-major-precedent-indigenous-peoples-land-rights/

representation in various meetings where the Maasai have expressed the need for the African Commission on Human and Peoples' Rights, the Maasai have not made real progress on that front (MCSF, 2005). The possibility for the Maasai to use the African Commission on Human and Peoples' Rights will depend on how they organize themselves and develop a consolidated front to pursue their case.

International Instruments

Since independence, Kenya has signed and ratified forty-nine treaties and acceded to about eighty-nine others. The conventions relate to the United Nations Human Rights, African Charter, Refugees, International Humanitarian Law, Narcotics, Trade, Transport and Communication, Civil Aviation, East African Community, Law of the Sea, and many others. The 2010 Constitution of Kenya contains a provision in Article 2(5) 2(6) stating that:

> "Any treaty or convention ratified by Kenya shall form part of the law of Kenya under this Constitution." (ROK,2010, p.14). Regarding Article 261 (1 & 4) and the 5th schedule of the Constitution, the Ratification of Treaties Bill, 2011, has been submitted to the Attorney General for drafting and subsequent publication (ROK, 2010). The Bill is for an Act of Parliament to make a provision for the ratification and domestication of international instruments and related matters." (ROK, 2010).

International Labour Organization Convention No. 169 on Indigenous and Tribal Peoples (ILO)

Convention No. 169 of the International Labour Organization (ILO) provides a set of subjective and objective criteria that are jointly applied to guide the identification of Indigenous Peoples (ILO, 1989). The Maasai, by their unique cultural practices and attachment to their land, have been identified as Indigenous people. Once a country ratifies it, it has one year to align legislation, policies, and programmes to the Convention before it becomes legally binding (ILO, 1989). Countries that have ratified the Convention are subject to supervision regarding its implementation. The Convention recognizes and protects tribal people's land ownership rights and sets minimum UN standards regarding consultation and consent (ILO, 1989).

The International Labour Organization Convention Number 169, Articles 14 and 15, gives the right of ownership. Possession of the people concerned over the land that they traditionally occupy (ILO, 1989, Art. 14). Also, Article 14 provides measures that shall be taken in appropriate cases to safeguard the right of the people concerned to use lands not exclusively occupied by them, but to which they have traditional activities. It calls for particular attention to be paid to the situation of nomadic peoples and shifting cultivators, and urges governments to take steps, as necessary, to identify the land which the people concerned traditionally occupy, and to guarantee effective protection of their rights of ownership and possession through the adoption and establishment of adequate procedures within the national legal system, and to resolve land claims by the people's concerned (ILO, 1989. Art. 14). In Article 15, the Convention provides for safeguards for natural resources associated with Indigenous people' land and territories including the right to participate in the use, management, and conservation of such resources (ILO, 1989. Art. 15).

Accordingly, the ILO Convention No. 169 can play a significant role in arguing the Maasai case in any local court of law or policy environment, by stating that people have the right to and protection of land that they historically and currently hold, and in light of the current constitution's provisions, the Maasai have tried to use such constitutional provisions to argue their cases. As it is, the Kenyan Constitution gives the Maasai a legitimate chance to frame their case (ROK, 2010), but this will require the translation of the provisions of the convention into Kenya's legal instruments. This also needs a judicial system that recognizes and supports international human rights instruments.

The United Nations Declaration on the Rights of Indigenous Peoples (UNDRIP)

The Maasai are globally acknowledged and considered Indigenous people due to their unique way of life, culture, and relationship with their land. The lack of recognition of their traditional land-use practices by Kenyan national legal frameworks has contributed to the continuous appropriation of their land and other natural resources. The United Nations Declaration on the Rights of Indigenous People (UNDRIP), Article 26 provides for the recognition of Indigenous people as having the right to own, develop, control and use their land and territories, including the total environment of their land, air, waters, coastal seas, sea-ice, flora and fauna, and other resources that they have traditionally owned or otherwise occupied or used. This includes the right to the full recognition of their laws, traditions, and customs, land-tenure systems and institutions for the development and management of resources, and the right to effective measures by States to prevent any interference with, alienation or encroachment of these rights" (UN, 2008).

While Kenya has not ratified the United Nations Declaration on the Rights of Indigenous Peoples (UNDRIP), relevant law provisions could be invoked to give legal credence and meaning to Indigenous peoples' land and resource rights. The Kenyan legal framework is inadequate in terms of the protection of these communities. Still, the law can be adequately interpreted, as well as other case laws adopted to file claims of land appropriation. The Maasai have, on several occasions, raised the issue of land appropriation and the impact it has had on local land governance institutions and courts in Kenya. Still, its interpretation by the Kenyan policy makers and the tribunals has been a constant challenge (Koissaba, 2013).

Case Laws

Case laws are a set of legislation that are established by following earlier judicial decisions and are based on judicial precedents rather than statutory laws of any country or state. In using case laws to seek redress, it should be noted that case laws are persuasive but not controlling. Such cases that may have a bearing on the Maasai case include the cases in Kenya such as the Environment and Land Court at Nairobi (ELC) Civil Suit no. 821 of 2012 (OS), (Kenya Law Review, 2014); the African Commission on Human and People's Rights (ACHPR) and the Endorois case; (ACHPR, 2009); Australia, such as Mabo v Queensland (No 2) (1992) 175 CLR 1; John Cecil Clunies-Ross v. The Commonwealth of Australia, Thomas

Uren and John Joseph Brown (1984) HCA 65; 155 CLR 193, and Gerhardy v Brown (1985) 159 CLR 70; Botswana, Sesana and others v Attorney General (52/2002) (2006) BWHC 1; some examples in Canada that can be cited are the Chippewas of Sarnia Band vs Canada (Attorney General), 195 D.L.R. (4th) 135, and Tsilhqot'in Nation v. British Columbia 2014 SCC.

44. Most of the cases filed by the Maasai in several courts in Kenya has used such case laws to argue their case regarding land appropriation.

While the above mechanisms may be instrumental in the Maasai case in either seeking justice or putting a stop to the increasing land losses, the greatest challenges lie in the individualization of land titles, the commodification of what was once community land, an increase in non-pastoralists' land-use systems, and a lack of supportive national policy. The interpretation of legal instruments by the judiciary and domestication of international legal statutes will also contribute as a helping factor.

PART VII:

MANIFESTATION OF MAASAI LAND APPROPRIATION

Introduction

The land puzzle in Kenya emanates from the processes through which the colonial government was established (Sorresnson, 1965; Okoth-Ogendo, 1991). The establishment of the colonial state at the beginning of the twentieth century has continued to impact land use, access, and control in diverse ways. First, the system established a capitalist development economy through a process that favoured colonialism, hence the foundation for land hitches in Kenya. The Colonial administration used a set of legal instruments and force to alienate land, often through compulsory acquisitions, for settlement.

One of the outstanding characteristics of Kenya, and indeed most African governments, is that they conduct globalization affairs as if the countries were homogeneous. Even though they are made up of different nationalities, minorities, indigenous communities, and cultural groups, this has had a debilitating effect on the whole scope of minorities and indigenous peoples' lives. In turn, this has become one of the major causes of marginalization, impoverishment, exploitation, commercialization, neglect, abuse, and disenfranchisement that continue to hamper the realization of their basic rights and fundamental freedoms as enshrined in national constitutions and other regional and international legal instruments. It is common practice in Kenya and elsewhere in Africa where government bureaucrats reserve the right to determine who should form social movements, engage in lucrative economic activities, vote and be voted for, and, to a large extent, who should enjoy what kind of rights and freedoms. It is this trend that makes it almost impossible for minorities and indigenous people to realize any tangible benefits brought about by such exercises because ethnic minorities and indigenous communities form an insignificant fraction of the populace and, as such, are often ignored by governments on this basis.

The Maasai, like other indigenous communities in Africa and the world over, depend on land for survival, and any loss of their land leads to a myriad of negative effects. Community land represents the backbone of their life and livelihoods. Its loss, whether due to expropriation, appropriation, conquest, conflict, infrastructure projects, private investments, or natural disasters, has grave consequences. Just like every other disposed community, it has felt negative consequences. There is consensus among many indigenous communities in Kenya that past land appropriation has had devastating effects and outcomes for the Maasai in Kenya. The dispossession of land not only reduced the amount of land that the Maasai owned, but it also led to numerous conflicts among the Maasai themselves and between the Maasai and other non-Maasai who occupied the alienated land. This is affirmed by the 2003 Report of the Working Group on Indigenous Populations/ Communities (WGIP) of the African Commission on Human and Peoples' Rights (ACHPR, 2004). The report recognized the existence of multiple indigenous people in Africa, primarily consisting of pastoralists (e.g., Pokot, Maasai, Barbaig, Karamajong, Samburu, Turkana, Afar, Borana, Tuareg, and Fulani) and hunter-gatherers (e.g., Batwa, Hadzabe, Ogiek, and San). According to the report:

"Dispossession of land and natural resources is a major human rights problem for indigenous people. They have, in so many cases, been pushed out of their traditional areas to give way to the economic interests of other, more dominant groups and to large-scale development initiatives that tend to destroy their lives and cultures rather than improve their situation. The establishment of protected areas and national parks has impoverished indigenous pastoralist and hunter-gatherer communities, making them vulnerable and unable to cope with environmental uncertainty and, in many cases, even displacing them. Large-scale extraction of natural resources, such as logging, mining, dam construction, oil drilling, and pipeline construction, has had very negative impacts on the livelihoods of indigenous pastoralists and hunter-gatherer communities in Africa. So has the widespread expansion of areas under crop production. They have all resulted in the loss of access to fundamental natural resources that are critical for the survival of both pastoral and hunter-gatherer communities, such as grazing areas, permanent water sources, and forest products. This is a serious violation of the African Charter (Article 21,1 and 21,2), which states clearly that every person [sick] has the right to natural resources, wealth, and property... theright to existence (Article 20,1) ... and] the right to their economic, social and cultural development with due regard to their freedom and identity and in the equal enjoyment of the common heritage of mankind (ACHPR, 2004, p11)"[1]

Consequences and Outcomes for the Maasai

Erosion of the Maasai Culture and Cultural Values

The Kenyan Constitution of 2010 recognises culture as the foundation of the nation and as the cumulative civilization of the Kenyan people and nation (ROK, 2010). Further, other international instruments also recognize culture and its connection to land as a human right. The connection between cultural rights and land rights has been acknowledged by the Human Rights Committee (HRC) in its interpretation of Article 27 of the International Covenant on Civil and Political Rights (ICCPR), which concerns cultural rights for minorities. Article 27 does not allude to land rights per se, but puts an emphasis on the connection between cultural rights and land rights. The HRC has thus developed specific protection for indigenous peoples' land rights by acknowledging the evidence that, for indigenous communities, a way of life is associated with the use of their lands. In an often-quoted general comment on article 27, the HRC stated:

"With regard to the exercise of the cultural rights protected under article 27, the Committee observes that culture manifests itself in many forms, including a way of life associated with the use of land resources, especially in the case of indigenous people. That right may include such traditional activities as fishing or hunting and the right to live in reserves protected by law". (Human Rights Committee, 1994)

The emergence of an indigenous people's right to

---

1   Report of the Working Group on Indigenous Populations/Communities (WGIP) of the African Commission on Human and Peoples' Rights (ACHPR, 2004), p. 11.

cultural integrity marks the establishment of a connection between access to ancestral territories and freedom of religion, cultural rights, and the right to access natural resources. Whilst land rights are not as such affirmed in the African Charter, the regional human rights bodies have acknowledged the protection of land rights as a crucial human rights issue for indigenous people as part of a larger bundle of rights, which include property rights, cultural rights, and social rights. This approach is one of the most developed forms of recognition of land as a human right.

A parallel law-making effort that culminated with the adoption of the UN Declaration on the Rights of Indigenous Peoples in 2007 has amplified this jurisprudential evolution. The declaration dedicates several of its articles to land rights, making land rights an essential human rights issue for indigenous people (Gilbert & Doyle, 2011). Article 25 of the Declaration affirms that:

> "Indigenous people have the right to maintain and strengthen their distinctive spiritual relationship with their traditionally owned or otherwise occupied and used land, territories, waters and coastal seas and other resources and to uphold their responsibilities to future generations in this regard" (UNDRIP, 2007, art. 25).

While the Declaration is not a treaty, the rights articulated in it are reflective of contemporary international law as it pertains to indigenous peoples and indicate a clear international recognition of the importance of a human rights-based approach to land rights for indigenous peoples. The International Labour Convention No. 169 on the Rights of Indigenous and Tribal Peoples also integrates a human rights-based approach to land rights. It notably affirms that, in applying the Convention,

> "governments shall respect the special importance of the cultures and spiritual values of the people concerned of their relationship with the land or territories, or both as applicable, which they occupy or otherwise use, and in particular the collective aspects of this relationship". (ILO 1989, art. 13).

Overall, within the larger perspective of a human rights approach to land rights, the affirmation of land rights as a key human rights issue for the Maasai shows that the traditionally individualistic approach to property rights can be challenged. Further, individualistic approaches to property rights are not enough for the Maasai as they do not integrate their specific cultural attachment to their traditional territories. Land rights, particularly in the context of the Maasai traditions and culture, are inextricably linked with the right to life. Displacement, therefore, disrupts community structures and traditions. It also means the loss of sacred and cultural sites. These intangibles can be irreplaceable. The Maasai attachment to land and nature is better explained by this quote: "Nature has programmed human beings as cultural beings" (Grossmann et.al. 2005, p.91).

This implies that culture is a key ingredient not only in cognitive development but in the development of all aspects of the life of a human being. Culture gives identity, and there is a connection between cultural practices, patterns, and cognitive styles. Culture enables socialization, which, even though universal, is different from culture to culture (Bornstein &Lansford, 2010). This difference calls for an approach that is more inclusive of different cultures, and a need for appreciation of how different cultures conceptualize development and how cultural beliefs determine the nature of parenting, family type, nature, and timing of children's entry to the cultural curriculum.

Culture plays an important role in human development. The role of culture in the theorist's view of human development is emphasized by Gardiner & Kosmitzki (2011), who states that culture is "the cluster of learned and shared beliefs, values, practices, behaviours, symbols, and attitudes that are characteristic of a particular group of people and that are communicated from one generation to another" (p.5). Berry et.al. (2002) defines culture as "the complex whole which includes knowledge, belief, art, morals, laws, customs and any other capabilities and habits acquired by man as a member of society" (p.42). According to Gardiner & Kosmitzki (2011); "human development is changing in physical, psychological, and social behaviour as experienced by individuals across the lifespan from conception to death" (p.4). Human development can be thought of as how humans mature (physically). It can refer to psychological maturation. About Bronfenbrenner's (2005) ecology of human development, human development can be measured by the degree to which humans interact with the environment and subsequent mutual accommodation throughout life. Gardiner & Kosmitzki (2011) emphasize the role played by cultural and environmental contexts in studying human development (p.22).

Both mainstream and traditional theories of human development have their basis in the system theory of human development, which is based on the principle of interconnectedness between community social structures, from the smallest unit (family or the individual) to the larger community (Bertalanffy, 1968). The system theory involves many factors in the process of human development, including power and influence as well as intergroup dynamics and relationships. According to Tamas et.al. (2000), a system is "a set of elements standing in interaction"; in other words, a group of things which have something in common. This includes any grouping with any sort of relationship - a collection of people, a forest, the planets, and rabbits on a hill-side, a pile of rocks, or anything else -- if it is possible to identify a group of things, this cluster becomes a «system"(p.2). According to Stackhouse (2007), culture is the power that drives the formation of civilizations; each "power" is organized by institutional clusters sharing primary norms and common ends, which he calls "spheres," (Stackhouse, 2007). Each sphere has a distinct role in today's social and historical life and functions in accordance to its own pattern of "best practices"; yet each interacts with every other sphere to form a society guided by a central faith-based worldview and an implicit ethos (Stackhouse, 2007).

The traditional communal Maasai culture provided for an opportunity for socialization, which, according to Gardner & Kosmitzsky (2008), "is a process by which individuals become members of a particular culture and take on its values, beliefs, and other behaviours in order to function"

(p. 54). Bronfenbrenner (2005) in Ecological Systems Theory enumerates how the relationships between a growing individual are influenced by the microsystem, mesosystem, exosystem, and macrosystem. The microsystem of a typical Maasai child comprises parents (both biological and others), siblings, peers, and the community as defined by the Maasai social structure. As the child grew up, there was interaction with all members of the community who had specific roles in childcare, and each child was treated as "our" child by all members of the community (Tarayia, 2004). The child's socialization process was a collective responsibility of all members of the community who had defined roles in the socialization process (Tarayia, 2004). According to Super & Harkness (1994), the developmental niche provided a framework for connections between culture, socialization, and ecology. The developmental niche concept (Super and Harkness 1982) delves into a child's physical and social settings, customs of childcare, and the psychology of caregivers as critical for the process of socialization.

New definitions for family, caregiving, and parenting have evolved and changed the dynamics of the Maasai culture and, hence, the family setting. Families are becoming smaller as many men abandon polygamy and embrace Christianity and modernity. All these changes can be described as effects of the microsystem, exosystem, and macrosystem according to Bronfenbrenner's ecological model of human development (Bronfenbrenner, 2005). Language and behaviour that were indicative of community are now emerging where parents are talking more of 'my children', 'my home', 'my land', 'my cows', etc.; in other words, individualism has crept in gradually taking the place of the older systems where everything was viewed from a communal perspective.

Though the Maasai have struggled to maintain their traditional way of life for a long time, it is now evident that they can no longer resist the pressure of the modern world. The survival of the Maasai culture has ceased to be a question. The truth is, the traditional way of life is disappearing rapidly. According to Drinkwater (2010), the Maasai are currently struggling to maintain their traditions and are instead seeking alternative means of survival by engaging in other forms of livelihoods and practices that are unfamiliar to them. Mol (1996) also confirms that the Maasai are gradually losing their traditions by arguing that the Maasai culture is under great stress and pressure from the present-day demands of life. Sindiga (1984) agrees with most pastoral observers that before the advent of the colonial government, the lifestyle of most pastoral groups was spatially designed to provide a stable cultural and ecological foundation that supported their culture and economy.

The agreements of 1904 and 1911 had devastating effects, which included loss of life for both humans and livestock, separated families, and triggered the disintegration of the social fabric of the Maasai in general. To date, the Maasai still lament the tragedy of having been forced to move from some of the best lands to drier areas that could not support their livelihoods. The non-consultative way laws related to the land and the lack of communication by the government (both in the colonial and post-independence periods) about these decisions related to land appropriation further led to the loss of Maasai land to the government and individuals without the consent of the Maasai. Statements from study participants have alluded to the reality that there are numerous negative consequences to the Maasai. For example, "The agreements have affected the Maasai economic activities, forcing others to adopt other economic activities such as trade and cultivation."

> "The agreements, laws, and decrees in Kenya have had tragic impacts among the Maasai. Social Impact: it separated the various Maasai clans/nations by pushing some to the South and others (Samburu) to the north of the country. It also caused a rift among the various nations that sided with Lenana, the man who signed the agreements. Economic: It exacerbated the continuous fall of the Maa nation by reducing grazing lands. It was the beginning of the end."

The study participants also raised issues about how the agreements, laws, and decrees have immensely affected the Indigenous Maasai way of life by reducing the movements of livestock and people to seasonal grazing areas, hence making them vulnerable to droughts and hunger, as captured in the following comments:

"The freedom of movement of the Maasai people, as well as the loss of community organization and territorial controls, was affected by the agreements."

"All land that was officially gazetted as Trust Land in Maasai land was appropriated by the presidents [in post-independent Kenya], especially the former president Daniel Arap Moi, who used the land as a political tool. The Maasai have lost all livestock market holding grounds, urban centres, and forests, which were subdivided without the consent of the local communities, and titles were issued to politicians who sold out the land to others or used the titles to get loans. A good example in Narok is the Mau Forest, where the then-President Arap Moi was allocated thousands of acres of land in the forest."

Loss of Livelihoods

The Maasai Agreements of 1904 and 1911 ushered in a long period of untold suffering for the Maasai, which is still being felt to date. The sacred sites and traditional venues were equally taken over, thereby denying the Maasai the rites to exercise their traditional, cultural, and religious rights. The human population was reduced drastically due to epidemics and anthrax that wiped out a large proportion of both livestock and people. Their political and military prowess was compromised, and the two agreements marked the beginning of the weakening and vulnerability of the Maasai as a people. The consequences are evident to this day. The Maasai have no claim to Nairobi and the outlying areas, they lack claim to Laikipia and outlying areas, they lack claim to Eldoret/Ilwuasinkishu (Wuasi Gishu), and outlying areas, they lack claim to Nyahururu/ Enaiuruur, Nakuru, Elburgon/Olpurkel, and Oldama Orropil (Eldama Ravine). First, upon the first moves as a result of the Agreements, and as the Maasai were moving towards the reserves, a lot of livestock was lost along the way. The Ilpurko who took the route towards Mao[2] mostly lost their lives and livestock as they entered the Mau because of the cold climatic conditions. The elderly and young children were the most affected because they were not used to such cold and hard conditions. The losses were insurmountable,

---

2   Note: I am using Mao instead of Mau which is commonly used in discussions about. The Maasai pronunciation is Mao.

and oral history has it that some families were completely wiped out. This was a big blow, which made some of the remnant families seek refuge in other communities, mainly the Kikuyu, as servants and wives.

A section of Ildalalekutuk followed the Ilkeekonyokie, but a larger portion of their population used the Eastern route around the slopes of Mount Kenya and through Meru[3]. This was also tragic to them because of the weather. They lost many herds and people along the way. The two groups later reunited after they reconverged in their current location in Kajiado. Some of their families, though, are found mainly among the Ilkeekonyokie[4].

After the land in group ranches was subdivided into individually owned pieces, the land could no longer sustain pastoralism. Further, the subsequent sale of the land reduced grazing areas, hence decreased the numbers of livestock that families needed to sustain their livelihoods. This has been exacerbated by the impacts of climate change, which have led to long dry spells, reduced pasture, and water scarcity. Displacements from community land have also exacerbated existing inequalities. The freedom of movement in search of pasture has been reduced, further threatening the survival of the livestock. In the recent past, the Maasai have faced more pressure in life than ever before.

The Maasai in Narok and Kajiado have also been faced with the problem of urbanization, which has led to the subdivision of the land into small units that do not support pastoralism. The Kenyan Maasai have had to cope with all the problems associated with urbanization. The threat of population growth and loss of pasture land to emerging urban centres is real. The challenges that come with urbanization today are threatening the way of life that has proved in the past to be a highly adaptive food production system in arid lands. Urbanization has resulted in declining mobility of livestock, thus placing the sustainability of both rangeland resources and pastoral

3   This is where the name Kangere is derived because many of them settled in Meru and to date there are Meru names that are also among the Maasai.
4   I have relatives in Ildalalekutuk and Ilpurko from my great grandfather's 5th wife "Siranka" their families are still named by her name.

livelihoods in jeopardy, hence threatening the livelihoods of the Maasai (Society for Applied Anthropology, 2003). The ability of most Maasai to achieve self-sufficiency through livestock production alone is being lost, mainly because of urbanization and the other factors cited before. In response, Maasai have increased farming numbers.

In discussing livelihood sustainability among the Maasai, it is important to understand that change is an inevitable part of life. It happens whether we're ready or not, and in most cases, is influenced by factors beyond one's control. Change affects everyone differently, and it comes up in two different forms, external and internal. In the Maasai context, external factors are those factors like government policies, immigrant culture, and climate change, among others, while internal factors are grazing patterns, cultural practices, and many others. Livelihood sustainability for the Maasai now means having access to alternative practices such as the cultivation of crops, alternative businesses, and livestock resources. These changes do not come overnight and are part of the learning that takes time for communities to adopt. While many pastoralists have adopted new ways and means of adapting to new trends, this will not be at the same pace.

Due to the increasing loss of the Maasai land, the Maasai situation may be more extreme than for pastoralists living in other less populated and more arid regions, such as northern Kenya, where the rate of urbanization is slower. This has affected resources that are channeled to the Counties through the devolved system. A case in point is Kajiado County, where the increased migration and proliferation of urban habitats in Kiserian, Ngong, Ongata Rongai, and Kitengela, Kajiado County, were rated as having 11.6% wealth as compared to the national average of 45.9% (KNBS, 2009). This is misleading because 90% of the county is rural, and this is where the Maasai live. This has denied them resources that would have been otherwise available to them if the statistics were not skewed to include urban centres that are included in the Nairobi Metro Area.

Over long periods since independence, there has been inequitable resource allocation that is skewed and unfavourably balanced against the Maasai and other pastoralists. The lopsided distribution of government resources introduced during colonial times continues to date. This discriminatory way of resource allocation led to economic marginalization, neglect, and abject poverty for pastoralist communities. There is also a poor market for livestock products, and due to constraints imposed by poor physical and industrial infrastructure, the terminal market is not easily accessible. Little, if any, effort is being made by the government to put in place mechanisms to access the national and international markets. They are made to rely on relief handouts, which perpetuate a culture of economic dependence and destitution.

Increased Risk of Conflict

Anthropologists and other social scientists have long been interested in the subject of violence and conflicts (Sponsel, 1996: 96; Vanhanen, 1999). This has led to an increase in attention for studies on conflicts over land and water in Sub-Saharan Africa, both in the social sciences and in the media (Derman, Odgaard & Sjaastad, 2007). Literature indicates that there is focus on the search for root causes of violence, and the linkages and interactions between specific social dynamics like the politicization of ethnicity (Montalvo &Reynal-Querol, 2005; Vanhanen, 1999; Sambanis, 2001), the militarization of profit-seeking elites and consequent grievances (Collier &Hoeffler, 2004), competition for scarce resources (Homer-Dixon, 1994), social exclusion (Le Billon, 2001), and contested entitlements (Brass, 1985). This general tendency to focus on the causes of violence has often implied neglect of non-violent conflict management strategies (Sponsel, 1996).

In addition, situations where prior violence turned into peaceful interaction have attracted little attention, though the analysis of such transitional phases holds the promise of contributing to applicable knowledge on conflict resolution. Community displacement places new pressures on surrounding land and resources, increasing competition and heightening the risk of conflict. This can create immediate tensions between communities or re-emerge as an escalating factor in broader violent conflicts. This has been the case with the Maasai since the infamous Maasai Agreements. The Maasai who were moved from Entorrorr (Laikipia) and Kinopop, who, as indicated before, were mainly Ilpurko, Ilkeekonyokie, and Ildalalekutuk, have had conflicts with the Maasai communities that were already living in the Southern Reserve. Due to the moves, Ilkaputiei, Iloodokilani, Ildamat, Ilmatapato, Ilkisonko, and Iloitai lost considerable land to the new immigrants who outnumbered them. These conflicts, which arose from access to natural resources, mainly for grazing, have pitted Maasai against each other in Laikipia County, where the remnants of the Laikipia-Maasai and Samburu have been having running conflicts over raids and counter raids; the Ilpurko have had conflicts with Ildamat, Ilkeekonyokie and Iloitai, Ilmatapato and Ildalalekutu, and Ilkisonko versus Ilkaputiei.

The Maasai have also experienced conflicts with other non-Maasai communities. Instances of violent conflicts between the Maasai are still inherent to date, with the most recent clashes between two Maasai clans along the Nkararo-Enooretet boundary have now escalated to several villages, raising tension in the region. The Maasai in Narok County have had continued conflicts with the immigrant Agikuyu community. Such cases include the Maasai and the Agikuyu in Enoosupukia and Mau Narok, as well as the Maasai and the Kalenjin in the areas bordering Mau Forest. There have also been conflicts between the Ilkaputiei and the Akamba, as well as between Ilkisonko and the Taita in Njukini over boundaries. With the proliferation of urban centres and the influx of non-Maasai to land that was held by the Maasai before, there has been conflict about the control of businesses within urban towns in both Narok and Kajiado counties. Instances of control of market areas have resulted in conflicts in Kitengela and Narok towns, where local Maasai communities clamoured for control and ownership of market stalls, which were corruptly allocated to non-Maasai. In Narok, for instance, there have been conflicts in the ownership and running of the Matatu business[5]. The clashes between the Kikuyu and Kisii managed companies and the emergent Maasai business people resulted in bloody confrontations that have led to the loss of lives and property (Daily Nation, March 30th, 2019)[6].

Political and Developmental Marginalization

Historically, the British colonial government demarcated the country into high-potential and marginal lands and favoured the high-potential in all respects, a practice which was adopted by post-colonial regimes. The pastoralists who occupied high-potential areas were forcefully evicted (e.g, with respect to the Maasai treaties of 1904 and 1911) to make way for British settler farmers. After the departure of the colonialists, the former Maasai land remained the property of other communities who assumed power. To date, the return of the Maasai land, or restitution in one form or another, remains a thorny issue that no government wants to address. To the Maasai and other pastoralists in Kenya, marginalization means being at the edge, being far removed from the centre, being on the periphery, having no voice, being neglected by the powers, having no representation, and being excluded from mainstream social engagement.

Political power is required to carry out social ideals. In a country where national goodies are denied or conferred by one's closeness to the centre of power led by the president, extreme exclusion is the reserved share of pastoralists. The government fears large numbers and a united voice. These are lacking with respect to pastoralists. Even efforts by the government to initiate projects ostensibly to improve the lives of pastoralists fail because the conception and execution of those programmes are not participatory.

Power is a means or a tool for implementing clear economic programmes, and pastoralists simply lack these powers. Historically, there were very few in government, Ministers, Permanent Secretaries, Directors of Parastatals, Ambassadors, and CEOs of reputable organizations from pastoralist

---

5   Matatu business is the privately-owned transportation system which was mainly controlled by non-Maasai but the Maasai want to run their own public transport business.
6   See Daily Nation, March 30th, 2019. https://www.nation.co.ke/kenya/ counties/ narok/chaos-in-narok-town-as-rival-matatu-saccos-fight-for- stage-153258

communities. Local voices from pastoralist communities are suppressed, and the government turns a deaf ear to the cries from these communities. While the new Constitution, which was promulgated in 2010, created new positions and the Maasai have seen an increase in representation, most of the representatives owe allegiance to the political parties that fronted them for election and the powers than the people they represent.

While the constitution of Kenya provides that any Kenyan can live and own property anywhere in the country and can also participate in the political process where they reside or own property, this poses a threat of political marginalization to the Maasai. This has been experienced in both Kajiado and Narok counties. In Kajiado, for instance, a new constituency, Kajiado North, was created, and its population is made up of immigrants who bought land or work in Nairobi. In Narok, Emurua Dikirr was hived from the greater Transmara. This constituency is predominantly a Kalenjin constituency. Narok North leadership is under threat of being taken over by others if the Maasai allow themselves to be divided along political lines.

Despite the above challenges, the Maasai in Narok and Kajiado need to take advantage of the new constitutional dispensation through devolution and provision of services that have been devolved to the counties. Public participation is a requirement of the constitution, and the community needs to up their game to make sure they are heard; as well, more awareness is needed to ensure that they can vote for leaders that stand for their interests rather than those of the country's political elite. The Maasai should also learn from other ethnic groups in Kenya, where not only do other communities unite to front their political and economic aspiration collectively, but they invest in areas where they see both political and economic opportunity.

PART VIII:

THE CONVERSATION ABOUT MAASAI LAND APPROPRIATION

Introduction

As previously mentioned in the preceding parts of this book, the contents of this book are informed by a case study of Kajiado and Narok County titled: *A Critical Analysis of Factors that Contribute to Maasai Land Appropriation; The Case Study of Narok and Kajiado County in Kenya* (Koissaba, 2016). In order to refine this conversation, the reader needs to know the processes that I used to gather the information that informed the content. This case study aimed to analyze events, practices, laws, and decrees that have contributed to Maasai land appropriation and acquisition from the perspective of the Maasai to make policy recommendations. This case study was both intrinsic (how the Maasai understood the situation of land appropriation and acquisition) and instrumental (what can others learn from the situation of the Maasai).

Significance of the Policy Conflict

In this century, the issue of public policy is complicated due to many factors. There are multiple definitions of what public policy is, how it is made, and who makes it. Public policy is ordinarily construed by the general public to mean whatever government or institutions choose to do or choose not to do. However, according to Anderson (2011), public policy can be defined as a relatively stable, purposive course of action or inaction followed by an actor or set of players in dealing with a problem. According to Cloate & Conning (2011), policy refers to statements of intent or an action plan to transform a perceived problem into a future solution. This implies that since nation-states are the custodians of land within the national boundaries, all activities that relate to the land must be policy-driven. Since this study was meant to contribute to policy decisions that relate to the Maasai situation, a critical analysis of policy and other factors that contributed to land appropriations and acquisition was of great significance.

The statement "one does not sell land upon which people walk" was made by Tashunka Wikto, a leader of the Lakota (USA) in 1800. Similarly, there exists a Maasai saying that states that "it is only a son and land that can never be given away." Both statements reflect the datum that people live on land and off the land. Globally, the relationship that people have with land varies considerably. The Maasai people of Kenya and Tanzania are pastoralists who live sustainably by practicing their traditional methods of subsistence that were bound by traditional collective land ownership practices. There were customary rules about the rights to use the land, and no rules that said an individual or corporate entity could own land outright according to the Maasai culture.

From a world-historical viewpoint, the history of capitalism begins with the transformation of land rights. From the perspective of the modern system, it is easy to take the concept of land property rights ownership for granted. But to do so would be missing the massive social transformation that involved centuries of struggles for and against the establishment of property rights in land and its usage. The forms of transformation are complex and varied over time and place. Maasai land appropriation and acquisition in Kenya provides both an intrinsic case study (exploration is driven by a desire to know more about the uniqueness of the case rather than to build theory or how the case represents other cases), and instrumental (because the case study will be used to understand more than what has been seen as obvious about the phenomenon) (Stake, 1995).

As discussed elsewhere in this work, in August 2004, the Maasai in Kenya held countrywide demonstrations to commemorate the centenary since the signing of the first Maasai agreement with the British government in 1904. In 2010, for the first time, the Maasai land issues and historical injustices became a national debate due to the inclusion of clauses related to land use and land ownership in the Kenyan Constitution (GOK, 2010) and the National Land Policy (GOK, 2009). For the Maasai, this became an opportunity to seek redress for land that the Maasai lost through the Maasai agreements of 1904 and 1911. The addition of the new clauses had an impact on the Maasai perceptions of land sale in both Kajiado and Narok counties. The inclusion of these provisions has been associated with an upsurge of Maasai civil society demanding the return of the land that was either part of the 1904 and 1911 agreements, and other lands that the Maasai believe were unlawfully appropriated or acquired.

This case study was further strengthened by the Report of the Truth, Justice and Reconciliation Commission (GOK, 2014). In this case study, one can examine the process of the Maasai over time. The case study also enabled an examination of the role of the state in controlling land as well as the inner workings of the state in shaping new understandings and articulations of territory, sovereignty, authority, and subjects. Land appropriation from the Maasai in Kenya also features the salient components of the current problems in the global crisis in land acquisition. First, in 1930, Kenya experienced the transformation from the system of customary rights of land usage to a system of legal and written titles of land ownership through the Kenya Land Commission. Second, was the transformation of a concept of property concretely defined by physical space (i., boundaries). The third was the use of land as a form of capital and expanded capital consumption, and the fourth was the increasing privatization of land. The outcome was the acquisition of land through such actions as forced long-term leases for large parcels of land or outright seizure of land using both legalized and highly unconventional methods. As presented elsewhere, the results for the Maasai have been displacement, poverty, loss of identity, and self-determination (Lyman & Kew, 2010).

Akram-Lodhi & Kay (2009) divide the complex history of the process of the commodification of land rights into four historical periods: primitive accumulation, colonialism, developmentalism, and globalization. This study focused on the appropriation and acquisition of Maasai land in Kenya during the last fifteen years, but uses historical facts in order to link current trends and the historical processes used in Maasai land appropriation. Understanding what occurred from the Maasai perspective, the principal actors involved, and the outcomes is critical to understanding the policy issues faced today and to identifying a way forward.

Some of the most urgent and strategic policy issues centre on governance and globalization. The role of the state and land appropriation in Kenya has been a major concern for years (TJRC, 2013). Key policy issues are related to addressing indigenous claims to the land, state processes in acquiring the land, legal barriers to indigenous rights, transparency, community dialogue in the governance of the land, tenure security, and the view of land as a commodity. Globalization policy issues are related to the political economy that is driving the commodification and the financialization of land (Akram-Lodhi and Kay 2009).

International land rights advocates are now recommending the development of a global land policy like the global approach to climate change (World Bank, 2014). By interrogating the events, practices, decrees, laws, and policies both at the national, regional and international level from the Maasai context, and the effects that such events, practices, decree-laws, and policies have contributed to Maasai land appropriation, this case study was aimed at informing future policies in Kenya that have a direct influence on Maasai land.

Study Design

This study used a qualitative research method known as a case study, and used both intrinsic and instrumental case study designs (Denzin and Lincoln, 2006; Stake, 1995). The goal of the intrinsic component of the case study was to better understand land appropriation from the Maasai: Research Question 1- What do you know about Maasai land appropriation in the past? Research Question 2- What is your understanding of what is currently occurring regarding Maasai land appropriation? Research Question 3- What do you think needs to be done about Maasai land appropriation in the future? The intent for instrumental components of this study was to gain more insight into the past and future policy elements of Maasai land appropriation (how can the lessons learnt from Maasai land appropriation be useful in addressing the increase in land grabs in developing countries?). Both approaches were considered appropriate for the analysis, and themes derived from an exploration of events, practices, laws, and decrees that have been associated with Maasai land appropriation and acquisition (Hughes, 2006). The instrumental component of the study was not possible without information from the intrinsic part.

The choice of the two types of approaches was guided by 1) the need to put aside prior theories and assumptions about Maasai land appropriation (Fairhead, Leach, and Scoones, 2014) and let the participants and data 'speak' in order to allow themes, patterns, and concepts to emerge; and, 2) the need to understand a variety of underlying factors that contributed to Maasai land appropriation and acquisition beyond the typical reasons such as government annexation, encroachment by urbanization, establishment of parks and forest reserves, and high levels of illiteracy among the Maasai. To understand the contextual background of Maasai land appropriation and acquisition, I used historical documents (laws, decrees, policies) from 1904, the year the Maasai in Kenya commemorated the centenary since the first Maasai agreements were signed in 1904 and 1911.

To gain a deeper and richer understanding of what land appropriation and alienation experience mean to the Maasai, it was necessary to engage in open dialogue and to allow the Maasai to simply share their experiences, tell their stories, and reveal their individual narratives. This inductive, participant-centred methodological approach allowed participants to reveal what is important to them, with the researcher following the leads presented by the respondents. This allowed for the personal meaning to emerge from the respondents themselves.

According to Denzin and Lincoln (2011), "qualitative research involves an interpretive, naturalistic approach to the world. This means that qualitative researchers study things in their natural settings, attempting to make sense of, or interpret phenomena regarding the meanings they bring to them" (Denzin & Lincoln, 2011, p. 3). Further, this study fitted into the framework of "naturalistic" ontology (Lincoln & Guba, 1985). In this study, I used data collected from semi-structured interviews and literature review (reports data related to policies, decrees, and laws) that have a bearing on land ownership and land use, policy decisions that have an impact on land and property access, ownership and control, and materials from the news media that have highlighted past and current land-related issues in Kenya, and the territories occupied by the Maasai.

To avoid biases in the interpretation of the data collected, I used an expert review of both sources (participants and subject matter experts) and methods (semi-structured interviews that were conducted by phone) to seek clarification. Creswell (2013) described the use of triangulation to improve the study's validity. The comparison and corroboration helped to determine if the data accurately reflected what was being studied. This process compared the information provided by the research participants and the other data sources. The continuum in the reflection and comparison of data from various sources during the research process facilitated the emergence of pertinent issues that helped in communicating and articulating the participants' expressions and feelings about the phenomenon that the researcher is studying.

Table 5: Ontological and epistemological questions

Type of Research Question	Meaning	Examples
Ontological question	Studying the nature of participants' realities and their lived lives	What is it like being a Maasai in the current Kenyan political dispensation? What are the lived experiences of the Maasai regarding land ownership, control, and access? What is the nature of the legal and policy landscape in relation to Maasai land?

Epistemological question	Knowing and understanding the phenomenon of Maasai land appropriation and acquisition in Narok and Kajiado counties	What factors do the Maasai know as contributing to Maasai land appropriation and acquisition?
		How does Maasai land appropriation affect the well-being of the Maasai in Narok and Kajiado counties?

Potential Research Bias

I was born and brought up in Kenya. I was active in human rights and civil society activities. I worked directly with Maasai communities who had land-related grievances. In my position as the national coordinator for MCSF, we were mandated to research, document, and disseminate information on the processes used to appropriate Maasai land. I was instrumental in facilitating public dialogue at national, regional, and international levels. I worked to redress both historical and current losses of land. When conducting this analysis, as the researcher, I identified where to fit between the etic and the emic. In the emic, I analyzed schemes and categories regarded as meaningful and appropriate by the Maasai, while in the etic, I analyzed the conceptual schemes and categories regarded as meaningful and appropriate in the community of scientific observers.

The researcher-participant relationship, as well as the relationship of the researcher to the topic, were placed on this continuum (Creswell, 1998). Etic characteristics were more detached relationships where I acted like an outsider viewing the subject and interpreting the phenomenon. The emic, on the other hand, was characterized by the researcher becoming one with the subject and experiencing the phenomenon. Researchers place themselves on this continuum based on the needs and purposes of the study. I approached this study using both perspectives.

For the objectivity of the study, the etic (outsider) approach eliminated cultural biases by the researcher becoming culturally neutral, limiting any ethnocentric, political, or alienation of the Maasai culture, and perspectives on land appropriation. I critically analyzed the data and compared it with perspectives from other cultures and similar case studies, and the researcher had a broader understanding of the phenomenon under discussion without prejudice to any situation. In order not to influence the study outcomes, the etic of the study was undertaken before the emic approach. In taking an emic approach, as the researcher and insider, I tried to put aside previous theories and assumptions to let the participants and data speak to them and to allow themes, patterns, and concepts to emerge. This enabled the respect for local viewpoints and their potential to uncover unexpected findings.

Limitations of the Study

The study examined the nature of land appropriation and the type of processes used, as well as the principal actors who have been involved in the processes of appropriating the land and those seeking to redress land appropriation in Kenya. The study had the following limitations:

1. The period covered was comprehensive, and since most of those involved with the first and second Maasai moves in 1904 and 1911 have died, the availability of first-hand narratives was limited to reports and second-hand information. This can be subject to misrepresentation of the facts.

2. Existing books, journals, magazines, and reports about Maa land appropriation and acquisition are limited. They are also biased towards general perspectives of the Maasai culture, and other aspects that relate to changes affecting the Maasai, or biased towards the Kenyan government and Western researchers who have, over time, misrepresented facts about the Maasai.

3. Sampling bias was also another limitation because the information is only available from those who have participated in land appropriation processes, either through advocacy or litigation.

4. I did not return to Kenya to collect data. The phone and generic surveys were used to conduct the interviews. This could lead to a distortion that is imposed by the limitations in the means of communication.

5. The time difference between the locations for the researcher and the research participants limited the time the researcher had for each participant. There is a difference of between 7 and 8 hours, which meant that the researcher had to wait until ten o'clock at night to call Kenya. The researcher was only able to interview participants during the early morning hours before the participants started their daily chores.

6. The ability to obtain government records that reflect fraudulently acquired or grabbed land was very difficult.

Boundaries of the Study

The purpose of this study was to examine a social phenomenon, the appropriation and acquisition of land from the Maasai people in Kenya, to understand the factors that contributed to the continued land loss among the Maasai in Kajiado and Narok Counties; it was not about whether the Maasai have been victims of land appropriation. The focus was on the processes involved in land appropriation and acquisition, as well as the outcomes for the Maasai. Yin (2003) and Stake (1995) suggest that the spatial and temporal boundaries of the phenomenon being studied need to be made clear. Suggestions on how to bind a case study to include 1) by time and place (Creswell, 2013); 2) by time and activity (Stake, 1995); and 3) by definition and content (Miles and Huberman, 1994). Components from these authors were used to bind this case. The period that was studied was from 2004 to the present, but informed by events that emanated from 1904 and 1911.

The year 2004 was chosen because that is the time the Maasai in Kenya held a country-wide demonstration to commemorate 100 years since the signing of the first agreement with the British in 1904. The demonstrations triggered a renewal of interest and activity among the Maasai about the land that had been appropriated or acquired from them. Since 2004, for the first time, clauses related to land use and ownership have been added to the Kenyan Constitution (GOK, 2010) and the National Land Policy (GOK, 2009). The report of the Truth, Justice and Reconciliation Commission (GOK, 2014) also examined previous land appropriation from Indigenous people in Kenya. Thus, the past 15 years have been an important period for the Maasai and the Kenyan government's activities related to land use and land ownership. Land remains a crucial element in conflict and post-conflict contexts in the country. When the conflict ends, the restitution of housing, land, and property rights for returning refugees and internally displaced persons constitutes a fundamental part of peacebuilding.

Current Trends about Maasai Land Appropriation

Land is an emotive issue in Kenya, and while I am using the Maasai as an example, the issue of land affects the whole country. It was therefore my intention to use the findings of this study to identify the players in Kenya, more so the players on land matters in Kajiado and Narok counties. In Kajiado and Narok, which were the areas of focus, the study participants expressed their concern that there is still massive land appropriation through individual sales and/or government-supported projects. Here are some of the comments:

> "The land brokers who sold land in Kajiado have now shifted to the newly subdivided Group Ranches in Narok. We have seen an increase in private surveyors in Narok town whose offices are used by cartels to sell land in Narok."

> "There is a crisis of land appropriation in most Sub-Saharan African countries. The land is being taken away in order to set up new plantations, factories, or conservation areas. This is especially in Maasai land, where grazing land is considered idle land."

> "It is very sad that we recently witnessed a policeman and a student die in Imbirikani Group Ranch in Oloitokitok when students demonstrated against an illegal lease agreement of land to unknown people."

In Kenya, land governance issues remain complex despite planning and local government laws that guide urban planning and management. As in many other East African countries, the rapid growth of urban areas has taken a toll on the ancestral land of pastoralists, where much of the new development is taking place. Kenya has undergone unprecedented urban growth, which has led to an increased demand for land, further exacerbated by a growing middle-class population. In 2019, 27.51 percent of Kenya's total population lived in urban areas and cities (Pletcher, 2020).

A push by middle-class Kenyans to own property amid soaring land prices has led financial institutions, developers, and speculators to target land in satellite towns around Nairobi. Currently, pastoral land is being lost through acts of state appropriation (i.e., Green Energy, the Standard Gauge Railways (SGR), etc.), the progressive encroachment of farmers, or by outside interests. In Kajiado County, land has become a contentious issue as fraudsters have duped thousands of buyers into purchasing Maasai communal land (e.g., Iloodoariak, Elangata Wuas, and Mosiro), which is then converted into private land.

The influx of outsiders and increase in buildings on land that belongs to indigenous communities have caused tension with the Maasai pastoralists, who say urbanization has led to evictions, forced displacement, and increased violence. Potential risks for communities in semi-urban and rural areas near cities were often disregarded when weighing the pros and cons of urbanization, resulting in poorly conceived plans. If land developers do not factor in human rights, the Maasai way of life will completely change as they may be forced to turn to crop and other farming-related livelihoods.

Key Players in Land Issues in Narok and Kajiado

The Government and the Constitution

Due to the sensitivity of land-related matters in Kenya and despite the powers that are bestowed on the National Land Commission by the Constitution of Kenya, the government has continually frustrated the National Land Commission (NLC) and inhibited its functions. There has been a jurisdictional conflict between the Ministry of Land and Physical Planning due to conflicts of roles between the National Land Commission as to whose responsibility it was to undertake key functions, such as extension and renewal of leases. On its part, the National Land Commission has variously been accused of corruption and self-gain by its management. The former chair of NLC is in court facing charges of corruption.

From the study participants' perspective, the Kenyan government has contributed to the land grabbing of Maasai land. The participants indicated that the Government of Kenya has been the greatest culprit regarding the appropriation of Maasai land and hold the view that pastoralism is not an economic and productive system worthy of practice in the modern world. Their view was that privatization and individualization of all land in the country, ostensibly, meant placing such parcels for productive use and forming collateral for bank loans. Due to high levels of illiteracy, lack of knowledge or experience in modern commercial land use, and the absence of mediation mechanisms that would assure fair value in land sales, given that the sales are based on 'willing buyer-willing seller principles, the land owner is substantially disadvantaged.

> "The government is doing very little to communicate land issues to the Maasai. However, the NGOs and the NLC have been partnering to discuss and sensitize the Maasai on this land-related issue, particularly on communal land issues or sometimes on historical land injustice, but very little has been done, as there is no government will."

> "The government is not only sleeping on its job by not protecting the Maasai from Massive land losses, but it is also a facilitator in the process. Government officials are becoming catalysts for land selling."

> "Currently, land in Kenya is controlled by the government, and they have made decisions on land through the National Land Commission since the 2010 constitution."

From the participants' responses, the government has been accused of being the major catalyst for Maasai land appropriation. The culture of corruption and impunity in the government and among the political elites, facilitated by rich people from outside the two counties, accelerated the pace at which Maasai land was being lost to outsiders. While the participants were aware of all the directives about processes of land management, there was a general agreement that the processes used to appropriate Maasai land were corrupt and illegitimate.

"When I worked for the Ministry of Lands in Narok and Kajiado, I witnessed land being transferred from the Maasai by the special land board, which was illegal. I was sometimes forced to write blank title deeds in the middle of the night, which the District Lands Registrar and the Chairman of the Land Control Board, who was either the District Commissioner or the District Officer, sold to senior government officials and politicians. That is how the Maasai from Iloodoariak and Mosiro lost their land. Maps were drawn in the office of the District Surveyor without even visiting the land. All the title deeds from such transactions were later used to acquire loans. I am sure all those who got the land do not even know the physical locations of the land they hold title to. My experience was very bitter, as I had to do what I was told to do while being threatened with negative consequences if I dared not to do so, or even sharing the information (former employee of the Department of Lands).

"The last 10 years were generally characterized by continued misappropriation of land, unabated corruption in the land ministry/ offices, and increased influx of immigrants into Maasai land. There has been a lack of deliberate effort in the form of political goodwill to correct or sow this trend. However, the last 10 years also provided a much better legal framework than ever before, including the 2010 constitution and the national land policy."

The processes that were used to acquire and transfer land were equally viewed by the participants as corrupt. According to the participants, they have contributed to the Maasai land appropriation and acquisition. The participants expressed their view that since independence in 1963, the country's leadership has contributed to Maasai land appropriation through legislating laws that did not recognize Indigenous Maasai land tenure and abetting corruption.

"Previous and current presidencies and regimes continue to use their powers and the gullibility of the Maasai community to misappropriate the Maasai land. They use the same land to trap and woo the Maasai community to vote for them. The Maasai do not have a major role in the appropriation of land; however, in most instances,"

> "[Land is obtained] mostly through corrupt deals where money changes hands between a few leaders and investors or land grabbers."

In their responses, the Maasai expressed understanding of the role played by the Kenyan government and the constitution in addressing issues about Maasai land appropriation and alienation.

> "To respect the constitution and allow the Maasai to participate in decision-making regarding control and use of their land. It should also recognize the Maasai land rights and protection from further discrimination on land issues. The government should give the Maasai the right to possess documents recognizing the community ownership of their piece of land."

> "The government should respect the constitution and immediately stop the special boards that are used to sell land, and at the same time, the government needs to entrench the Community Land Act, which is a product of the Kenyan civil society that collected views from all over the country."

> There is a need to change the policy of land title holding so that all members of the family are included as joint title holders. This will stop the men from selling land."

> "Put a stop to all land transactions and do an inventory of various land categories in the counties. Put measures that discourage careless selling of land without major reasons, civic education to the people about the value of their land, and more so if they hold on to it for future better gains."

Overall, the participant's perspective about the role of the government in Maasai land appropriation and acquisition is that the government played the role of a facilitator for the past and present land losses. The government, through the enactment of laws and the use of presidential decrees on matters related to land, has led to the untold loss of land through the enforcement of the laws and adherence to the presidential decrees. Corruption by land officials in collaboration with land brokers, Maasai elites, and rich people from outside Narok and Kajiado counties was also cited as a major conduit for land losses. In summary, the independent Kenyan government actively contributed to the appropriation and privatization of land in a manner that was a continuation of what the colonial government did. The government also continued with land reforms that did not recognize pastoralism, which is the Maasai way of life, or offer restitution for losses occasioned by the reforms. As noted above, all aspects of land tenure were brought under the Registered Land Act of 1963. The formalization of land rights was adopted by the Kenyan government to achieve both political and economic goals.

The National Land Commission and the Community Land Management Boards

The National Land Commission (NLC) is a constitutional body whose existence came to be after the then-President Kibaki approved a national dialogue about the formulation of the national land reform process in Kenya, which culminated in the development of the National Land Policy in 2009. This came through a national consultative process where most stakeholders participated. The NLC was to drive a process of land administration reforms that would redress historical land grievances, rid the land sector of corruption, and curtail manipulation of land acquisition by the elites, politicians, and land prospectors.

In Narok, for instance, due to the absence of a fully-fledged Community Land Management Board (CLMB) and the manipulation by the county government, the NLC was accused of abetting or yielding into pressure for the state to acquire 880 hectares of land near the Maasai Mara Game Reserve in Narok County for the setting up of a military base[1]. The residents said the targeted parcel of land at Nkairowuani, within the Lemek Group Ranch, was acquired fraudulently by the alleged owner. The group, with a registered membership of more than 1,000, vowed to block the acquisition of what they termed as their ancestral land. The way the land was acquired and gazetted by the NLC without consultation of the community was also questioned by the Narok North MP, Moitalel Ole Kenta, who opposed the sale of the land, arguing that the sale and establishment of a military camp would have far-reaching

---

1   Comments from Fredrick Kariankei.

negative environmental implications[2] (Comments in Maa Unity Agenda social page). According to the community representatives, through their spokesperson Fredrick Kariankei, failure to observe the Public Procurement and Asset Disposal Act No. 33 of 2005 made the whole transaction between the government and the private developer shady. More so, the requisite Environmental Impact Assessment, individually done, was inadequate.

While the community believed they had all the right reasons to stop the land acquisition, their quest was curtailed by the partisan politics at the Narok County Assembly because the community could not raise money to file the case in court. On its part, the NLC had been reigned in by a Supreme Court advisory opinion in 2016 and could not take any action. As well, the Elangata Wuas Group Ranch had long-standing disputes over misuse of office by the Group Ranch Committee. The last NLC was disbanded in 2019 without having a concrete solution to the problem.

According to Lemayian Ole Taiko:

> "Much power is vested in the National Land Commission, but with the new bill in Parliament, the role of the Cabinet Secretary is increasing, for the government prefers the Ministry of Land to the NLC. (Ole Taiko).[3]"

The Role of the Maasai

According to the study findings, 25% of the participants were conversant with events that led to Maasai land appropriation and alienation in the past. 98% of the participants understand the current events regarding the Maasai land appropriation and alienation. Regarding the issue of what needs to be done about Maasai land appropriation and alienation, the participants gave varied views. Further, 45% percent of the participants said that the implications of the Maasai land appropriation and alienation case will inform policy on the ongoing global land grabs.

While it is not possible to ascertain the size of land that the

---

2   The Gazzatement of the land was not available to the community members who made this observation.

3   Interview with Lemayian Ole Taiko.

Maasai have lost in Kajiado and Narok counties, there was a common consensus among the study participants that the Maasai had a minimal and passive role in the appropriation and alienation of their land either by the governments of the day or by non-indigenous people in Kajiado and Narok counties. The primary role of the Maasai, according to the study, has mainly been fighting back to regain the land that was appropriated from them and raising awareness about land-related issues through advocacy and using the courts. The Maasai have faced many challenges in the past and are currently facing more such challenges, as most of the laws about land in Kenya are guided by title ownership. Since all the appropriated land has been titled, the Maasai must occupy unoccupied land, ask for adverse possession of the land, or file litigation in the courts, which are long and expensive processes. This was expressed by some of the Maasai people who were interviewed:

> "The settlers did not consult the community leadership structure during the signing of the agreements, but rather used a divide and rule mechanism and convinced Olonana (who was a medicine man) to sign the agreement on behalf of the Laikipia Maasai. As a result, this raised suspicion and feelings of betrayal by Olonana, leading to conflicts, mistrust, and a polarized tribe."

> "Maasai attempts to go to the Colonial Court of Appeal were thwarted through a combination of strategies that included intimidation, manipulation, and non-cooperation. Therefore, the hearing was unfair to the Maasai."

> "We, the Maasai in Kedong, have lived here for as long as we can remember. We have been having court cases against people who claim to have titles to this land, yet the land is ours. Now that the SGR and geothermal are here, everybody wants Kedong. Unfortunately, an agreeable restitution process is reached when a few of us have sold the land for Ksh 10,000,000 and a token of 4,000 acres."

The sustained protests by the Maasai about land that was appropriated and illegally acquired in the past were expressed as an ongoing and unending process until the time when the Maasai will get their grievances heard. The comments below affirm the Maasai resilience and sustained arguments about pursuing their lost lands: -

"The Maasai [who] protested and refused to sign the Constitutional Draft [before independence] like Dr. Tameno, Dr. Likimani, and others were persecuted while the ones who signed like Ole Tipis, J. Keen, and Ole Sompisha were rewarded handsomely with cabinet positions and tracks of land."

"I have been involved with research and advocacy in Kajiado; I am also a founder member of Maa Civil Society Forum, which is involved in advocacy and land rights."

"I have participated in Maasai land-related issues in Kenya for many years. Currently, as a member of the Maasai Council of Elders, other council members and I are aggressively involved in raising awareness about land-related issues, especially in Narok County."

In their pursuit of redress for the land issues, some Maasai members from civil society have had the opportunity to participate in various national land-related forums to represent the interests of the Maasai. They have also been involved in organizing processions and awareness meetings in Maasai counties in Kenya to demand redress of land-related issues.

"I am a member of the National Land Commission, which is a Constitutional body responsible for all matters related to land. Being a Maasai, I am responsible for overseeing all matters related to land in Narok County at the Commission."

"As a founder member of Maa Civil Society Forum and the National Coordinator for Pastoralists Development Network of Kenya, I have participated in various activities that address Maasai land issues. I have been active as the media liaison person and have organized several peaceful demonstrations by various Maasai groups."

Since the land has been used as a political tool, the participants also raised issues on how their local elites have been enticed to engage in land appropriation in return for political gains. The government has been instrumental in appointing some Maasai leaders to government positions and supporting certain individuals to win the elections so that they can be used in plans to appropriate Maasai land, according to respondents. Such was expressed in statements made by the Maasai below: -

"After independence, some Maasai leaders sold out their people in exchange for power and riches. It also gave rival communities a chance to take over the land that was left by the colonialists."

Some of our own people have become brokers and middlemen and are involved in the selling of our own land and dispossessing many families. They are being used by land buyers who collude with land officers to sell the land without consulting family members".

"It is unfortunate that some of our politicians in Narok South are colluding with politicians from Bomet to buy land in Narok South to settle the Kalenjin who were evicted from Mau so that they can get votes. They are selfish and do not have the interest of the Maasai at heart".

There is a common understanding among the Maasai that while there are many players in the land sector, their main concerns were around decision-making processes after the National Land Commission and the County Land Management Boards were formed. There were mixed feelings as to how the two would manage and streamline matters of land in the two counties.

"The National and County Governments have an interest in land, and the County Assemblies, the National Land Commission, the Senate and National Assembly, as well as the Ministry of Lands."

"These are key actors on matters of community land from a policy and legal framework perspective. The other key actors are private corporates, quasi-government institutions-parastatals, Vision 2030 Secretariat, the local leadership/MPs and Senators, County Land Management Boards, the community, and NGO."

According to the study participants' narratives, decision-making on matters relating to land has been confusing and not participatory, and where the community was the rightful decision-maker, their decisions were manipulated by the Ministry of Land officials.

"Currently, the main decision-making bodies concerning Maasai land are the community as identified through membership to the former Group Ranches, Community Land, the County Land Management Boards, the County Executive in charge of Land, and the National Land

Commission and the Ministry of Lands."

"Lack of adherence to community land laws makes this hazy, however, the setting according to the constitution is such that there is a Ward Land Committee comprising of individuals from the community who address land issues at that level, then there is the Constituency Land Committee representing the community and County Land Management Board who are key in decision making regarding community land. However, the existence of these bodies is not clear—the County Land Executive, in liaison with the County Land Management Board and the National Land Commission, has the prerogative to communicate with the Maasai on any matters touching land appropriation."

The decision-making processes on matters related to land were also raised with participants, who were concerned about the lack of involvement of the local communities.

"We do not understand how decisions about our land are made. They are made in boardrooms with very little community participation. Where the community is consulted, the government has the prerogative to ignore their suggestions."

"It is hard to say who makes decisions because there are a lot of players who work with the government officers to make decisions. Mainly, the government, the land owners, the land brokers, and people with money have the power to buy land."

"The NLC can also play a critical role, as well as friendly county governments, like Kajiado County and its governor. The Brokers and corrupt Members of the County Assembly are, however, a major stumbling block."

"Decisions are made in boardrooms with very little community participation. Where the community is consulted, the government has the prerogative to ignore their suggestions."

While comments from study participants point out that the Maasai have played a minimal role in land appropriation, I posit that this perspective is self-defeating on the part of the Maasai for various reasons. Once the Maasai have apportioned blame on others, forgetting that they have elected leaders who are in positions that can play roles in securing the land. Secondly, the Maasai have not been innovative enough to develop mechanisms and systems that will protect their lands. Thirdly, the Maasai have representatives in most of the boardroom meetings held to deliberate or transact land, and it is their own representatives who become the go-between the prospecting buyers and the sellers. As a matter of fact, it is their own representatives who become brokers of the land. Dealing with land, especially where the land is privately owned, is challenging, even when there are legal instruments and processes; they are substantially limited by factors like absolute ownership, legal agreements, compulsory acquisition by the government, and many others.

Land Prospectors

The population explosion in highly populated parts of Kenya has necessitated other Kenyan communities to seek land for settlement in the Maasai land, where land is seen to be available. This has created an exponential increase in property agents in urban centres in Narok and Kajiado. In the two towns, land selling has become a very lucrative business because land agents and government officials conspire to buy land from the Maasai at cheap prices and sell to prospecting clients at much higher prices, thereby making very high profits. This migration to Narok and Kajiado counties has also altered the perspective of political representation by the immigrant communities. In order to have a political voice, rich immigrants buy large tracks of land, which they subdivide into smaller portions and then sell to many people, hence increasing the numbers. In return, this will influence the voting patterns. Immigrant communities like the Kikuyu and Kisii have also formed both local and diaspora land-buying groups to buy land in the Maasai land. While they do have the constitutional right to buy land, settle, and engage in political and economic activities in their newly acquired lands, this poses a threat of political and economic dominance among the Maasai.

National Investors

With overcrowding, poor planning, and a lack of adequate infrastructure to spur industrial growth in Nairobi, Kajiado has become a target for industrial development. While the development of industries brings economic development to Kajiado County, such projects come with unintended consequences. Such consequences are industrial (water, air, etc.) pollution, reduction of pastureland for the Maasai pastoralist, an increase in sexually transmitted diseases such as HIV/AIDS, and increased use of drugs that are introduced by the workforce in the industries. Such investments have contributed to the inflation process of land, food, housing, and other services that are out of reach for low-income people who, in the long run, are forced to sell their land in order to meet their daily needs.

Multinational Investors

Since 2009, infrastructure financing in Africa has seen unprecedented growth. Chinese financing, Official Development Financing (ODF), and Private Participation in Infrastructure (PPI) investments have been key sources in this rapid growth, in the same way as the national African governments and their domestic resources. In 2018, Kenya received a total of United States Dollars 2.488 billion in Net Official Assistance (World Bank, 2019). Kenya has seen such growth in the development of renewable energy in the form of geothermal development, infrastructure development like the Standard Gauge Railway (SGR), wind, and oil exploration. While this has been the case, most of the projects that have been implemented have raised major concerns of a lack of proper protocols for community involvement, irregular and skewed compensation for communities, and, more so, forceful evictions of local communities that live within project sites (Koissaba, 2014).

Such glaring examples of the projects and the impacts they have on the Maasai are the Kedong and Narasha communities in Nakuru County. The local community has variously faced forced evictions accompanied by mass destruction of property due to the contestation of land ownership by the Maasai and other groups that claim to legally own the land, which is historically the home for thousands of Maasai families. In Kajiado, and as mentioned in the preceding parts of the book is the Tata Chemicals Magadi which has had conflicts with the Iloodokilani Maasai over the concession area; abstraction of clean water for the exclusive use of the company at the expense of the community, and lately the diversion of seasonal rivers to reduce the siltation of the lake that affects the quality of soda ash.

The proliferation of flower farms in Kajiado and Naivasha has also been evident in the last twenty years and has had its adverse effects on the health of the community arising from the use of chemical sprays and discharges into the groundwater system, which have sometimes been reported to have caused deaths to livestock (Gitonga, 2013). Since most of these industries use land agents to buy land from mostly illiterate Maasai people, they end up getting exploited, with others being rendered landless because men who are the title holders sell the land in exclusion of other family members. Further to the discussion about the SGR and the Dry Port in Kedong, which were discussed earlier, there are many areas of contestation about multinational investment in areas occupied by the Maasai in Kenya.

Commitment to Action

Since issues relating to land are in the hearts of the Maasai, the Maasai have anger and bitterness that the land has continued to be appropriated, with some of them making personal commitments on what they will personally do to address the issue.

> "I will personally work to discourage the selling of land and claim for past injustices for appropriate compensation since the land taken has benefited the wrong people after independence."

> "As part of my job, I will continue with the dissemination of information that relates to land."

> "I will take a keen interest and aspire to stop land selling. There should be guardians of public land who are prone to grabbing. I will safeguard public lands, advocate against land selling, and lobby for a favourable land policy."

> "I will support any legal action directed in the efforts to recover the Maasai land, as well as working with other like-minded people to sustain pressure to demand compensation and put a stop to land sale."

> "The Maasai have faced many challenges at any time they stand up and address land issues. Some people have been

arrested, and even some killed. There is a lot of intimidation from the government, and I will keep talking to people and use the Maasai Council of Elders as a platform to address issues related to land."

In summary, the Maasai have contested all the agreements and laws that have contributed to Maasai land appropriation through the local courts, demonstrations, and occupying the land. This has led to conflicts between the Maasai and the land grabbers, as well as the government. While many Maasai people were against the manner and nature of land appropriation processes, the Kenyan law on land in the old constitution was an inhibiting factor. While the new constitution is more favourable, the problem is the implementation of the latter, corruption in the NLC and CLMB, and a lack of political will to accept (even if in principle) that those who lost their land need restitution. Further, the Maasai expressed their concerns about how decisions about the land were made and hope that with the involvement of the NLC and the CLMB, all land-related matters will be streamlined to reduce corruption and illegal land appropriation. Whereas there are high hopes about the new bodies and the roles they will play in land management, there seem to be concerns about the role of the Ministry of Lands, which is still the same body that will issue land titles. The government needs to be more active in protecting the land by implementing and enforcing relevant legislation and reports of past land-related commissions.

PART IX:

CONCLUSION

Background

The purpose of this part is to interpret and describe the significance of the study findings, considering what is already known about Maasai land appropriation and alienation, and to provide a new understanding and new insights about the phenomenon. As indicated elsewhere, the research sought to understand:

1. Common Maasai beliefs about land ownership;
2. current events and activities that are related to Maasai land appropriation and acquisition, key actors, and the roles they are playing regarding Maasai land appropriation;
3. views, suggestions, and recommendations about addressing Maasai land appropriation and acquisition;
4. How lessons learned from the Maasai land appropriation can be used to address global land appropriation.

This discussion is guided by the themes and topics that emerged after the data were analyzed. This approach enabled both research participants and the researcher to contextualize all responses to daily real-life experiences of the Maasai, how the phenomenon of land appropriation and acquisition is affecting them, how they are responding, and how their responses are contributing to mechanisms that mitigate the impacts of the loss of land. It gave room for the expression of true emotional experiences of the Maasai that led to the unearthing of the pains, bitterness, and the struggles that they underwent (and are still undergoing) due to the impact of appropriation and acquisition of their land. The narratives helped demonstrate strong connections between the land, the people, and how they feel about the continued loss of their land. It brought about their regrets and aspirations on issues related to land, and how they will, in the future, respond to the effects of land appropriation.

In this study, the argument was that the dominant actors, the British at the onset of colonialism, sought to maximize and establish their hegemony, a dependency structure as defined by Dos Santos in his work: *The Structure of Dependence,* implying a situation in which economies of certain states were conditioned by the development and expansion of another economy to which the former is subjected. The British had core economic interests rooted in a certain structure of their colonies. Their overriding objective was to ensure sustenance, critically, upon which was the need to set up political, economic, and social structures that would retain Britain's dominance. The process of negotiation (both in colonial and post-independence periods) became core to ensuring the incorporation of the new elite whose interests would sustain the economic and social realms of production (Dos Santos, 1970).

According to Klopp & Lumumba (2016, p.4), "the Colonial Land Administration system was set up in the early 1900s largely to expropriate and manage land for a privileged, politically powerful foreign minority within the conquest of territory. The highly centralized, opaque and bureaucratic system that was born in this political context was never created for the transparent public of regulation of land for broad, inclusive societal interests". They further argue that, "the Colonial land tenure system thus entrenched inequality of rights and access to land between 'settlers' and 'natives' and gave opaque administrative structures linked to the most powerful office (Governor and the Commissioner of Lands); enormous discretionary power to manipulate land rights blatantly" (p. 5).

As alluded to in the previous sections, the acquisition of land in Kenya was based on the Land Acquisition Act of India of 1894. According to Okoth-Ogendo (1991), by 1902, all land within the protectorate was declared Crown Land, whether or not the land was reserved for the natives or occupied by the same, which in effect made all Africans become tenants of the Crown (Okoth-Ogendo, 1991). Crown Land was defined as all public lands within the East African Protectorate that, for the time being, were subject to the control of His Majesty by virtue of any agreements or treaties, and all land that had been or may have been acquired by His Majesty under the Land Acquisition Act of 1894. Further, the Crown Lands

Ordinance No. 21 of 1902 gave powers to the Commissioner to identif and sell freehold land to desiring European settlers without giving due cognizance to customary and indigenous land tenure systems (Kanchorry, 2006). According to Mortensen (2004), by 1914, nearly five million acres (two million hectares) of land had been taken away from Kenyan Africans, mostly from the Agikuyu, Maasai, and Nandi communities (Okoth-Ogendo, 1991).

The main objective of the colonialists was to bring the tribal groups under British rule and to pacify their agitation. To do so, the colonial administration used force (Okoth-Ogendo, 1991). Acting Commissioner Sir Arthur Hardinge advocated for the use of force as the only way to contain the natives, who] the natives had to learn submission through the bullet. Legal segregation, through fixing the boundaries of the Native Reserves and the White Highlands, as recommended by the Report of the Kenya Land Commission (1934), effectively removed the African natives from the White Highlands and gave the European settlers assurance of permanency on their new settlements (Syagga, 2011). Restricting the movement of the Indigenous communities and denying them access to their natural habitat amounted to an apparent infringement of their rights by the imperial regime. The Crown Ordinance, which regulated how government land was to be distributed, gave powers to the Governor, and, without consultation, to distribute the land through auctions to individuals and corporations for development (Okoth-Ogendo, 1991).

The removal of the natives from their ancestral land in the East African Protectorate to create room for European settlement was the driving force behind the Africans' struggles for independence. It was also the beginning of land-related conflicts in the territory that later came to be known as Kenya, before and after independence in 1963. Major challenges are evident today in how some political elites want to maintain the status quo, reverse gains, and manipulate the pace and nature of changes recommended in the new constitutional order. As is evident by recent actions and decisions by the president and parliament, some of the Maasai land-related grievances (e.g., Kedong) have fallen on deaf ears among the political leaders as well as in courts. At the behest of President Uhuru Kenyatta, who has established a dry port, extended the SGR, and offered the President of Uganda space for transit goods, the Maasai, who have been claiming Kedong, have been evicted and property destroyed to give room for the infrastructure development[1] (Daily Nation, July 14th, 2019). Because the Maasai had no title deeds for the land, they were not compensated. This gave rise to several demonstrations by the Maasai, resulting in several injuries.

Figure 22: Maasai demonstrate along the Narok -Mai Mahiu road against evictions in Kedong to give room for the establishment of a dry port

© Jackson Shaa. November 13th, 2019

Land disputes are frequently some of the causes of violent conflict and place obstacles to restoring sustainable peace. In short, the human rights aspects of land affect a range of issues, including poverty reduction and development, peace building, humanitarian assistance, disaster prevention and recovery, and urban and rural planning, to name but a few. Emerging global issues, such as food insecurity, climate change, and rapid urbanization, have

1   See Daily Nation. July 14th, 2019. Uhuru's Naivasha dry ports deal triggers debate https://www.nation.co.ke/kenya/business/uhuru-s-naivasha-dry- ports-deal-triggers-debate--185960.

also refocused attention on how land is being used, controlled, and managed by states and private actors. An increasing number of people are forcibly evicted or displaced from their land to make way for large-scale development or business projects, such as dams, mines, oil and gas installations, or ports. In many countries, the shift to large-scale farming has also led to forced evictions, displacements, and local food insecurity, which in turn has contributed to an increase in rural to urban migration and consequently further pressure on access to urban land and housing. A considerable portion of this displacement is carried out in a manner that violates the human rights of the affected communities, thus further aggravating their already precarious situation.

Urban development projects have led to socio-economic polarization in cities owing to escalating costs of land and housing, as well as the depletion of low-income housing. Measures taken to protect the environment are also, at times, in conflict with the interests and human rights of populations that depend on land for subsistence and survival. Failure to effectively prevent and mitigate environmental degradation and the negative impact of climate change could drastically reduce access to land, especially for marginalized groups.

For the Maasai people of Kenya, the land goes beyond being an economic asset; it provides social capital in the form of social status among the community and confers cultural and religious identity. Among the Maasai, land is sacred, a gift from God, and meant for the use of all without individual ownership. They also believe that land is life, as it provides water, grass, plants, and air, which people and livestock need for survival. The land also has sacred places that the Maasai use to communicate with God (Enkai) and perform other essential rituals, including rites of passage. Since the land was meant for all the people, the Maasai had a set of rules that were used to govern and manage the land. The Maasai had no monetary value attached to their land, as land was never meant to be sold. It was preserved as a safety net for children (present and future), family, livestock, and the whole community. Land was considered the source of peace and provided food for all people. Land and livestock defined the Maasai as people, gave them identity and prestige. As such, they defended it from encroachment by non-Maasai tribes. According to the Maasai, their land was not transferable and could not be appropriated to individuals, especially to non-Maasai. It was considered sacred and had to be owned communally. It was both for the rich and the poor to be held in trust for future generations.

As captured elsewhere in this work, the historical dispossession of land by colonial powers through the infamous 1904 and 1911 Maasai agreements, and subsequent post-independence land-related laws, led to severe losses of land by the Maasai. Before the advent of colonialism, the Maasai knew the extent of their land, and any encroachment by outsiders was repulsed by force of arms. To obtain more land, the Maasai raided their neighbours, pushed them out, and took over that land. Historical examples are in the Uasin Nkishu region, where the Maasai forced the Kalenjin to move northwards, leaving the Maasai to occupy the rich plain of Uasin Nkishu. This is the reason why many areas had, and still bear, Maasai names (Lotte, 2006). There is evidence that, just like the colonial settlers, other communities, like the Kalenjin, Kisii, Kikuyu, and Baluhia, came into the picture long after the Maasai inhabited most places that have Maasai names in Kenya. Places such as Nakuru (Nakuro in Maa), Uasin Gishu, Eldoret, Molo, and elsewhere were all part of the expansive Maasai land by 1890. The names the community gave to certain areas signified broad and specific, unique geographical formations therein.

Being pastoralists, the Maasai held their land under communal tenure (Migot-Athola et al., 1991; Galaty, 2013). This communal property regime created pastoral rights of access and control, which provided a framework for the Maasai to exploit available resources across various ecological zones, thereby reducing their levels of vulnerability (Niamir-Fuller, 2005; Nori, 2007). This customary form of tenure, which was characteristically communal, ambiguous, and with negotiable boundaries, provides a sustainable economic system for the Maasai. Traditionally, as noted by the study participants, the Maasai considered land to belong to God, and therefore human beings could only claim temporary ownership as a basis for survival. Further, land to the Maasai can only be claimed collectively either by a family (Olmarei), clan (Olgilata), sub-nation/ section (Olosho), or the entire Maa-Nation. There were clear boundaries that were marked by natural features like valleys, rivers, ridges, mountains, and trees. The land and natural resources form the basis of Maasai unity, which is demonstrated by the communal utilization of the bush pharmacy (herbs to treat many diseases), trees, honey, grasses, and water.

The privatization of land and natural resources was an alien concept that the Maasai were hesitant to adopt, as land formed the platform that bridged the gap between man and God. Maasai believe that land is life, as it provides water, grass, plants, and air for their survival and that of their livestock and wildlife.

The study participants discussed land as an ancestral heritage and were clear about the important relationship between the land, their culture, and way of life. They were equally clear about the devastating impact of the loss of their land on the Maasai. This study's findings related to the importance and impact of the loss of ancestral land by indigenous people were supported by other studies about the dispossession of indigenous people (Ahmed, Booth, Njogo & Stephanou, 2014; Anaafo, 2015; Caromody & Taylor, 2016; and Little, McPeak, Barrett & Kristjanson, 2011). In addition, other studies and reviews asserted that traditional culture and language are associated with the health and well-being of indigenous people and noted a connection between spiritual ties to ancestral land and health.

Some studies found that indigenous people's relationship with the land helped to maintain the balance necessary for health. The belief that land is alive and contributes to positive emotional and physical health has also been affirmed by others (McIvor, Napoleon & Dickie, 2009). The land was found to be a source of traditional medicine and traditional foods that supported health (Milburn, 2004; Waldram, 2000). Food insecurity and poor nutrition are now problems for the Maasai, and this was tied to the issue of land grabbing or the poor quality of land the Maasai now occupy (Fenton, Hatfield & McIntyre, 2012; Pilla & Dantas, 2016; Galvin, Beeton, Boone & BurnSilver, 2015). The study participants' responses to research questions two and three described the long process of disassembling the Maasai land.

Another key area that will determine whether the injustices meted out to the Maasai by post-colonial governments is the independence of the judicial systems. The past has seen the interference in the affairs of the judiciary by the executive branch that resulted in the infringement of the rights of many citizens, some of whom were detained without trial, fired from government jobs, while others disappeared after court hearings. The imminent fear is that those with vested interests in the land claims may again see the wheels of justice being manipulated to favour the political elites. It is, therefore, a 'wait and see' situation given the bitter rivalry between pro-land reform advocates and the elites who want to maintain the status quo.

It is important to note that Kajiado County has put in place measures to address historical and contemporary issues regarding land appropriation. The country has developed a land management plan that, hopefully, will address the intrigues of the land brokers, local political elites who use the land equation for their gains, and the National Government, which drives its agenda on migrating communities to Kajiado and Narok for numbers in every election. While the Maasai of Kajiado County are yet to realize the effectiveness of the county policy on land, there is imminent fear that the policy will not see the light of the day due to the influence of the political elites, land grabbers, and land prospectors in Kajiado County (Kajiado County, 2014).

In concluding this section, it has become clear in this study that many factors contributed to Maasai land appropriation and alienation in Narok and Kajiado counties: treaties and agreements; laws and decrees; high levels of illiteracy; land sales; corruption and impunity; globalization and conservation and tourism. The colonial and post-colonial governments have been accused of being the major catalyst for Maasai land appropriation. The culture of corruption and impunity in the government and among the political elites, facilitated by rich people from outside the two counties, accelerated the pace at which Maasai land is being lost to outsiders.

While the Maasai themselves, due to high levels of illiteracy and without knowledge of the cash economy, voluntarily sold their land, corrupt government officials and land brokers played a major role in working as a go-between for potential land merchants, and either individual land owners or Group Ranch Representatives. Local politicians have also either abetted the vice of illegal land transactions or not taken steps to stop them. The infamous Maasai agreements in 1904 and 1911 ushered in a long period of untold suffering for the Maasai, which is still being felt. The sacred sites and traditional venues were equally taken over, denying the Maasai the right to exercise their traditional, cultural, and religious rights. The human population was drastically reduced due to epidemics such as anthrax that wiped out a large proportion of both livestock and people. The Maasai's political and military prowess was compromised, and the two agreements marked the beginning of the weakening and vulnerability of the Maasai as people.

Further evidence of how the agreements and treaties contributed to Maasai land appropriation during the Kenyan independence negotiations, commonly known as the Lancaster Conference, was also presented. It was common knowledge to all who attended this conference that the Maasai had a genuine claim to the land lost to the white settlers. The conspiracy between the British and the KANU delegation led by Jomo Kenyatta to deny the Maasai the return of their land forced them to walk out of the conference in protest. Retaining colonial laws related to land after independence facilitated further land appropriation from the Maasai. One argument the Maasai have posited is, "What would have happened if the Maasai delegation never walked out of the Lancaster deliberations? Would they have had an opportunity to argue their case as opposed to what happened, where issues about land were discussed in their absence?" I want to say that walking out of the conference took the Maasai agenda off the table, hence the Maasai lost.

The introduction of group ranches, which later were subdivided into individually owned parcels of land, led to the extensive sale of land by the Maasai. The land sale was being facilitated by government officials and land brokers financed by rich individuals from other regions and politicians. I argue that there was no adequate preparedness or strategies to educate the Maasai about group ranches. The process was government-initiated, without considering the impacts it posed on the Maasai. It later became an elite project where the majority were disfranchised by their elites.

High levels of illiteracy among the majority of the Maasai individual land owners were also a significant contributor to land sales among the Maasai in Narok and Kajiado. Lack of background in formal employment by the majority of the Maasai population limited them from accessing outside employment. This also contributed to poor animal husbandry skills in managing their livestock in the smaller parcels of land that they individually owned. The factors mentioned above are further compounded by the persistent encroachment of Maasai land by migrants from other areas with burgeoning populations. The lack of economic opportunities and threats of climate change drive the Maasai to sell their lands. That is further exposing them to social-cultural-economic and political domination by migrant tribes within their own lands.

Importance of the Discourse about Land

Globally, land has remained a contentious issue, more so where governments have used their authority to displace communities or where there is a lack of requisite legislation to address land-related concerns. In the past few decades, several countries have adopted drastic land reforms to deal with such issues as poverty, equity, restitution for past expropriation, investment, and innovation in agriculture or sustainability.

Arable land is becoming extremely valuable due to greater investors'interest, changes in agricultural production systems, population growth, migration, and environmental change. Such lands are also under pressure due to urbanization.

This includes large-scale foreign agricultural investments in developing countries labelled as land-grabs. Over the past 15 years, large investors in developing countries have acquired tens of millions of hectares of land. The Land Matrix documented 1,037 transnational land deals covering 37,842,371 hectares during this period, while many remain undocumented (Land Matrix, 2015).

This has raised new issues regarding the respect of the right to land of local populations by depriving them of essential lands to sustain their access to food. For example, the Indian-owned Siva Group amassed a farmland portfolio of nearly one million hectares for oil palm plantations in only a few years. The company is now facing bankruptcy proceedings in the Seychelles. In another example, Foras, the private sector arm of the Islamic Development Bank, which was on its way to acquiring 700,000 hectares of farmland across Africa for a massive rice project, has folded up. Karuturi, which had flower farms in Kenya, has a 300,000-hectare concession in Ethiopia but now has nothing to show. Karuturi flower business in Kenya has been liquidated, and its Ethiopian farms have been sitting idle for the past two years.

The recent focus on climate change-offsetting measures, which has generated the acquisition of large tracts of land to plant palm oil or other sources of biofuels, is likewise creating a pattern of acquisition of land for economic gains to the detriment of the local populations who are losing their land to international investors (GRAIN, 2014).

While the land is increasingly commodified as an exclusively commercial good, a human rights-based approach to land rights brings another perspective to the value of land, as a social and cultural asset and, more importantly, a fundamental right. For those with the right to land, otherwise, if everyone were to have a right to the land, there wouldn't be enough of it to go around. It said, everyone has a right to enjoy that which comes from the land – food, clean air, biodiversity, etc., and when indigenous people's land is appropriated for common benefit, they should be compensated accordingly. As traditional access and ownership rights for women, minorities, migrants, and pastoralists are ignored or reduced within the current context, these populations see trampling of their land rights as a trampling of their fundamental human rights. Under this banner, land rights are human rights. For them, land is not only a valuable economic asset but also a source of identity and culture.

Overall, within the larger perspective of a human rights approach to land rights, the affirmation of land rights as a key human rights issue for the Maasai shows that the traditionally individualistic approach to property rights can be challenged. Further, individualistic approaches to property rights are not enough for the Maasai as they do not integrate their specific cultural attachment to their traditional territories. Land rights, particularly in the context of the Maasai traditions and culture, are inextricably linked with the right to food, work, and other human rights. In many instances, the right to land is bound up with a community's identity, livelihood, and thus its very survival. It is therefore from this standpoint that I suggest that continued loss of land by the Maasai is not only a threat to their culture but an imminent threat to their livelihood and eventual existence.

Good governance and land rights are excellent goals, but the results of this study found that these goals are not implemented in a vacuum. To understand land appropriation or land grabbing, we need to understand the state's nature, the various actors' motivations, the government's capacity, and the political cultures that will shape the path from policy to implementation. As noted in the study, the focus should not just be on the land or a specific act of land grabbing, but rather on the many processes such as narratives of legitimation, the state's development policy, the role of the courts, the partnerships, foreign capital involvement, patterns of power within the state, and the motivations of the various state and non-state actors. The results of this study provided a good understanding of Kenya's political ecology related to land appropriation by illustrating, through the participants' comments, the state's role in shaping land deals, and providing some new understandings about the relationships among the concepts of territory, sovereignty, authority, and people.

The depth, scale, and pace of land appropriation from the Maasai and other native communities globally are of concern. There is increased interest in land as an economic asset by governments, private investors, and transnational corporations. There is a demand for agricultural commodities, space for growing populations, agro-fuels, and raw materials (trees, minerals, etc.). There is also the 'green economy' where land is appropriated for alleged environmental ends such as the establishment of natural reserves, game parks, or carbon trade schemes, as well as geothermal and wind energy. In addition to these economic factors, states have played a major role in facilitating land appropriation through national legislation or corrupt practices. If this pattern is not reversed, land appropriation, or land grabbing, will deprive the Maasai and other global rural populations of their access to and control over their land and its resources. This will deepen the existing patterns of inequality, discrimination, social and cultural instability, and peace of rural societies such as the Maasai.

In moving forward, the state and international policy responses to land appropriation, or land grabbing, need careful attention. Many of these policy instruments fail to address the underlying economic and political drivers to obtain land. The notable exception is the Minimum Principles formulated by the Special Rapporteur (DeSchutter, 2009). The current complex nature of land appropriation cuts across local, national, and international actors, norms, and governing institutions. Thus, it is unlikely that a single institution or policy could regulate land appropriation comprehensively.

One answer to this dilemma is to make the right to land operational in an international human rights treaty. Some International human rights treaty laws already exist that recognize the right to land for indigenous and tribal people. The ILO Convention 169 and the UN Declaration of the Rights of Indigenous Peoples comprehensively treat indigenous land issues. Both instruments contain provisions requiring governments to recognize indigenous peoples' rights under pre-colonial customary law to own the natural resources and land they have traditionally used and occupied. There has also been some action in international human rights advocacy groups that, for people and communities, land is essential for the enjoyment of economic, health, social, political, and cultural rights (DeSchutter, 2009, 2010; Gelbspan & Nagarai, 2012). Thus far, a human rights approach to land appropriation, or land grabbing, has not been specifically described in the international human rights framework that would apply to all people, and not just indigenous populations. Relying on other human rights, such as health or food, to resolve land grabbing issues is risky because they do not include land rights; hence, land rights are pushed to the periphery when discussing human rights. Globalization and global land grabbing make it necessary to pay attention to the international dimensions of the human right to land.

International legal approaches might also offer a way for Kenyan indigenous people, such as the Maasai, to gain leverage against the Kenyan government. However, with no mechanism to enforce international tribunals' final decisions and recommendations, the state would control implementation. The Kenyan government is likely to be a reluctant partner to the negotiations proposed above and would probably not ratify a human rights treaty related to the right to land. A more promising solution may be to continue to work for a negotiated agreement between the Maasai and the Kenyan government.

This study described territory as a physical manifestation of the land that has abstract and symbolic meanings. Interactions with the Maasai and review of literature described a very complex history of land deals involving their ancestral lands. They also described the histories of state developmentalism and tourism-related environmental actions. The participants' comments described land

appropriation differently, but all highlighted the state's role and various actors involved in negotiating and acquiring the land.

The concept of sovereignty was addressed indirectly by the study as it focused on the ability of the Maasai to control their fate through the retention of their land. With the loss of their land, they lost control of their economic situation (herding livestock) and food production. The loss of their ancestral land also led to the displacement of the Maasai community to multiple locations, so their ability to govern themselves was disrupted. The participants also discussed what happened when local-level elites exercised access and control over the land. The literature review on sovereignty focused on sovereign rulers and the political relationships within the state. Thus, when examining sovereignty associated with land appropriation, one deals with complex inter-relationships between property control and autonomy, land appropriation and sovereign power, and fragmented sovereignty when land is ceded to outsiders.

I also discussed aspects of authority regarding decision-making power concerning various components of land appropriation. Currently, in Kenya, an increasing number of actors authorize land deals. I noted that authority took many forms, that there were multiple and overlapping arenas in which political and economic elites operated in Kenya, and that this has complicated attempts to organize land claims.

Perhaps the most important contribution of this study is the focus on the Maasai people, who had to deal with the outcomes of a series of appropriations of their ancestral land. For the Maasai, the land was more than a physical resource or an area for commerce. The land was life, livelihood, and culture. Their identity was constituted through the relationships on and with the land. Some of the articles reviewed argued that the Maasai and other pastoralists were unproductive or lazy; therefore, land appropriation was common sense. What was not described in these articles, but was described by the participants, was that the loss of land led to marginalization, reduced productivity, poverty, loss of a sense of belonging, and well-being. Studies of land appropriation, or land grabbing, need to use a holistic perspective to fully examine the outcomes of land loss by people.

The Maasai lag in education given the day's changes, dynamics, and politics. Their educational rates are below those of most of the Kenyan population. Thus, another action is to increase the number of children who complete secondary education, including the number of girls in school. Financial support for education for the Maasai should be given priority, and the Maasai should have access to provincial and national schools. In addition, models of education delivery that do not constrain pastoral mobility are important to pursue.

The Maasai need political empowerment and independence from mainstream political parties to have bargaining power in the national political arena. There is a need for Maasai political representation to influence the policy-making process. This can only be achieved when the Maasai are united politically and requires addressing the stereotypes that have impeded Maasai pastoralist voices for years, where pastoralists have been described as environmentally destructive agents of the land, uneducated, and disinterested in development. These descriptions tend to decrease the importance of their political input. This has also fostered the long-standing intervention to transform pastoralism through outside intervention 'for their own good' because, ostensibly, they cannot manage the land (the tragedy of the commons). New forms of misguided external interventions are likely without the Maasai receiving increased responsibility and authority over their own development agenda. The Maasai are attempting to cope with the common-pool resource dilemma described in *Governing the Commons* (Ostrom, 1990). Ostrom notes that "humans have a more complex motivational structure and more capacity to solve social dilemmas than posited in earlier rational-choice theory" (p. 435). The core goal of Kenyan public policy is to facilitate the Maasai's development as individuals and as a community. Since communities in Kenya are not homogeneous, there is no one-size-fits-all policy; policies should be made to suit each community's interests. Policies should be facilitators and not barriers to each community's development aspirations.

Implications and Recommendations

Research implications refer to the impact that this study might have on future research or policy decisions, or the relevant field of interest of the study. On the other hand, recommendations are based on the results of this study, which indicate the specific measures or directions that can be taken to address issues arising from the study. The study aimed to critically analyze factors contributing to Maasai land appropriation. This limited the study in several areas, first: the study did not examine the impacts of land appropriation on the total well-being of the Maasai in Narok and Kajiado counties, nor did it disaggregate data to find out who among the study population was most affected and the degree of these effects. The study also did not go into an in-depth analysis of the key players and their roles in the phenomenon since the goal was to analyze the factors that contributed to Maasai land appropriation. Therefore, as a way forward, in future research and policy development, I recommend unbundling the four concepts of territory, sovereignty, authority, and people to better understand the implications of land appropriation or land grabbing. We need research that leads to a relational understanding of power in which various actors (state government officials, local elites, investors, indigenous people, and communities) play a role in land appropriation politics and its outcomes.

Policy Recommendations

Policies provide guidance, consistency, accountability, efficiency, and clarity on how an organization (in this case, the National and County governments) operates. This offers leadership guidelines and principles. Policies define the goals of an organization and hence the objectives and activities, and give projections of expected outcomes. The five-year election cycle drives the development agenda in Kenya's policy context. After every election, the elected leaders (from the President, Members of Parliament, Senators, Governors, and Members of the County Assembly) come with new visions and plans to entrench political clout. This has resulted in the abandonment of projects, duplication, and inconsistencies in the development agenda. To be able to have consistency and sustainability in development, the following are suggested:

i. That Kajiado and Narok Counties undertake resource mapping to validate availability, accessibility, quality, and quantity of all resources available in the county (while the study was done in Kajiado and Narok, the same recommendations can apply to Laikipia, Samburu, and Baringo Counties where Maasai live);

ii. The counties should develop short-term (5 years), medium-term (10 years), and long-term (15 years) strategic development plans that will guide the development path regardless of the change in the county's political leadership. These plans should be ward-based and are arrived at through a community participatory process devoid of elite capture.

iii. To avoid duplication, all devolved funding should be administered through a county development committee comprised of the Governor, Members of Parliament and Members of the County Assembly.

Recommendations for Further Research

The National and County governments should invest in research that will inform policy in each county. The research should be done in collaboration with reputable research institutions and institutions of higher learning based in both Narok and Kajiado counties. The recommendations from the research findings should inform decisions about priorities that require investment in each county and provide high-value returns and appropriate long-term outcomes for the community. This means the county government should include research in its budgetary planning. Future studies need to:

i. identify and describe the social, political, economic, and spiritual impacts that the Maasai of Narok and Kajiado have experienced over time due to land appropriation;

ii. explore the severity of land appropriation among Maasai women and children, as they are the most vulnerable groups in society;

iii. explore the role education has played in either contributing to or stopping land appropriation in Kajiado and Narok counties;

iv. The impact of Christianity, which has taken over from Maasai traditional practices, thus contributed either to abetting land appropriation or helped to stop and mitigate the effects of Maasai land appropriation. This will also lead to new knowledge about how the loss of cultural values, which has been associated with Christianity, may have contributed to the current situation among the Maasai; and

v. Use case studies to demonstrate the risks confronting Maasai land from a social, economic, ecological, and political perspective, and the role that community leaders should play in intervening when concerns arise.

Recommendations about Land

Recommendations to the National Government

The recommendations to the National Government are summarized as follows:

i. The government should adopt and implement a human rights-based approach to land governance to enhance transparency, participation, and accountability, and to democratise tenure governance systems.

ii. that the government, the President and Parliament, implement as required by the law, the roles of the NLC by adequate funding, cease the interference with the work of the Commission, and provide security of tenure for all officials;

iii. that the National Government provides adequate funding, knowledge, and skills to permit the CLMBs to function effectively;

iv. The National Government implements recommendations of the various commissions formed to investigate land-related grievances. In addition, there is a need for the government to address the injustices meted out to the Maasai (and other communities) in connection with their lands and territories. These remedies will address the following: 1) acknowledging the injustices committed by all concerned; 2) restitution all illegally expropriated Maasai land through legal processes where courts are used to give orders about the same; 3) adequately compensating the Maasai for all loss suffered and sufficiently developing the land presently occupied by the Maasai to make them as ideal and habitable as the lands from whence they were moved from by giving back to the Maasai land equivalent in size or value to the land they lost; and, 4) reversing and annulling all corrupt and illegal processes of land adjudication, subdivision of Group Ranches, registration, and individual pieces that were illegally sold;

v.   Since continued subdivision of land impacts the economics of scale, which are associated with the productivity of the land, research and capacity building on alternative livelihoods need to be undertaken to address the impacts of continued land fragmentation.

vi. Respect the Constitution and allow the Maasai to participate in decision-making regarding control and use of their land. It should also recognize the Maasai land rights and protection from further discrimination on land issues. The government should give the Maasai the right to possess documents of their land that show the community's ownership of the piece of land.

vii. The government should respect the Constitution and immediately stop the special boards used to sell land. At the same time, the government needs to entrench the Community Land Act, a product of Kenyan civil society that collected views from all over the country.

viii. There is a need to change the policy of land title holding so that all members of a family are included as joint title holders. This will stop men from selling land without consultation.

ix.   That adequate community involvement of those affected by the government projects through processes that allow for the use of the principles of Free Prior and Informed Consent before such projects are implemented;

x.   The government and multinational investors ensure safeguards and the principle of Free and Prior Informed Consent in all projects undertaken on land belonging to the Maasai and other Indigenous communities.

xi.   The government should review and ensure that all trade and investment rules, plus those coming up for negotiation, revision, or renewal, include explicit clauses stating that they prioritize compliance with human rights, legitimate tenure rights, and other environmental, social, and labour rights, standards, duties, and obligations.

xii.   The government should review all land, property, and tenancy-related laws and customary systems to ensure and enforce equal rights for women and men to access, use, control, own, bequeath, and inherit all legitimate tenure rights.

Recommendations to the County Governments

i.   Professional human resource companies should be retained to advertise and shortlist the candidates for CLMB positions in consultation with the NLC to entrench transparency. After shortlisting, the applicants should be subjected to public vetting before being appointed to the positions, and they should be the representatives of the face of the county.

ii.   The County Assemblies need to empower CLMB by enacting legislation that requires all family members to be adequately consulted before any land sale transaction is approved.

iii.   Both Narok and Kajiado counties establish a land fund and bank to purchase land from disparate community members who are genuinely pressed by their livelihoods to buy the land and keep it for prosperity.

iv.   Enact legislation that requires that all family

members be adequately consulted before any land sale transaction is approved.

v. An inventory of all land claimed to have been illegally appropriated should be established, and an investigation should be conducted to authenticate all transactions.

vi. The digitization of all land records in Kajiado and Narok counties.

vii. A partnership between the NGOs and County governments needs to be strengthened to play complementary roles in safeguarding community land.

viii. play a role in ensuring that existing Group Ranches do not exclude legitimate claimants, especially widows and children;

ix. enact laws to protect pastoralist land from being subdivided into uneconomic acreage that will not support family livelihoods;

x. Expand its social services and extension programmes that are targeted at issues related to land.

xi. Facilitate and financially support the establishment of Iloshon-based land and natural resource cooperatives that buy land and manage it as business ventures, with the profits used to buy any land offered for sale within the County.

Recommendations to the Maasai and Maasai NGOs

i. The Maasai should consult local, regional, and international legal instruments to institute litigation for reparation and compensation;

ii. Maasai political leaders seek opportunities to create a united political front free from political, clanism, age group, and County influence that will spearhead the issues that relate to land appropriation.

iii. The formation of men, women, and youth groups at the village level, which becomes whistleblowers of any injustice meted out upon the Maasai, either by local politicians or external forces;

iv. limiting the change of user procedures on all agricultural land;

v. reviving the traditional approaches like Ilamala to educate Maasai and punish truant members of the community; and

vi. strengthening the traditional institutions by using the Maasai age group structure, not as a tool for dividing the community, but using it, as was intended, as a cultural leadership succession plan.

Recommendations about Land-Related Cross-Cutting Issues

Poverty Alleviation

Devolution has brought about various funding opportunities to the counties. Such funding should be consolidated and managed through a County Financial Resource Management Board where representation from the Governor, Members of Parliament, Women Representatives, and Senators collectively develop county short-term, mid-term, and long-term strategic plans informed by research findings. This will help reduce the duplication of projects and the wastage of resources. Here is a summary:

i.   establishment of community-based producer and marketing associations;

ii. facilitating and promoting entrepreneurship and small and medium enterprises;

iii. promoting and supporting community-based cottage industries;

iv. building Public-Private Partnership with potential investors in each county that will leverage the availability of local natural resources; and

v.   establishing county-based local resource processing industries that will create jobs, add value to local produce, and reduce capital flight.

Food Security

Despite being endowed with various natural resources, Narok and Kajiado have repeatedly faced food insecurity, with whole communities entirely depending on relief food. Part of this is due to climate change, reduced lands for pasture, inadequate infrastructure, and poor or lack of planning by the responsible National and County governments. Here are recommendations to address food security:

i. Provide support, including supplying irrigation equipment and training of community members in crop farming to reduce overreliance on livestock trading;

ii. Creating dams and other forms of reservoirs for water harvesting during peak rain season to (a) stem floods and (b) have water for use in dry months; some of the water could be used for irrigation.

iii. establish livestock processing, storage, and food banks to buy and process livestock products, package and sell them back to communities;

iv. train large-scale farmers in hay planting, harvesting, and baling for marketing to needy farmers during times of drought;

v. discourage local farmers from selling green maize to outside traders by supporting local farm producers and marketing groups to establish local food banks;

vi. Stock livestock sale yards with weighing scales to prevent exploitation of local livestock producers by middlemen who buy live animals;

vii. enhance livestock disease monitoring and control systems; and

viii. disseminate Early Warning System information to communities

Conflict Mitigation

Most of the inherent politics in both Narok and Kajiado counties are land-related, be they conflicts between the Maasai themselves or between the Maasai and other communities. Perceptions of history, identity, and past or present discrimination, which may motivate Maasai sub-clans that have achieved political power to adopt self-protective offensive strategies to ward off future suffering before it takes place, while those communities that perceive that their rights have been trampled on take a self-preservation stand. To address such conflicts, the National and County governments need to:

i.   delineate the conflicts from clan politics;

ii.   Re-establish boundaries between communities that have current feuds.

iii.   Use indigenous conflict resolution mechanisms;

iv.   Regarding conflict between the Maasai and the immigrant communities, land sale should be streamlined, and all transactions should be transparent, with vetting of all land surveyors who have become conduits of land surveying and transfers.

v.   Entrenching Indigenous conflict resolution mechanisms in all national and county by-laws.

ENDNOTES

1. See Sabelo J., Ndlovu-Gatsheni: *Decolonization, Decoloniality and the Future of African Studies.*

2. The rights enjoyed by citizens should be evident across the whole structure, as those rights that grant free opportunities of free choice to the citizens. See Harbamas 1996, p. 83.

3. This group of mixed young Maasai tried their luck in getting rich by stealing from the European Settlers.

4. See the Maasai social structure section for the meanings

5. Some others, like Isalei, are also sometimes referred to as Masai, but I have not confirmed that from reliable sources

6. See Ministry of State for Planning, National Development, Kenya Population and Housing Census, 2019. https://www.knbs.or.ke/

7. Known in Maasai as Iloshon, they are the Ildamat, Ilpurko, Ilkeekonyokie, Iloitai, Ilkaputiei, Ildalalekutul (Ilkankere), Isiria, Ilmoitanik, Iloodokilani, Iloitokitoki, Ilarusa, Ilmatatapato, Ilwuasinkishu, Kore, Parakuyu, and Ilkisonko.

8. Maasai Association Website: http://www.maasai-association.org/maasai.html (last accessed January 20, 2019).

9. This is elaborated further in the section about the Maasai religion

10. This translates in Maa as "Kule e Kaiyiam nairowuo naaruko Olaburra"

11. Emanaa enanyokie- First light

12. If you are brave enough, hit him below the lower lobe of the ear, and if you are not, let us know so we can run for our lives.

13. Note that I am capitalizing the name God to denote my belief that, contrary to some Christian beliefs, any

belief in any other divine name denotes a lesser god. As a Maasai, and having observed the Maasai faith, I am convinced that the Maasai worshiped a true God, not a lesser god.

14. Lemareka Kibasisi (2011). *A Comparative Study of Maasai and Biblical Traditions on God and Origins.*

15. Hans-Egil Hauge: *Maasai Religion and Folklore,* Nairobi: City Print Works, 1979), p. 42. The Maa stand on the side of God while cannibalistic; monsters were fought against and detested as enemies of God and humanity. On monotheism and the religion of Olmaa, see Merker, *Die Masai* 195-203; 249-251; Vincent J. Donovan, *Christianity Rediscovered*, p. 21.

16. It is interesting to note that the thought of feminine attributes can also be described in masculine names and variants as Mol puts it: "olosira kumok: he of many stripes, God is indescribable [my translation would be 'God of variant colours' (glory)] oloonmuain kumok: he of diverse colours, God is indescribable" [here I would translate 'God with multiple glory']. Mol, *MAA: A Dictionary of the Maasai Language and Folklore*, p. 75. This applies also to the rainbow, which the Maasai girls would call *olkila le papa,* "the cloth of my father!" Because it is the father who offers blessings to the young members of the family is highly respected, his robe is an icon that reflects the covenant bond of Maa with Enkai symbolized by the rainbow "There is something which the Masai call the rainbow (Olokirr Ai), and if one is seen in the heavens whilst rain is falling, it is a sign that the rain will shortly cease. Children call a rainbow 'Father's garment' because of its many colours, one part being red, another white, and a third variegated. They also say: 'I will give it to father for he will like it.'" Hollis: *The Masai*, p.277. Furthermore, the word "*olkila le papa*" is a sacred name used by girls in oath-like confirmation of truth.

17. *Enkakenya sirwa* is God's name in feminine form but masculine in its function, and it was the name of the ideal time chosen for the confrontation of the Maa armies.

This may correspond with entoros, a feminine word that depicts supreme warriors.

18. This has changed a lot since many Maasai communities have abandoned warriorhood. In some cases, many young Maasai men do not even know their age group or clan because circumcision has become more of a family affair.

19. This is mainly done by the rest of the Maasai Iloshon, except for Ilkisonko and Ilkaputiei, who have their warriors stay for longer periods of warriorhood.

20. 20. The fines ranged from a heifer, the highest price one would pay, to a goat, depending on the nature of the act that one performed.

21. Lately, this has greatly changed due to the influence of school and the decline of younger generations' adherence to the Maasai culture.

22. This has since gradually changed, but one can still find some pockets of communities that maintain the practice. However, the periods have drastically reduced to between 3 and 4 years.

23. The cases of Iltareto and Ilterioto are all dead, while the living Ilnyankusi were senile at the time of writing the manuscript.

24. Case study courtesy of Mainyioito Pastoralist Integrated Development Organization.

25. Tyranny of numbers is a term used to express a political situation where the majority or more numerous communities subject others to their rule through the use of numbers in a democratic environment.

26. Notes of Dr. Tameno's daughter, Mary Tameno.

27. Daily Nation, October 2nd, 2019. Ruto sucked into controversy over purchase of 900 acres. https://www.nation.co.ke/kenya/news/ruto-sucked-into-controversy-over-purchase-of-900-acres-209586

28. See Kamau Ngotho, 2017, Daily Nation, SUNDAY, JANUARY 1, 2017

29. See Daily Nation 14/01/88

30. See Daily Nation 10/02/88

31. Joseph Ole Lenku's comments about the diversion of a river by Tata Chemicals Magadi

32. Governor Joseph Ole Lenku, with other Maasai leaders, addressed the press regarding the displacement of the Maasai in Kedong.

33. See Weekly Review 31/01/97

34. Daily Nation, January 13th, 2015. Money and politics: How the 2013 poll tsunami haunts Narok. https://www.nation.co.ke/kenya/news/politics/money-and-politics-how-2013-poll-tsunami-has-come-to-haunt-narok-1064768

35. Interview with Hassan Ole Kamwaro, May 23rd, 2019, Oklahoma City.

36. Committee on Economic, Social and Cultural Rights (CESCR), General Comment 14, *The right to the highest attainable standard of health* (Art. 12), 27 (Nov. 8, 2000).

37. The date for signing the 1911 agreement is contested because it is said either Lenana signed it on his deathbed, his fingerprints were used after his death, or his son, Supeet, signed.

38. There have been disagreements and misinterpretations about whether the actual Agreements were leases that had an expiration time or if the leases were done after the Agreements between the then land owners who were awarded the land by the Crown Ordinance.

39. These Agreements have variously been referred to as Anglo-Maasai Agreements.

40. It is estimated that 29% of the land occupied by protected areas in Kenya forms part of the Arid and Semi-Arid Lands (ASALs) that are occupied by pastoral communities (Kenya Land Alliance, 'Fact Sheets on Human Wildlife Conflict in Kenya', Fact Sheet 1)

41. Patricia Kameri-Mbote, 2002: *Property Rights and Biodiversity Management in Kenya; The Case of Land Tenure and Wildlife.* Nairobi: ACTS Press, p. 86

42. A Kenya Human Wildlife Conflict Network has been formed to advocate for the protection of community interests against the destruction caused by wildlife, and in January 2005, Kenya Land Alliance launched Fact Sheets on this problem as part of its campaign for an appropriate land policy.

43. See the East African, August 30, 2004

44. See Daily Nation, August 25, 2004

45. See https://reliefweb.int/report/kenya/kenya-least-14-killed-clashes-over-water

46. See Kenya Maasai land claims rejected BBC News Monday, 16 August, 2004 http://news.bbc.co.uk/2/hi/africa/3570656.stm

47. See why Maasai's BBI demands are unworkable, especially on land. Daily Nation Thursday, February 27th, 2020

48. See https://www.refworld.org/pdfid/4ca571e42.pdf

49. See https://minorityrights.org/2017/05/26/huge-victory-kenyas-ogiek-african-court-sets-major-precedent-indigenous-peoples-land-rights/

50. Report of the Working Group on Indigenous Populations/ Communities (WGIP) of the African Commission on Human and Peoples' Rights (ACHPR, 2004), p. 11

51. Note: I am using Mao instead of Mau, which is commonly used in discussions about. The Maasai pronunciation is Mao.

52. This is where the name Kangere is derived because many of them settled in Meru, and to date, there are Meru names among the Maasai.

53. I have relatives in Ildalalekutuk and Ilpurko from my great-grandfather's 5th wife, "Siranka"; their families are still named after her name.

54. The matatu business is a privately owned transportation system that was mainly controlled by non-Maasai, but the Maasai want to run their own public transport business.

55. See Daily Nation, March 30th, 2019. https://www.nation. co.ke/kenya/counties/narok/chaos-in-narok-town-as- rival-matatu-saccos-fight-for-stage-153258

56. Comments from Fredrick Karlankei.

57. The Gazetteer of the land was not available to the community members who made this observation.

58. Interview with Lemayian Ole Taiko.

59. See Daily Nation. July 14th, 2019. Uhuru's Naivasha dry ports deal triggers debate. https://www.nation. co.ke/ kenya/business/uhuru-s-naivasha-dry-ports-deal- triggers-debate--185960

GLOSSARY OF MAASAI TERMS USED IN THE BOOK

Maasai Terms	Meanings
Aayel	Adoption but also used to depict smearing/Anointing
Aibiribirr	Critical Thinking/Reflection/Meditate
Enegilat	Clannism
Eneporori	Age-groupism
Embuata	The gap after the removal of the two lower teeth
Emuratta	Circumcision
Empus Oshoke	God of the blue stomach (belly)
Enkai	God
Enkai Narok	The Black God
Enkai Nanyokie	The Red God
Enkakenya Sirwa	The God of the bright morning
Enkang oo-nkiri	Meat-eating ceremony after warriorhood which allows the young men to eat meat at their mothers' and wives' houses without the accompaniment of others.
Enkeene-E Nkai	The rope of God.
Enkoteyiai	The Mother God
Enkiama	Marriage
Enkipaata	The pre-circumcision ceremony for boys
Enkipolosa	Warrior morning prayer during meat camps
Enkitupukunoto Tiaji	Traditional baptism or naming ceremony
Entaloishi e-tatene	The right side of the cattle entrance
Entaloishi e-kedienye	The left side of the cattle entrance
Entiamasi	The dragon
Entidiyai	Malaria
Esegerua	The lower ear lobe

Eokoto e-kule	The milk-drinking ceremony which permits the young men to drink milk by themselves after the Eunoto ceremony
Eunoto	The warrior shaving ceremony where warriors graduate to junior elders
Esuguroi	Traditional liquor made from honeycombs mostly referred to as ilchankaro
Ilaikitalak	Spies
Ilarinkon (Olarinkoi-singular)	Mythological people (giants) that the Maasai conquered
Ilkalikal	The senior right-hand circumcision group of Ilnyankusi
Ilkamaniki	The junior left-hand circumcision group of Ilnyankusi
Ilkiragarien Imiet	Five Sleep Overs
Ilkipirat	Fire tattoos on the legs and the upper hand
Ilpuli	Meat camps
Iltorobo	The hunter-gatherers
Iseuri	The age set after Ilnyankusi
Ilkunono	The Blacksmiths
Ilmeek	Non-Maasai/Heathen
Inkangitie (Enkan'g-Singular)	Homesteads
Inkasis	Spiritual and traditional leaders
Inkidongi	The medicine men
Inkoon	Stories, Idioms, and narratives about the past wisdom and culture
Iran'giran'g	The junior left-hand circumcision group of Ilkitoip
Irampaun	The senior right-hand circumcision group of Ilkitoip- the term is mainly used by Ilkeekonyokie.
Kopikop	South
Moikuape	North
Murrano	Warriorhood
Nalakua Etaana Ai	My God who is far yet so near

Napik neitayu	My God who puts and removes
Naori oriki Ai	The God who distributes and allocates gifts and resources
Noonkipa	The God of the embryonic fluid- provider of fertility
Noosaen Ai	My God of many bracelets
Olaigueanani	The Chief/ Chief Counsellor
Olaitoriani	The ruler
Olamal	A ceremonial group formed to initiate an important community event
Olgesherr Loo Inyankusi	Ceremony ushering in Ilnyankusi as junior elders by holding a ceremony between the right and left circumcision group Ilkalikal and Ilkamaniniki
Olgilata (Ilgilat in plural)	Clan /clans
Oloboru Enkeene	One who is honored with a leather strap with a knot that symbolizes his age set.
Olodua	Rinderpest
Oloontoluo	West
Oloosaen	East
Olotuno	One who is chosen to be responsible for the ending of the ceremony; warriorhood.
Oltikana	East Coast Fever
Olosira Nkumok	The God of many colours
Olkiu-(Ilkiushin- Plural)	Meeting points or sometimes referred to as the heap
Olporror/ Olaji	Age-Set/Age Group
Olpul	Meat eating-hideout or camp
Olpurkel	Arid and Semi-Arid Land
Orkitipet	The upper ear lobe
Oloiboni	Medicine man/ Seer
Olosho	Subtribe
Oodo Mongi	The Red Cow Clan
Orok Kiteng	The Black Cow Clan

Orngesherr	Junior elder ceremony where the right and the left-hand circumcision groups are made one age-set
Parmuain	The God of many colours
Partulusoo	The over provider, the generous God
Pasai [Parsae]	He who is worshiped

BIBLIOGRAPHY

Allen, B. & Reser, D. (1990). *Content analysis in library and information science research.* Library & Information Science Research, 12(3), 251-260.

Ahmed, Z., Booth, L., Njagi, L., & Stephanou, E. (2014). *The warrior's dilemma: Can Maasai culture persist in a changing world? Consilience:* The Journal of Sustainable Development, 13(1), 300-31.

Anaafo, D. (2015). *Land reforms and land rights change: A case study of land-stressed groups in the Nkoranza South Municipality, Ghana.* Land Use Policy, 42(6), 538-546.

Akram-Lodhi, A. H., & Kay, C. (2010). *Surveying the agrarian question (part 2): current debates and beyond.* The Journal of Peasant Studies, 37(2), 255-284.

Asiema, J.K. & Situma, F.D. (1994). *Indigenous people and the environment. The case of the pastoral Maasai in Kenya:* Colorado Journal of International Environmental Law and Policy, 5, 149-171.

Atuahene, B. (2009). *Things Fall Apart: The illegitimacy of property rights in the context of past property thefts.* Arizona Law Review. Vol. 52, No. 4.

Barsade, S.G.; Brief, Arthur P.; Spataro, S.E., & Greenberg,

J. (eds.), (2003). *"The effective revolution in organizational behaviour: The emergence of a paradigm." In Organizational Behaviour:* The State of Science (2nd ed.), pp. 3-52. Mahwah, NJ: Lawrence Erlbaum Associates Publishers.

Barume, A. K. (2009). *Land Rights of Indigenous People in Africa;* International Work Group for Indigenous Affairs (IWGIA).

Bedelian, C. (2012). *Conservation and ecotourism on privatized land in the Mara, Kenya. The case of conservancy land leases.* LDPI Wording Paper 9. The Land Deal Politics Initiative.

Berry, J.W., Segall, M. H., & Dasen, P.R. (2002). *Cross-cultural psychology* (2nd ed.). Cambridge, England: Cambridge University Press.

Bertalanffy von, L. (1968). *General System Theory.* New York. George Brazilia

Boone, C. (2014). *Property and constitutional order: Land tenure reform and the future of the African state.* Oxford Journals, Vol. 106, Issue 425, pp. 557-586.

Boone, C. (2007). *"Africa's new territorial politics: regionalism and the open economy in Côte d'Ivoire."* African Studies Review, 50(1).

Bowen, G.A. (2009). *Document Analysis as a qualitative research method.* Qualitative Research Methods Journal, Vol. 9, No. 2.

Bornstein, M. H., & Lansford, J. E. (2010). *Parenting. In M. H. Bornstein* (ed.), HANDBOOK OF CULTURAL DEVELOPMENTAL SCIENCE (pp. 259–277). Psychology Press.

Borras, S.M., Hall, R., Scooners, I., White, B., & Wolford, W. (2011). *Towards a better understanding of global land grabbing: An editorial introduction.* The Journal of Peasant Studies, 38(2), 209-216.

Brass, P. R. (ed.), (1985). *Ethnic groups and the state* (p. 27).

London: Croom Helm.

Brennan, J. (1993). *The Australian case of Mabo v. Queensland (No. 2) 1* LRC 194, p. 219.

Catley, A., Lind, J., & Scoones, I. (Eds.). (2013). Pastoralism and development in Africa: dynamic change at the margins. Routledge.

Bronfenbrenner, U. (2005). *Ecological systems theory. In U. Bronfenbrenner (ed.), making human beings human: ecological perspectives on human development* (pp. 106-173). Thousand Oaks, CA: Sage.

Bronfenbrenner, U. & Morris, P.A. (1998). *The ecology of the developmental process.* In W. Damon (ed.), Handbook of Child Psychology: Theoretical models of human development (5th ed.), Vol. 1, pp. 993-1028. New York: Wiley.

Carmody, P. & Taylor, D. (2016). *Globalization, land grabbing, and the present-day colonial state in Uganda:*

Ecolonization and its impacts. Journal of Environment and Development, 25(1), 100-126.

Creswell, J.W. (2013). *Qualitative Research Methods: Choosing Among Five Approaches.* London: Sage Publications.

Collier, P., Hoeffler, A., & Soderbom, M. (2004). *On the duration of the civil war.* Journal of Peace Research, 41(3), 253-273.

Crotty, M. (1998). *The Foundations of Social Research: Meaning and Perspective in the Research Process.* London: Sage Publications.

Davis, K.F., D'Odorico, P., & Rulli, M.C. (2014). *Land grabbing: a preliminary quantification of economic impacts on rural livelihoods.* Population Environment, 36, 180-192.

DeBlij, H.J. (2003). *Geography: Realms, Regions, and Concepts* (11th ed.). New York: John Wiley & Sons.

DeHaven-Smith, L. (1988). *Philosophical Critiques of Policy Analysis: Lindblom, Habermas, and the Great Society.* Gainesville, FL: University of Florida.

DeSchutter, O. (2010). *The emerging human right to land.* International Community Law Review, 12(3), 303-334.

DeSchutter, O. (2009). *Large-Scale Land Acquisition Leases: A set of Minimum Principles and Measures to Address Human Rights Challenges.* Addendum to the Report of the Special Rapporteur on the Rights to Food to the Human Rights Council. (A/HRC13/33/AAdd2) (Geneva Human Rights Council).

Denzin, N.K. & Lincoln, Y.S. (2005). *The Sage Handbook of Qualitative Research (3rd ed.)* Thousand Oaks, CA: Sage Publications.

Denzin, N.K. & Lincoln, Y.S. (2011). *Introduction: The discipline and practice of qualitative research.* The Sage Book of Qualitative Research. (4th ed., pp. 1-19). Thousand Oaks, CA: Sage Publications.

Dillman, D.A., Smyth, J.D., & Christian, L.M. (2009). *Internet, Mail, and Mixed-mode Surveys: The Tailored Design Method* (3rd ed.). Hoboken, NJ: John Wiley & Sons.

Derman, B., Odgaard, R., & Sjaastad, E. (2007). *Conflicts over Land & water in Africa.*

Dos Santo, T. (1970). *The Structure of Dependence.* The American Economic Review, Vol. 60, No. 2 (1970): 231-6.

Dunn, W. & Kelly, R. (1992). *Advances in Policy Studies.* Brunswick, NJ: Transaction Books.

Drinkwater, M. A. (2010). *Critical democratic pedagogy through the arts in indigenous/Maasai rural schools in Kenya.* In the 2nd World Conference on Arts Education (UNESCO), Seoul, Korea.

Fairhead, J., Leach, M., & Scoones, I. (2014). *Green Grabbing: A New Appropriation of Nature.* Routledge.

Fenton, C., Hatfield, J., & McIntyre, L. (2012). *A qualitative pilot study of food insecurity among Maasai women in Tanzania.* Pan African Medical Journal, 12, 81-86.

Forester, J. (1993). *Critical Theory, Public Policy, and Planning Practice.* Albany, NY: State University of New York Press.

Galaty, J.G. (2011). *The Modern Motility of Pastoral Land Rights: Tenure Transitions and Land-grabbing in East Africa.* Paper presented at the International Conference on Global Land Grabbing, Sussex, UK.

Galaty, J.G. & D.L. Johnson. (1990). *Introduction: Pastoral systems in a global perspective. In the world of pastoralism: herding systems in comparative perspective.* New York: The Guilford Press.

Galaty, J.G. (1999). *The rhetoric of rights: Construing Maasai land claims. The Arid Lands and Resource Management Network in Eastern Africa.* ALARM Working Paper No. 7. Kampala, Uganda Centre for Basic Research, p. 1-13.

Galaty, J.G. (2013). *The collapsing platform for pastoralism: Land sales and land loss in Kajiado County, Kenya.* Nomadic People, 17(2), 20-39.

Galvin, K.A., Beeton, T.A., Boone, R.B., & BurnSilver, S.B. (2015). *Nutritional status of Maasai pastoralists under change.* Human Ecology, 43, 411-424.

Gelbspan, T. & Nagaraj, V. (2012). *Seeding hope? Land in the international human rights agenda: Challenges and prospects.* (ESCR Net and International Council on Human Rights).

Gilbert, J., & Doyle, C. (2011). *A new dawn over the Land: Shedding Light on Indigenous Peoples' Land Rights. In: Allen, Stephen; Xanthaki, Alexandra* (eds.), 2011. Reflections on the UN Declaration on the Rights of Indigenous Peoples. Oxford; Portland, Or: Hart Pub.

Gitonga, G.S. (2013). *Effects of flower farming on workers' welfare in Ketengela Area, Kajiado County, Kenya.* Unpublished Dissertation.

Grandin, B. de Leeuw, P., & Ole Pasha, I. (1991). *The Study Area: Socio-spatial organization and land use.* In Bekure, S., de Leeuw, P., Grandin, B., & Neate, P. (Eds.), *Maasai Herding: An analysis of the livestock production system of Maasai pastoralists in eastern Kajiado district, Kenya.* ILCA *Systems study no.* Addis Ababa, Ethiopia, pp. 57-70.

GRAIN. (2014). *The global farmland grab in 2016: how big, how bad.* Retrieved from https://www.grain.org/article/entries/5492-the-global-farmland-grab-in-2016-how-big-how-bad]

Green, M. & Houlihan, B. (2004). A*dvocacy coalitions and elite sports policy change in Canada and the United Kingdom.* International Review for the Sociology of Sports, 39(4), 387-403.

Gribich, C. (2007). *Qualitative Data Analysis: An Introduction.* London: SAGE Publications Ltd.

Groody, D.G. (2007). *Globalization. Spirituality and Justice.* New York: Maryknoll.

Grossmann, K. E., Grossmann, K., & Keppler, A. (2005). *Universal and culture-specific aspects of human behaviour: The case of attachment.* In W. Friedlmeier, P.Chakkarath,

&B. Schwarz (eds.), *Culture and human development: The importance of cross-cultural research to the social sciences* (pp. 75-97). New York: Psychology Press.

Habermas, J. (1996). *Between Facts and Norms: Contributions to a Discourse Theory of Law and Democracy.* Cambridge, MA: The MIT Press.

Habermas, J. (1989). *The Structural Transformation of the Public Sphere.* Cambridge, MA: The MIT Press.

Hardin, G. (1968). *The tragedy of the commons. Science,* 162, 1243-1248.

Hatch, J. (2002). *Doing Qualitative Research in Educational Setting.* Albany, NY: State University Press of New York.

Hauge, H. (1979). *Maasai Religion and Folklore, Nairobi:* City Print Works.

Headand, T.N., Pike, K.L., & Harris, M. (eds.). *Emics and etics: The insider/outsider debate.* Frontiers of Anthropology, V7. Newbury Park, CA: Sage Publications.

Hedges, S., Mulder, M.B., James, S., & Lawson, D.W. (2016). *Sending children to school: Rural livelihoods and parental investment in education in northern Tanzania.* Evolution and Human Behaviour, 37(2), 142-151.

Hill, C.E., Williams, E.N., & Thompson, B.G. (1997). *A guide to conducting consensual qualitative research.* Counselling Psychologist, 25, 517-572.

Hill, C.E. et al. (2005). *Consensual qualitative research: An update.* Journal of Counselling Psychology, 52, 196-205.

Hodgson, D.L. (1999). *Once Intrepid Warriors: Modernity and the Production of Maasai Masculinities.* Pittsburgh, PA: The University of Pittsburgh Press.

Hodgson, D.L. (2004). *Once Intrepid Warriors: Gender, and the Cultural Politics of the Maasai Development.* Bloomington, IN.: Indiana University Press.

Hughes, L. (2006a). *Moving the Maasai: A Colonial Misadventure.* Basingstoke, UK: Palgrave.

Hughes, L. (2006b). *"Beautiful beasts" and brave warriors: The longevity of a Maasai stereotype.* In Romanucci-Ross, L., De Vos, G.A., & Tsuda, T. (Eds.), *Ethnic Identity: Problems and Prospects for the Twenty-first Century.* Lanham, MD: Altamira Press, pp. 264–294.

Homer-Dixon, T. F. (1994). *Environmental scarcities and violent conflict: evidence from cases. International Security, 19*(1), 5-40.

IRIN. (2005). *Kenya: At least 14 killed in clashes over water.* Retrieved from https://reliefweb.int/report/kenya/Kenya-least-14-killed-clashes-over-water

Israel, G. (2010). *Using Web-hosted surveys to obtain responses from extension clients: A cautionary tale.* Journal of Extension, 48(4). Article 4FEA8. Retrieved from http:// www.joe.org/joe/2010august/a8.php. Accessed on 12/25/14.

IWGIA. (2019). *Landmark ruling provides compensation to indigenous people in Australia.* Retrieved from https://www.iwgia.org/en/australia/3336-compensation-australian- indigenous-peoples.html#:~:text=In%20 a%20landmark%20decision%20on,the%20town%20of%20Timber%20Creek.

Kamau, J. (2009). *Daily Nation Special Reports,* 11 and 12 November.

Kanchorry, S.O. (2005). *The Proposed Maasai Land Case Brief.* Report Prepared with the Authority of and upon Commissioning by the Maa Civil Society Forum (MCSF).

Karanja, F., Tessema, Y., & Barrow, E.G. (2002). *Equity in the Loita/Purko Naimina Enkiyio Forest in Kenya: Securing Maasai rights to and responsibilities for the Forest* (No. 11).

Kantai, P. (2005). I*n the grip of the vampire state: Maasai land struggles in Kenyan Politics.* Reuters Foundation Paper No. 250.

Keiwua, M. (2002). *Maasai Land: Part 1—A History.* Whose land.

Kenta, M.O. (2015). *Maasai Mau Forest. Letter to the Cabinet Secretary, Interior and Coordination of National Government,* dated 26 June 2015.

Kibugi, R.M. (2009). *A failed land use legal and policy framework for the African Commons.* Reviewing range land governance in Kenya. Journal of Land Use, 24(2).

Kiereini, D. (2019), *How the 1934 Morris-Carter land report set the stage for Mau Mau.*Retrieved from https://www.businessdailyafrica.com/lifestyle/society/-land-report-set-stage-for-Mau-Mau/3405664-5097794-ba4c7tz/index.html.

Kieya, J. (2007). *Indigenous people's land rights in Kenya. A case study of the Maasai and Ogiek people.* Penn State Environmental Law Review, 15(3), 397-437.

Kibasisi, L. (2011). Enkai and YHWH. A comparative study of Maasai and biblical traditions on God and origins. Friedensau Adventist University. Master's Thesis.

Klopp, J.M. & Lumumba, O. (2016). *The state of Kenya's land policy and land reform: A political and institutional analysis.* Paper presented at the 2016 World Bank Conference on Land and Poverty. Washington, DC, 14-18 March 2016.

King, K. (1971). *The Kenya Maasai and the Protest Phenomenon, 1900-1960,* The Journal of African History Vol. 12, No. 1 (1971), pp. 117-137.

Koissaba, B.R. (2016). *A Critical Analysis of Factors that Contribute to Maasai Land Appropriation: The Case of Maasai Land Appropriation in Kajiado and Narok Counties in Kenya. Dissertation.* Tiger Prints

Koissaba, B.R. (2012). *Local Advocacy to National Activism: Maa Civil Society Forum, Kenya.* LAP, LAMBERT Academic Publishing.

Koissaba B.R. Ole (2014). *Legitimization Crisis: Laws, policies, and decrees as tools for Maasai land appropriation.* Intercontinental Cry.

Koissaba, B.R.(2014). *Elusive Justice: The Maasai contestation of land appropriation in Kenya. A historical and contemporary perspective.* Cultural Survival.

Krapf, J. L. 1860. *Travels, research, and missionary labours during an 18-year residence in Eastern Africa.* London: Trübner & Co. Repr., London: Frank Cass, 1968.

Kvale, S. (1996). Interviews: An *Introduction to Qualitative Research Interviewing.* Thousand Oaks, CA: Sage Publications.

KWCA (2016). State of Wildlife Conservancies in Kenya Report 2016. Retrieved from https://kwcakenya.com/wp- content/uploads/2018/01/SoC-Report.pdf

Laker-Ojok, R. (1980). *An analysis of structures implemented to resolve land use conflict and overstocking by Masai pastoralists in Kajiado District, Kenya.* Doctoral dissertation, Michigan State University.

Land Matrix (2015). Available at the Land Matrix Website. Retrieved from https://landmatrix.org/

Lawson, D.W., Mulder, M.B., Ghiselli, M.E., Ngadaya, E., Ngowi, B., Mfinanga, S.G.M., Hartwig, K. & James, S. (2014). *Ethnicity and child health in Northern Tanzania: Maasai pastoralists are disadvantaged compared to neighbouring ethnic groups.* Plos One, 9(10): e110447. DOI: 10.1371/ journal.pone.0110447.

Le Billon, P. (2001). *The political ecology of war: natural resources and armed conflicts. Political Geography, 20*(5), 561-584.

Lesorogol, C.K. (2008). *Land privatization and pastoralists' well-being in Kenya.* Development Change, 39(2), 309-311.

Lincoln, Y.S., Lynham, S.A., & Guba E.G. (1994). *Pragmatic Controversies, contradictions, and emerging confluences.* In N.K. Denzin & Y.S. Lincoln (eds.), *Handbook of Qualitative Research* (2nd ed., pp. 163-188). Thousand Oaks, CA: Sage.

Lincoln, Y.S. & Guba, E.G. (1985). *Naturalistic Inquiry.* Beverly Hills, CA: Sage.

Little, P.D., McPeak, J.G., Barrett, C.B., & Kristjansen, P. (2011). *Challenging orthodoxies: Understanding poverty in pastoral areas of East Africa.* Economics Faculty Scholarship, Paper 83. Syracuse University. Retrieved from http://surface.syr.edu/ecn/83.

Ludert, J. (2010). *Habermas revisited: Indigenous life world(s) today.* Indigenous Policy Journal, 21(4).

Lyman, A. & Kew, D. (2010). *An African dilemma: Resolving Indigenous conflicts in Kenya.* Georgetown Journal of International Affairs, 37-46.

McIvor, O., Napoleon, A., & Dickie, K.M. (2009). *Language and culture as protective factors for at-risk communities.* Journal of Aboriginal Health, 5, 6-25.

Margulis, M.E., McKeon, N., & Barros, S.M. (2013). *Land Grabbing and Global Governance. Critical Perspectives.* Globalizations, 10(1), 1-23.

Markakis, J. (2004). *Pastoralism on the Margin.* UK: Minority Rights Group International.

MCSF. (2004). *A Memorandum on the Anglo-Maasai Agreements. A Case of Historical and Contemporary Injustices and the Dispossession of Maasai Land.*

Merriam, S.B. (1988). *Case Study Research in Education.* San Francisco, CA: Jossey-Bass Publishers.

McCarthy, T.A. (1979). *The Critical Theory of Jurgen Habermas.* Cambridge. MA: The M.I.T. Press.

McCracken, G. (1988). *The Long Interview.* Newbury Park, CA: Sage Publications.

Milburn, M. (2004). *Indigenous nutrition: Using traditional food knowledge to solve contemporary health problems.* American Indian Quarterly, 28, 411-434.

Millar, M.M., & Dillman, D.A. (2011). *Improving response to Web and mixed-mode surveys.* Public Opinion Quarterly, 75(2), 249-269.

Miles, M.B. & Huberman, A.M. (1994). *Qualitative Data Analysis:* An Expanded Source Book (2nd ed.). Thousand Oaks, CA: Sage Publications.

Moiko, S.S. (2004). *The Vanishing Commons: Tenure Reforms, Individualization and Dispossession of Land in the Pastoral Range Lands of Kajiado District, Kenya.* Unpublished Dissertation.

Montalvo, J. G., & Reynal-Querol, M. (2005). *Ethnic polarisation, potential conflict, and civil wars.* American Economic Review, 95(3), 796-816.

Morgan, D.L. (2008). *The SAGE Encyclopedia of Qualitative Research Methods.* SAGE Publications, Inc.

Morrow, S.L. & Smith, M.L. (2000). *Qualitative research for counselling psychology.* In S. D. Brown & R. W. Lent

(Eds.), Handbook of Counselling Psychology (3rd ed., pp. 199–230). New York: Wiley.

MPIDO. (2011). *A memorandum submitted by the Maa speaking pastoralist community to the Truth, Justice, and Reconciliation Commission.* Brown & Lent (eds).

Mortensen, D.S. (2004). *The white man's country.* Partnernews, 4(3), 4–5. New York: Wiley.

Mwangi. E. (2007). *Subdividing the commons: Distributional conflict in the transition from collective to individual property rights in Kenya's Maasailand.* World Development, 35(5), 815-834.

National Science Foundation. (1997). *User-Friendly Handbook for Mixed Methods Evaluations.* Retrieved from http://www. nsf.gov/pubs/1997/nsf97153/. Accessed 3/26/2016.

Nyangira, N.1975. *Relative Modernization and Public Resource Allocation in Kenya.*

Ntuli, P.P. (2002). *Indigenous knowledge systems and the African renaissance.* In Odora Hoppers, C.A. & Claremont,

C.A. (eds.), *Indigenous Knowledge and the Integration of Knowledge Systems.* pp. 53-66. South Africa: New Africa Books.

Nyariki, D.M., Mwang'ombe, A.W., & Thompson, D.M. (2009). *Land-use change and livestock production challenges in an integrated system: The Masai-Mara ecosystem, Kenya.* Journal of Human Ecology, 26(3), 63-173.

Okoth-Ogendo, H.W.O. (1991). *Tenants of the Crown: Evolution of Agrarian Law and Institutions in Kenya.* Imprint unknown.

Olanya, D.R. (2013). *Indigenous people and customary land rights. Public policy discourse of large-scale land acquisitions in East Africa. US-China Law Review,* 10(6), 620-638.

One Hundred Years of Terra Nullius: Disassembling and other factors that contribute to Maasai land appropriation. A Case Study of Kajiado and Narok Counties in Kenya. In Maurice, N.A & Linnet, H. H. (Eds), Global Trends in Africa's Development. Publisher. Centre for Democracy, Research & Development.

Ostrom, E. (1990). *Governing the Commons: The Evolution of Institutions for Collective Action.* New York: Cambridge University Press.

Ostrom, E. (2009). *Beyond markets and states: Polycentric governance of complex economic systems. Nobel Prize Lecture,* 8 December 2009. Stockholm, Sweden.

Palys, T. (1997). *Research Decisions: Quantitative and qualitative perspectives* (2nd ed). Toronto, Ontario, Canada: Harcourt Brace Jovanovich.

Patton, M.Q. (2002). *Qualitative Research and Evaluation Methods* (3rd ed.). Thousand Oaks, CA: Sage Publications. Patton, M. (1990). *Qualitative Evaluation and Research Methods.* p. 169-186. Beverly Hills, CA: Sage.

Pilla, L. & Dantas, J.A.R. (2016). *Intra-household nutritional dynamics: A cross-sectional study of Maasai communities in Kenya.* Qualitative Health Research, 26(6), 793-806.

Pletcher, H.(2020). *Urbanization in Kenya 2019. Statista.* Retrieved from https://www.statista. c o m / s t a t i s t i c s / 4 5 5 8 6 0 / u r b a n i z a t i o n - in-kenya/#:~:text=Urbanization%20means%20the%20share%20of, in%20urban%20areas%20and%20cities.]

Priven, F.F. & Cloward, R. (1993). *Regulating the Poor. The Foundations of Public Welfare.* New York: Pantheon Books.

Prunty, J. (1985). *Signposts for a critical educational policy analysis.* Australian Journal of Education, 29(2), 133-140.

Rahaman, A.S., Lawrence, S., & Roper, J. (2004). *Social and environmental reporting at the V.R.A.: Institutionalized legitimacy or legitimization crisis.* Critical Perspectives on Accounting, 15, 33-56.

Rein, M, & Goodin, R.E. (Eds.) *The Oxford Handbook of Public Policy.* Oxford CIT: Oxford University Press.

Reisch, M. (2014). *Routledge International Handbook of Social Justice.* Toronto, Canada: Routledge.

Society for Applied Anthropology (2003). *Sustainability and Pastoral Livelihoods: Lessons from East African Maasai and Mongolia. Human Organization Vol. 62,* No. 2.

Sponsel, L. E. (1996). 4 *The Natural History of Peace: The Positive View of Human Nature and Its Potential.*

The Cross Section Between Policy, Climate Change, and Security among Indigenous People in Kenya. In Maurice, N.A. & Abel, M. (Eds), Dynamics of Sustainable Development in Africa. Publisher: Centre for Democracy, Research & Development.

The Republic of Kenya. (2002) *Report of the Commission of Inquiry into the Land Law System of Kenya (Njonjo Commission), Nairobi:* Government Printer.

The Republic of Kenya. (2004) *Report of the Commission of Inquiry into the Illegal/Irregular Allocation of Public Land (Ndung'u Commission), Nairobi:* Government Printer.

The Republic of Kenya. (2010). *The Constitution of Kenya.* Government Printer. Nairobi.

The Republic of Kenya. (2009). *Sessional Paper No. 3 of 2009 on National Land Policy.* Nairobi: Government Printer.

The Republic of Kenya. (2009). *Kenya Population Census. Central Bureau of Statistics. 2009 population & housing census results. Nairobi:* Government Printer.

The Republic of Kenya. (1968). *Group Representative Act. Nairobi:* Government Printer.

The Republic of Kenya. (1963). *Registered Land Act (Cap. 300). Nairobi:* Government Printer.

The Republic of Kenya. (1968). *Report of the Mission on Land Consolidation and Registration in Kenya.*

Roberts, M.J. (2009). *Conflict analysis of the 2007 post-election violence in Kenya.* Discussion paper for conflict recovery, *New Dominion Philanthropy Metrics.*

Sabatier, P.A. (2007). *Theories of the Policy Process* (2nd ed.). The University of California. Boulder, CO: Westview Press.

Sassen, S. (2013). *Land grabs today: Feeding the disassembling of national territory.* Globalizations, 10(1), 25-46.

Sellen, D.W. (1996). *Nutritional status of African pastoralists: a review of the literature.* Nomad People, 39: 107-134.

Schneider, A.L. & Ingram, H. (1997). *Policy Design for Democracy. Lawrence, KS:* University of Kansas Press.

Schwitzgebel, E. (2006). *"Belief," in Zalta, E. (Ed.), The Stanford Encyclopedia of Philosophy.* Stanford, CA: The Metaphysics Research Lab.

Sena, O.S. (1986). *Pastoralists and Education: School Participation and Social Change Among the Maasai.* Ph.D. Dissertation, McGill University, Canada.

Shenton, A.K. (2004). *Strategies for Ensuring Trustworthiness in Qualitative Research Projects.* Newcastle, UK: Northumbria University.

Sindiga, I. (1984). *Land and population problems in Kajiado and Narok, Kenya.* Africa Studies Review 27.

Silverman, D. (2000). *Doing Qualitative Research: A Practical Handbook.* Thousand Oaks, CA. Sage.

Skollerhorn, E. (1998). *Habermas and nature: The theory of communicative action for studying environmental policy.* Journal of Environmental Planning and Management, 41(5): 555-57.

Stake, R.E. (1995). *The Art of Case Study Research. Thousand Oaks, CA:* Sage Publications, pp. 49-68.

Syagga, P.M. (2011). *Public Land, historical land injustices, and the new Constitution.* Society for International Development (SID).

Szto, P., Furman, R., & Langer, C. (2005). *Poetry and photography: An exploration into expressive/creative qualitative research.* Qualitative Social Work: Research and Practice. Vol. 4, No. 2, 135-156.

Taiko, L. (2013). *Elangata Wuas Group Ranch scandals.* A report submitted to the National Land Commission by aggrieved Group Ranch members.

Tamas, A. Yukon, W. & Almonde. (2002). *System Theory in Community Development.*

Tarayia, G.N. (2004). *The legal perspectives of the Maasai culture, customs, and traditions. Arizona Journal of International & Comparative Law 186.*

Taylor-Powell, E. & Renner, M. (2003). *Analyzing Qualitative Data.* Madison, WI: University of Wisconsin Extension.

Retrieved from http://learningstore.uwex.edu/pdf/ G3658-12.pdf.

Thompson, J. (1885). *Through Masai land: A journey of exploration among the snowclad volcanic mountains and strange tribes of eastern equatorial Africa.* London: Sampson Low, Marston & Co.

Thompson, M., Serneel, S., Kaelo, D., & Trench, P.C. (2009). *"Maasai Mara – Land Privatization and Wildlife Decline: Can Conservation Pay Its Way? In Homewood, K., Kristjanson, P., & Trench, P.C. (Eds), Staying Maasai. Livelihoods, Conservation, and Development in East African Rangelands. Springer:* New York.

Tiampati, M. (2014). *The Maasai land dispossessions.* Partner NEWS Vol. 7 No. 3. Denmark: Action Aid Denmark.

Tignor, R. (1976). *The Colonial Transformation of Kenya: The Akamba, Agikuyu, and the Maasai from 1900 to 1939.* Princeton, NJ: The Princeton University Press.

T.J.R.C. (2013). *The Report of the Truth, Justice, and Reconciliation Commission.* Government Printers, Nairobi

Tobiko, K. (1989). *The Land (Group Representatives) Act: A case study of Ilkaputiei Maasae Group Ranches of Kajiado District.* (Unpublished LLB Thesis) in Rutten (1992:302-3).

UNDRIP (2007). *The United Nations Declaration on the Rights of Indigenous Issues.* Available at https:// indigenousfoundations.arts.ubc.ca/un_declaration_on_ the_rights_of_indigenous_peoples/.

UN Human Rights Committee (HRC). (19194). *Report of the UN Human Rights Committee (Volume II),* 1994, A/49/40, available at: https://www.refworld.org/ docid/3f4745ee2. html.

United Nations Human Rights. (2015). *Land and human rights. Standards and applications.* Retrieved from https:// www.ohchr.org/Documents/Publications/ Land_HR- StandardsApplications.pdf.

UNPO. (2005) M*aasai: State Censured Over Mai Mahiu Shootings.* Retrieved from https://unpo.org/article/2057.

Vanhanen, T. (1999). *Domestic ethnic conflict and ethnic nepotism: A comparative analysis. Journal of Peace Research, 36*(1), 55-73.

Wachira, G.M. (2008). *Vindicating Indigenous people's land rights in Kenya.* Doctoral dissertation presented to the University of Pretoria.

Waldram, J.B. (2000). *The efficacy of traditional medicine: Current theoretical and methodological issues.* Medical Anthropology Quarterly, 14, 603-625.

Western, D. & Nightingale, D.L.M. (2004). *Environmental change and the vulnerability of pastoralists to drought: A case study of the Maasai in Amboseli, Kenya. In Africa Environment Outlook Case Studies: Human Vulnerability to Environmental Change. Nairobi:* UNEP Review, 74, p. 316-337.

Wilson, R. (2001). *Assessing communicative rationality as a transportation planning paradigm.* Transportation, 28, 1-31.

World Bank. (2019). *Net official development assistance received (current US$).* Retrieved from https://data.worldbank.org/ indicator/DT.ODA.ODAT.CD.

World Bank. (2014). *Linking land policy with climate change: A Multi-dimensional landscape approach to territorial development with a focus on Europe and Central Asia (ECA) Region.*

Yannow, W.D. (1993). *The communication of policy meaning: Implementation as interpretation and text. Policy Sciences,* 26 (1); 41-61. Yin, R.K. (2013). Case study research: Design and methods (3rd ed.). Thousand Oaks, CA: Sage Publications.

Zommers, A. (2010). *Globalization and the foreignization of space: Seven processes driving the current global land grab.* The Journal of Peasant Studio.Thousand Oaks. CA: Sage Publications, Thousand Oaks.

ABOUT THE AUTHOR

Dr. Ben R. Ole Koissaba holds a Ph.D. in International Family and Community Studies from Clemson University, South Carolina, USA, a Post-Doctorate in Advanced Rehabilitation Research from Langston University, Oklahoma, an MA in Social Entrepreneurship from Northwest University, Kirkland, Washington, USA, and a Post-Graduate Diploma in Theology and Development from the Oxford Center for Mission Studies of the University of Leeds, UK. Dr. Koissaba is a Certified Development Project Manager and a holder of several professional certifications, including Occupational Safety and Health Administration, Project Information Management Systems, Project Design Monitoring & Evaluation, Financing for Development, and Advocacy and Human Rights, among others.

Dr. Koissaba has extensive experience working for non-profits and government agencies in Africa and the United States, as well as international institutions like USAID, AusAid, UNDP, DFID, the World Bank, and the European Union. Dr. Koissaba has contributed immensely to the work of global Indigenous Peoples through advocacy work and representation at global forums, including the United Nations, where he was the global co-chair for the United Nations Permanent Forum on Indigenous Popples during the 2009 session.

Dr. Koissaba's broad **research interests** are in indigenous societies of Sub-Saharan Africa, globalization, environmentalism and development, social justice, and human rights. Nevertheless, within these foci, there is a strong work, consultancy, and research experience in ***community-engaged research in community development as it pertains to the challenges facing the minorities and/or underrepresented indigenous peoples in other parts of the world***. Thus, he has researched, published, advocated for, and made many conference presentations on the land, ecological, and development challenges of the Maasai community of Kenya and other minority groups.

Dr. Koissaba has several publications, including a book *"Local Advocacy to National Activism: Maa Civil Society Forum, Kenya. ISBN 978-3-659-26221-0. Lambert Academic Publishing,* and book chapters *"Elusive Justice: The Maasai Contestation of Land Appropriation in Kenya: A Historical and Contemporary Perspective"* in *M. M. Kithinji, M. M. Koster, & J. P. Rotich (Eds.), "Kenya after 50: Reconfiguring historical, political, and policy milestones", Bassingstoke, U.K.: Palgrave Macmillan, several,* and E-learning Principles and Practices in the context of Indigenous Peoples: A Comparative Study. In M. Gitau, P. Mutisya, C. Kamau, C. Wieczorek, & J. Ngundi (Eds.), Kenyan Education System: *Are We Preparing Students to Meet Current Global Needs and Challenges.* BookBaby, among others

COVER PICTURE

These are photos of Ratik Ole Kuyiana, Ms Mary Simat, and Godfrey Ole Ntapayia during the Maasai processions in Nairobi on August 15th, 2004. Photographs courtesy of Michael Ole Tiampati

www.ingramcontent.com/pod-product-compliance
Lightning Source LLC
Chambersburg PA
CBHW051953270326
41929CB00015B/2643